STANDARD ENCYCLOPEDIA OF

CARNIVAL GLASS

4TH EDITION

Bill Edwards

COLLECTOR BOOKS
A Division of Schroeder Publishing Co., Inc.

Searching For A Publisher?

We are always looking for knowledgeable people considered to be experts within their fields. If you feel that there is a real need for a book on your collectible subject and have a large comprehensive collection, contact us.

Collector Books
P.O. Box 3009
Paducah, Kentucky 42002-3009

On the Cover:

Top left: *Loganberry*, 10" tall vase, base diameter 3¾", four marks, made by Imperial, amethyst. See price guide for value.

Top right: *Wild Strawberry*, 9" bowl, made by Northwood, amethyst. See price guide for value.

Bottom: *Jewels*, green candleholder, unpatterned iridized glass, made by Dugan. See price guide for value.

Printed by IMAGE GRAPHICS, INC., Paducah, Kentucky

Dedication

In Memory of Ellen Edwards
1909–1990
and Donald E. Moore

Acknowledgments

In this massive revision, I've been aided by the generosity of many collectors, and I wish to thank all of them from the bottom of my heart. But I would be remiss if I neglected to single out my very good friend, Don Moore, who gave me his help whenever I asked right up to the time he entered the hospital for the last time. Don was kind, thoughtful and generous, and not many like him come our way. We'll miss you, Don.

Others whom I owe my thanks for this book are: Dean M. Hanson, Russell Bibbee, Thelma Harmon, Pat and Bob Davis, Bill Stoetzel, Norman Archer, Eileen Moake, John Woody, Joe Cobb, Jim Halacz, Kathi Johnson, John and Jeanette Rogers, Lewis Price, Bob Gallo, Richard Conley, Carl and Eunice Booker, Florrie Grace Morehead Johns, Arlene and Joe Johannets, Ernie and Kathy Pyles, Linda Blanton, Raymond A. Johns, Mercedes Titus, Don Doyle, Frank Bounds, Gloria and Vicky Balander, R.G. Klein, Bill Banks, and Mark Sadowski.

Author's Note

I have spent a major portion of my life learning about, living with, and writing about Carnival glass. Let me say that aside from the pure pleasure of handling so much of this beautiful glass, I've met so many very wonderful people, I feel my life has been enriched beyond measure by the experience.

Introduction

For the benefit of the novice, Carnival glass is that pressed and iridized glass manufactured between 1905 and 1930. It was made by various companies in the United States, England, France, Germany, Australia, Sweden, and Finland.

The iridization, unlike the costly art glass produced by Tiffany and his competitors, was achieved by a spray process on the surface of the glass before firing, thus, producing a very beautiful product at a greatly reduced cost, giving the housewife a quality product well within her budget.

In addition, Carnival glass was the last hand-shaped glass mass-produced in America and remains as a beautiful reminder of the glassmaker's skills.

In this volume, we will show the variety of shapes and colors of Carnival glass and will also attempt to define the patterns by manufacturer and for the first time, put the entire field of Carnival glass into one reference book for the collector.

It is my hope that this effort will bring new interest to this truly beautiful glass and stimulate its growth as a collectible; and my only regret is a lack of space to show every known pattern.

The Dugan Story

The Dugan Glass Company of Indiana, Pennsylvania began production on April 14, 1892 calling itself the Indiana Glass Company with Harry White as its president and operating for less than a year before closing. The vacant plant was first leased, then purchased by Harry Northwood in 1895. For the next two years it poured out a stream of Northwood glass until Northwood decided to join the National Glass Combine and moved his main operation to the old Hobbs, Brockunier plant, leasing the Indiana plant to its managers, Thomas E. Dugan and W.G. Minnemeyer, who changed the name to the Dugan Glass Company (also called the American Glass Company).

They produced basically the same sorts of glass as Northwood until 1913 when the name was changed again to the Diamond Glass Company with John P. Elkin as president; H. Wallace Thomas, secretary; D.B. Taylor, treasurer; and Ed Rowland, plant manager. During this time, many Northwood molds were reworked, a trademark with a "D" within a diamond registered and most of the Carnival glass from the company was produced under the supervision of Thomas Dugan.

The plant operated until 1931 when it was destroyed by fire and never rebuilt because of the Depression that gripped the country and the industry.

The Fenton Story

First organized in April 1905, the Fenton Art Glass company didn't really materialize until the following July. At that time the glass decorating shop was opened in Martins Ferry, Ohio in an abandoned factory rented by Frank L. Fenton and his brother, John (who was later to found the famous Millersburg Glass Company).

The next few months were occupied in obtaining financial backers, glass workers, buying land to be plotted into lots as a money-raising venture, and construction of their own plant in Williamstown, West Virginia. At times, everything seemed to go wrong, and it wasn't until 1907 that the company was "on its way."

From the first, the design abilities of Frank Fenton were obvious, and each pattern seemed to bear his own special flair. He (along with Jacob Rosenthal who had come to the Fenton factory after fire had destroyed the renowned Indiana Tumbler and Goblet Company in Greentown, Indiana) was greatly responsible for sens-

ing what the public admired in glass ornamentation.

In 1908 friction arose between the two brothers, and John exited to pursue his dreams in Millersburg, Ohio. By this time, the Fenton process of iridization has taken the mass-scale art glass field by storm and "Carnival glass" was on its way.

For the next 15 years, the Fenton company would produce the largest number of patterns ever in this beautiful product, and huge amounts of iridized glass would be sent to the four corners of the world to brighten homes. While the company made other decorative wears in custard, chocolate glass, mosaic inlaid glass, opalescent glass, and stretch glass, nothing surpassed the quality and quantity of their iridized glass. Almost 150 patterns are credited to the company in Carnival glass alone, and many more probably credited to others may be of Fenton origin.

All this is truly a remarkable feat, and certainly Frank L. Fenton's genius must stand along side Harry Northwood's as inspiring.

The Imperial Story

While the Imperial Glass Company of Bellaire, Ohio was first organized in 1901 by a group of area investors, it wasn't until January 13, 1904, that the first glass was made; and not until nearly five years later the beautiful iridized glass we've come to call Carnival glass was produced.

In the years between these dates, the mass market was sought with a steady production of pressed glass water sets, single tumblers, jelly jars, lamp shades, chimneys, and a full assortment of table items such as salt dips, pickle trays, condiment bottles and oil cruets.

All of this was a prelude, of course, to the art glass field which swept the country, and in 1909 Imperial introduced their iridescent line of blown lead lustre articles as well as the Nuruby, Sapphire, and Peacock colors of Carnival glass.

Quite evident then, as now, this proved to be the hallmark of their production. Huge quantities of the iridized glass were designed, manufactured, and sold to the mass marketplace across America and the European Continent for the next decade in strong competition with the other art glass factories. Especially sought was the market in England early in 1911.

In quality Imperial must be ranked second only to the fine glass produced by the Millersburg company and certainly in design, is on an equal with the great Northwood company. Only the Fenton company produced more recognized patterns and has outlasted them in longevity (the Imperial Glass Company became a subsidiary of the Lenox Company in 1973).

Along the way came the fabulous art glass line called "Imperial Jewels" in 1916. This was an iridescent product often in freehand worked with a "stretch" effect. This is so popular today, many glass collectors have large collections of this alone.

In 1929 Imperial entered the machine glass era and produced its share of what has come to be called Depression glass and in the early 1960's, the company revived their old molds and reproduced many of the old iridized patterns as well as creating a few new ones for the market that was once again invaded by "Carnival glass fever." While many collectors purchased these items, purists in Carnival glass collecting have remained loyal to the original and without question, the early years of Carnival glass production at the Imperial Company will always be their golden years.

The Millersburg Story

Interestingly enough, if John and Frank Fenton hadn't had such adverse personalities, there would have been no Millersburg Glass Company. Both brothers had come to the Martins Ferry, Ohio area in 1903 to begin a glass business in partnership, but Frank was conservative and level-headed while John was brash and eager – a constant dreamer and the pitchman of the family. Each wanted to make a name in the business, and each wanted to do it his way.

By 1908 with the Fenton Art Glass Factory going strong, the clashes multiplied, and John went in search of a location for a plant of his own. He was 38, a huge strapping man with a shock of heavy brown hair and a pair of steely eyes that could almost hypnotize. He would sire five children.

After weeks of travel and inquiry, he came to Holmes County, Ohio and was immediately impressed with the land and the people. Here were the heartland Americans whose families had come from Germany and Switzerland. They were hard workers like the Amish that lived among them, good businessmen who led a simple life.

Word soon spread that John Fenton wanted to build a glass plant, and the people welcomed him. By selling his interest in the Fenton plant and borrowing, John secured option on a 54.7 acre site on the north edge of Millersburg. Lots were plotted and sold, and ground was broken on September 14, 1908. And like John Fenton's dreams, the plant was to be the grandest ever. The main building was 300' x 100', spanned by steel framing with no center supporting. A second building, 50' x 300', was built as a packing and shipping area as well as a tool shop. The main building housed a 14-pot furnace, a mix room, an office area, a lehr area, and a display area for samples of their production.

During construction gas wells were drilled to supply a source of power, and stocks were sold in the company, totaling $125,000.00

On May 20, 1909 the first glass was poured. The initial molds were designed by John Fenton and were **Ohio Star** and **Hobstar and Feather.** While at the Fenton, factory, he had designed others, including the famous "Goddess of Harvest" bowl as a tribute to his wife. The glass that now came from the Millersburg factory was the highest quality of crystal and sample toothpick holders in the **Ohio Star** pattern were given to all visitors that first week.

In addition to the crystal, iridized glass in the Fenton process was put into production the first month in amethyst, green, and soft marigold. A third pattern – a design of cherry clusters and leaves – was added and soon sold well enough to warrant new molds, bringing the **Multi-Fruit and Flowers** design into being as a follow-up pattern.

Early in January 1910 the celebrated "Radium" process was born. It featured a softer shade of color and a watery, mirror-like finish on the front side of the glass only; it soon took the glass world by storm and became a brisk seller. Noted glassworker, Oliver Phillips, was the father of the process, and it was soon copied by the Imperial company and others in the area.

In June of that same year, the famous **Courthouse** bowl was produced as a tribute to the town and to the workers who had laid the gas lines to the factory. These bowls were made in lettered, unlettered, radium and satin finish and were given away by the hundreds at the factory, just as the crystal **Ohio Star** punch sets had been given to all the town's churches and social organizations, and the famous **People's Vase** was to be made as a tribute to the area's Amish.

During the next years the Millersburg plant was at its zenith, and dozens of new patterns were added to the line from molds produced by the Hipkins Mold Company. They included the noted **Peacock** patterns as well as the **Berry Wreath, Country Kitchen, Poppy, Diamond, Pipe Humidor** and **Rosalind** patterns. By late March 1911 Hipkins wanted pay for their work, as did other creditors, and John Fenton found his finances a disaster. The plant was kept producing, but bankruptcy was filed, and Samuel Fair finally bought the works in October, renaming it the Radium Glass Company. In the next few months, only iridized glass in the radium process was produced while John Fenton tried to find a way to begin again.

But time soon proved Fair couldn't bring the factory back to its former glory, and he closed the doors, selling the factory and its contents to Frank Sinclair and the Jefferson Glass Company in 1913. Sinclair shipped many of the crystal and Carnival molds to the Jefferson plant in Canada for a run of production there which included **Ohio Star, Hobstar and Feather** and Millersburg **Flute.** The rest of the molds were sold for scrap despite the success of the patterns with the Canadians who bought the graceful crystal

6

designs for several years. Jefferson's production at the Millersburg plant itself was brief. The known pieces include a 6" **Flute** compote just like the famous Millersburg **Wildflower**, marked "Crys-tal" with no interior pattern.

In 1919 the empty plant was again sold to the Forrester Tire and Rubber Company; the great stack was leveled and the furnace gutted. The Millersburg Glass factory was no more. But as long as one single piece of its beautiful glass is collected, its purpose will stand, and the lovers of this beautiful creation will forgive John Fenton his faults in business and praise his creative genius.

The Northwood Story

An entire book could be written about Harry Northwood, using every superlative the mind could summon and still fail to do justice to the man, a genius in his field. Of course, Harry had an advantage in the glass industry since his father, John Northwood, was a renowned English glass maker.

Harry Northwood came to America in 1880 and first worked for Hobbs, Brockunier and Company of Wheeling, West Virginia, an old and established glass-producing firm. For five years, Harry remained in Wheeling, learning his craft and dreaming his dreams.

In 1886 he left Hobbs, Brockunier and was employed by the Labelle Glass Company of Bridgeport, Ohio where he advanced to the position of manager in 1887. A few months later, a devastating fire destroyed much of the LaBelle factory, and it was sold in 1888.

Harry next went to work for the Buckeye Glass Company of Martin's Ferry, Ohio. Here he remained until 1896 when he formed the Northwood Company at Indiana, Pennsylvania. Much of the genius was now being evidenced, and such products as the famous Northwood custard glass date from this period.

In 1899 Northwood entered the National Glass combine only to become unhappy with its financial problems, and in 1901 he broke away to become an independent manufacturer once again. A year later, he bought the long-idle Hobbs, Brockunier plant, and for the next couple of years, there were two Northwood plants.

Finally in 1904, Northwood leased the Indiana, Pennsylvania plant to its managers, Thomas E. Dugan and W.G. Minnemeyer, who changed the name of the plant to the Dugan Glass Company. In 1913 the plant officially became known as the Diamond Glass Company and existed as such until it burned to the ground in 1931.

In 1908 Harry Northwood, following the success of his student, Frank L. Fenton, in the iridized glass field, marketed his first Northwood iridescent glass, and Northwood Carnival glass was born. For a 10-year period Carnival glass was the great American "craze," and even at the time of Harry Northwood's death in 1919, small quantities were still being manufactured. It had proved to be Northwood's most popular glass, the jewel in the crown of a genius, much of it marked with the well-known trademark.

Other American Companies

Besides the five major producers of Carnival glass in America, several additional companies produced amounts of iridized glass.

These companies include: Cambridge Glass Company of Cambridge, Ohio; Jenkins Glass Company of Kokomo, Indiana; Westmoreland Glass Company of Grapeville, Pennsylvania; Fostoria Glass Company of Moundsville, West Virginia; Heisey Glass Company of Newark, Ohio; McKee-Jeanette Glass Company of Jeanette, Pennsylvania; and U.S. Glass Company of Pittsburgh, Pennsylvania.

The Cambridge Company was the "leader" of the lesser companies, and the quality of their iridized glass was of a standard equal to that of the Millersburg Glass Company. Actually, there appears to have been a close working relationship between the two concerns, and some evidence exists to lead us to believe some Cambridge patterns were iridized at the Millersburg factory. The Venetian vase is such an item. Known

Cambridge patterns are:

Horn of Plenty	Inverted Thistle
Sweetheart	Double Star (Buzz Saw)
Buzz Saw Cruet	Near Cut Souvenir
Cologne Bottle	Proud Puss
Forks Cracker Jar	Tomahawk
Inverted Feather	Toy Punch Set
Inverted Strawberry	Venetian
Near-Cut Decanter	

Many of the Cambridge patterns are beautiful near-cut designs or patterns intaglio; and while amethyst and blue are colors rarely found, most Cambridge Carnival glass was made in green and marigold.

The Jenkins Glass Company made only a handful of Carnival glass patterns, mostly in marigold color, and nearly all patterns in intaglio with a combination of flower and near-cut design. Their known patterns are:

Cane and Daisy Cut	Stork Vase
Cut Flowers	Fleur De Lis Vase
Diamond and Daisy Cut	Oval Star and Fan
Stippled Strawberry	

The Westmoreland Company also made quality Carnival glass in limited amounts. Known patterns are:

Checkerboard	Strutting Peacock
Footed Drape	Pillow and Sunburst
Footed Shell	Shell and Jewel
Basketweave and Cable	Wild Rose Wreath #270
Prisms	Corinth Vt.
Orange Peel	Carolina Dogwood
Fruit Salad	Little Beads

The Fostoria Company had two types of iridized glass. The first was their Taffeta Lustre line which included console sets, bowls and candlesticks; the second was their brocaded patterns which consisted of an acid cutback design, iridized and decorated with gold. These patterns include:

Brocaded Acorns	Brocaded Palms
Brocaded Daffodils	Brocaded Rose
Brocaded Summer Garden	

Heisey made very few iridized items and those found have a light, airy luster. Patterns known are:

Covered Frog	Heisey #357
Covered Turtle	Heisey Flute
Heisey Tray Set	Paneled Heisey

The McKee-Jeanette Company had a few Carnival glass patterns as follows:

Aztec	Rock Crystal
Heart Band Souvenir	Sea Gulls Bowl
Lutz	Snow Fancy
Hobnail Panels	

The U.S. Glass Company was a combine of 17 companies, headquartered in Pittsburgh, Pennsylvania. Their plants were usually designated by letters, and it is nearly impossible to say what item came from which factory. However, some of the patterns we have classified as U.S. Glass are:

Beads and Bars	Louisville Shrine
Daisy in Oval Panels	Rochester Shrine
Field Thistle	Champagne
Golden Harvest	Shrine Toothpick
New Orleans Shrine Champagne	Palm Beach
Feather Swirl	Vintage Wine
Cosmos and Cane	Butterfly Tumbler

In addition to all the glass produced by these minor concerns, specialty glass houses contributed their share of iridized glass in the large "Gone With The Wind" lamps, shades, chimneys, etc.; as well as minute amounts of iridized glass from Libby, Anchor-Hocking, Tiffin, Devilbiss, Hig-Bee, and Jeanette are known.

It is not possible in our limited space to show all these patterns from the smaller makers, but we'll try to give a sampling from many of them.

In addition, many patterns in Carnival glass have not been attributed to definite producers at this time, and so you will find a few items shown where we must say "maker unknown." While we wish this didn't have to be, sooner or later, these too will find their proper place in the history of Carnival glass.

Non-American Carnival Glass Makers

Besides the British and Australians, factories in Sweden, Finland, Denmark, Czechoslovakia, Holland, Mexico, France and Argentina are now known to have produced some amount of iridized glass. While it would be impossible for us to catalogue all these companies, I will list a few of the more prolific and their currently known patterns.

Finland
Finnish Carnival glass wasn't made until the early 1930's and was made primarily at four factories, including one at Riihimaki which seemed to specialize in copying some best-selling American patterns like Lustre Rose, Four Flowers, and Tiger Lily.

Czechoslovakia
Several researchers trace such patterns as Zipper Stitch, The Fish Vase and the Hand Vase to this country's production. If so, they also made some red for I have seen one red Hand Vase! Everything else named is in marigold including the Star and Fan Cordial set.

Sweden
Swedish Carnival glass was in the Varmland region at a factory called the Eda Glassworks with such patterns as Rose Garden, Curved Star, Sunk Daisy, and Sunflower and Diamonds. Colors are primarily marigold and blue, and I suspect the Sungold Epergne may have come from this factory.

Argentina
The Regolleau Cristalerias Company is in Buenos Aires, and here a handful of little-known patterns were made including the Beetle Ashtray and an ashtray I call CR since that is just how it is shaped. I've seen it in both marigold and blue.

Mexico
Recent information into the mysterious patterns of Votive Light, Ranger, and Oklahoma all point to a Mexican production by Cristales de Mexico in Nuevo Leon, Mexico. Each of these patterns is marked with the "M" inside a "C."

In addition, small amounts of iridized glass, often decorated with hand painting, was made in France, Germany, Holland, and Belgium. Some of these pieces are very intricate and the design top-notch. I have seen a very beautiful custard glass bowl in a bride's basket that has a candy-ribbon edge; it is iridized and has an enamel design. It was pretty enough to be in a museum, and I've envied the owner ever since I saw it.

English Carnival Glass

When iridized glass caught the buyer's fancy in this country, the major companies (especially Imperial and Fenton) began to ship Carnival glass to England, Europe, and Australia, and it wasn't long until the glass house there began to enter the iridized field. In England the chief producer of this glass was the Sowerby Company of Gateshead-on-Tyne. However, other concerns made some iridized glass, including Gueggenheim, Ltd., of London; and Davisons of Gateshead.

The movement of Carnival glass in England began later than in America and lasted about five years after sales had diminished in this country. Many shapes were made, including bowls, vases, compotes, and table pieces. However, water sets and punch sets were pretty much overlooked, and only a few examples of these have come to light. Colors in English glass were mainly confined to marigold, blue, and amethyst, but an occasional item in green does appear. The pastels apparently were not popular for few examples exist.

Here then is a list of known English patterns and its volume may surprise many collectors:

African Shield   Hobstar Reversed

Apple Panels
Art Deco
Banded Grape and Leaf
Beaded Hearts
Buddha
Cane and Scroll
Cathedral Arches
  (Hobstar and Cathedral)
Chariot
Covered Hen
Covered Swan
Daisy Block
Daisy and Cane
Diamond Ovals
Diving Dolphins
Fans
Feathered Arrow
Fine Cut Rings
Flute Sherbet
Footed Prism Panels
Grape and Cherry
Heavy Prisms
Hobstar Cut Triangles

Illinois Daisy
Intaglio Daisy
Kokomo
Lattice Heart
Lea (and variants)
May Basket
Moonprint
My Lady's Powderbox
Pineapple
Pinwheel
Pinwheel Vase
Sacic Ashtray
Saint Candlestick
Scroll Embossed Vt.
Signet
Spiralex
Split Diamond
Star
Stippled Diamond Swag
Thistle and Thorn
Tiny Berry Tumbler
Triads
Vining Leaf

Australian Carnival Glass

Just as England caught the "fever," so did the populace of Australia, and in 1918 the Crystal Glass Works, Ltd. of Sydney began to produce a beautiful line of iridized glass, whose finish ranks with the very best (mostly in bowls and compotes but with occasional table items and two water sets known).

Australian Carnival glass is confined to purple, marigold, and an unusual amber over aqua finish, and patterns known are:

Australian Swan   Banded Diamonds
Australian Grape   Beaded Spears

Blocks and Arches
Butterflies and Bells
Butterflies and Waratah
Butterfly Bower
Butterfly Bush
Crystal Cut
Emu (Ostrich)
Feathered Flowers
Flannel Berry
Flannel Flower
Golden Cupid
Interior Rays

Kangaroo (and variants)
Kingfisher (and variants)
Kiwi
Kookaburra (and variants)
Magpie
Pin-ups
Rose Panels
S-Band
Sun Gold Epergne
Thunderbird (Shrike)
Waterlily and Dragonfly
Wild Fern

ABSENTEE DRAGON

If you take a close look at this very rare 9" plate, you will see it is very different from the Dragon and Berry pattern it resembles. It is the only one known, and while I hate the name, I consider it a top rarity in Fenton glass. It has a Bearded Berry reverse pattern, and the color is excellent. It was, no doubt, an experimental piece.

ACANTHUS

An Imperial pattern found mostly on bowls and occasionally on plates, the Acanthus is quite graceful. Colors known are marigold, smoke, green, and blue, but certainly Imperial purple is possible. The exterior pattern is Wide Panel or Flute.

ACORN (FENTON)

It would be hard to imagine a more naturalistic pattern than this. Realistic acorns and oak leaves arranged in three groupings fill much of the allowed space and form a pleasing design. Acorn is found on bowls and plates in a wide range of colors including marigold, amethyst, green, red, vaseline, ice blue, and iridized milk glass.

ACORN (MILLERSBURG)

What a shame the Millersburg company didn't make this realistic design in other shapes; the compote is one of the best designed in all of carnival glass. Realistic acorns and leaves with an exterior of flute and the typical Millersburg clover base. Colors are marigold, amethyst, green, and a rare vaseline.

ACORN BURRS

Other than the famous Northwood Grape and their Peacock at Fountain pattern, Acorn Burrs is probably the most representative of the factory's work, and one eagerly sought by Carnival glass collectors. The pattern background is that of finely done oak bark while the leaves are those of the chestnut oak. The mold work is well done, and the coloring ranks with the best. Acorn Burrs is found in a wide range of colors and shapes and always brings top dollar.

ADAM'S RIB

This scarce Dugan-Diamond pattern dating from the 1920's can be found on tall, dome-shaped pitchers and stemmed and handled tumblers. This is actually a lemonade set. Colors are pastel in green, blue, and frosty white.

ADVERTISING ITEMS

These come in dozens of varieties, shapes, and colors, and it would be impossible in our limited space to show them all. Advertising items were a much-welcomed area of business by **all** Carnival glass makers, because they were a guaranteed source of income without the usual cost-lost factor of unsold stock. Also, they could often be made with less care, since they were to be given away; old molds could often be utilized to avoid expensive new molds. Many Northwood advertising items were small plates with simple floral designs.

AFRICAN SHIELD

This small vase-shape originally had a wire flower holder that held the stems of freshly cut blossoms in a neat arrangement. It is 2⅞" tall and 3¼" wide at the top, and while I can't be certain who made it, I believe it is English. Marigold is the only color reported so far.

Absentee Dragon

Adam's Rib

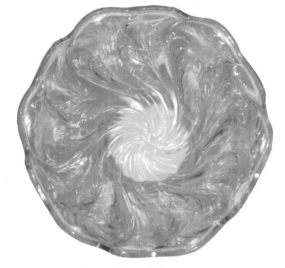

Acanthus

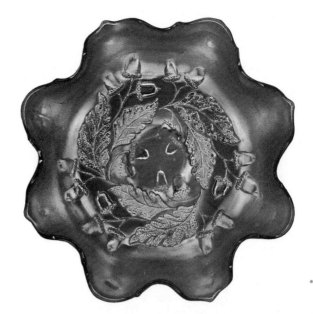

Acorn (Fenton)

Acorn (Millersburg)

Acorn Burrs

Advertising Items

African Shield

11

AGE HERALD

Another famous advertising pattern, known to have come from the Fenton factory, is found only in amethyst. Both bowls and plates are known, and the pattern was designed as a give-away item from the well-known Birmingham, Alabama newspaper. The exterior pattern is a wide panel.

AMARYLLIS

This unusual compote is a treasure for several reasons. First is the size (2¼" high, 5¼" wide). The shape is roughly triangular, rising from a slightly domed base. The underside carries the Poppy Wreath pattern, and the only colors reported are a deep purple, cobalt blue, and marigold.

Amaryllis is a rather scarce Northwood pattern and isn't often mentioned in Carnival glass discussions. It is, however, a unique and interesting addition to any collection.

AMERICAN

From the Fostoria Glass house the American pattern was one of their most important patterns in crystal, and it is no surprise to find it among their iridized items. The footed tumbler shown is slightly taller than most tumblers.

APPLE AND PEAR INTAGLIO

Like its cousin the Strawberry Intaglio, this rather rare bowl is a product of the Northwood Company and is seen mostly in crystal or goofus glass. The example shown measures 9¾" in diameter and is 2¾" high. The glass is ½" thick!

APPLE BLOSSOM (NORTHWOOD)

The tumbler shown is only part of a grouping, painted by the same artist that consists of water set, berry set, and table set. Usually found in blue, both amethyst and marigold are known in smaller quantities.

APPLE BLOSSOM TWIGS

This is a very popular pattern, especially in plates where the design is shown to full advantage. The detail is quite nice with fine mold work, much like that of Acorn Burrs. Found mostly in marigold, peach, and purple, Apple Blossom Twigs has as its exterior pattern, the Big Basketweave pattern. Shards in this pattern at the Dugan site have been identified.

APPLE BLOSSOMS

Found only in small bowls or plates, Apple Blossoms seems to be an average Carnival glass pattern, produced for a mass market in large quantities. Most often seen in marigold, it is occasionally found in vivid colors as well as pastels, especially white. A quarter-size chunk of this pattern in white was found at the Dugan dump site in 1975.

APPLE PANELS

Found only in the breakfast set shown so far, Apple Panels is an intaglio pattern. The design consists of two panels with an apple, stem and leaves; these are separated by panels of hobstars and fans. Colors are marigold and green but others may someday surface.

American

**Apple Blossom
(Northwood)**

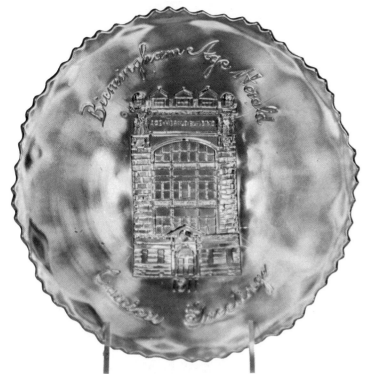

Age Herald

Amaryllis

Apple and Pear Intaglio

Apple Blossom Twigs

Apple Blossoms

Apple Panels

APPLE TREE

It certainly is a pity Fenton chose to use this realistic pattern on water sets only. It would have made a beautiful table set or punch set. Apple Tree is available in marigold, cobalt blue, and white, and I've seen a rare vase whimsey formed from the pitcher with the handle omitted. The coloring is nearly always strong and bright.

APRIL SHOWERS

Like the bubbles in a carbonated soft drink, the tiny beads seem to float over this very interesting vase pattern. Found in all sizes from 5" to 14", April Showers is sometimes found with Peacock Tail pattern on the interior. The colors are marigold, blue, purple, green, and white. The top edge is usually quite ruffled in the Fenton manner.

ARCS

This pattern is often confused by beginning collectors with the Scroll Embossed pattern, and it's easy to see why. Perhaps they were designed by the same person since they are both Imperial patterns. Arcs is found on bowls of average size, often with an exterior of File pattern and on compotes with a geometric exterior. The usual colors are marigold or a brilliant amethyst, but green and smoke do exist.

ART DECO

We don't often see such a plain Carnival pattern, but this one has a good deal of interest, despite its lack of design. The very modern look was all the rage in the Art Deco age so I've named this cute little bowl in that manner. I don't know who the English manufacturer was.

ASTERS

Recently, I've seen this very pretty intaglio exterior pattern on a 6" compote as well as a 10" bowl, both in a very strong marigold, and Mrs. Hartung lists it in a 6" bowl. I suspect this pattern is English, probably from Sowerby.

AURORA PEARLS

Since I first showed this beautiful iridized custard piece, I've seen a larger version that was 12½" wide as well as a version in red and one in cobalt, both iridized and decorated. All were beautiful! I'm sure this is European and bridges the space between art glass and carnival glass.

AUSTRALIAN FLOWER SET

Used like the Water Lily and Dragonfly flower set, this Australian beauty has no design except the slender thread border on the bowl's exterior. The iridescence is fantastic, as you can see.

AUSTRALIAN SUGARS

These two beauties are kissing cousins and both Australian. The marigold one is called Australian Panels and the purple one Australian Diamonds (not Concave Diamonds as previously listed). Other shapes may exist, but I haven't seen them.

Australian Sugars

Aurora Pearls

14

Apple Tree

Asters

Arcs

Art Deco

Australian Flower Set

April Showers

AUSTRALIAN SWAN

Pictured is the Australian Black Swan on a beautiful bowl design. The floral sprays remind us of lily of the valley but are probably some Australian plant. Colors are purple and marigold in both large and small bowls.

AUTUMN ACORNS

Apparently a spin-off pattern from the Fenton Acorn, Autumn Acorns has replaced the realistic oak leaf with the grape leaf used on the Vintage pattern bowls. Found mostly in bowls, an occasional plate is seen in green. The bowls are found in marigold, blue, green, amethyst, vaseline, and red.

AZTEC

While McKee didn't make much Carnival glass, the few existing pieces are treasures and certainly the Aztec pattern is one. Known only in a creamer, sugar, rose bowl, tumblers, and pitcher, the coloring ranges from a good strong marigold to a clambroth with a fiery pink and blue highlights. Each shape in Aztec is rare and important.

BALLOONS

Balloons is one of those borderline items that could be called either Carnival glass or stretch glass since it has characteristics of both. Found in various shapes, including vases of different sizes and shapes, plates with a center handle, compotes, and perfume atomizers. The colors are marigold or smoke. The design is ground through the luster and appears clear, and, of course, there is the stretch effect on many of the pieces.

BAND

Like most of the violet basket inserts, this one relies on a metal handle and holder for any decoration it might have. It was made by Dugan and probably came in marigold as well as the amethyst shown.

BAND OF ROSES

Besides this tumble-up and matching tray, a pitcher and tumbler are known in this pattern. It came from Argentina I understand, but is probably a product of a glass firm in Europe. At any rate, it is pretty and quite rare in any shape.

BANDED DIAMOND

Now known to be an Australian pattern, Banded Diamond is found in water sets and berry sets that are scarce. The colors are a very rich amethyst and a strong marigold.

BANDED DIAMONDS AND BARS

Three sizes of this Finnish tumbler are known thus far, and all have a deep, rich marigold color and strong iridization. The smallest one (shown) is only 2¼" high; the second one shown is the largest, and it is just slightly over 3½" high.

BANDED DRAPE

Banded Drape is another of Fenton's decorated water sets, but the shape is quite distinctive, being almost urn-shaped. The colors are very beautiful with much luster and are found in marigold, amethyst, cobalt blue, white, and ice green. The enameled flower seems to be a lovely calla lily.

Aztec

Band of Roses

Banded Diamonds and Bars

Australian Swan

Autumn Acorns

Balloons

Band

Banded Diamond

Banded Drape

BANDED GRAPE AND LEAF

Here is the only water set I've heard about in English glass. As you can see, the design is quite good, and the color is better than average. The only color I've seen is marigold, and at least two sets of this pattern are in American collections.

BANDED RIB

Another rather late pattern, this is one of the taller water sets, probably intended for iced tea or lemonade. The only color reported is the marigold, and the only shapes are tumblers and pitchers.

BARBELLA

Made by Northwood, this scarce tumbler is 3½" high. It has a collar base and has for a design, 14 panels on the interior. The Northwood "N" is on the inside of the base. The coloring is a strong, pure vaseline, but other colors may exist.

BARBER BOTTLE

While the drawing in the Hartung books vary somewhat from the actual bottle, the pattern isn't hard to confirm. Standing over 11" high with good marigold color, the bottle and stopper are trimmed in a black enameling much like Fenton used on some items.

BASKET

Novelty items are a very important area of glass production, and this little item is one of the best known. Standing on four sturdy feet, the Northwood Basket is about 5¾" high and 5" wide. Often the basket is simply round, but sometimes one finds an example that has been pulled into a six-sided shape. Made in a wide range of colors including marigold, purple, vaseline, cobalt, ice green, ice blue, aqua, and white. This is a popular pattern.

BASKETWEAVE (NORTHWOOD)

Here's a secondary Northwood pattern found often on bowls and now and then on compotes and bonbons. It's a pretty, all-over filler that does the job.

BASKETWEAVE AND CABLE

Much like the Shell and Jewel breakfast set from the same company, the Westmoreland Basketweave and Cable is a seldom-found pattern and surely must have been made in limited amounts. The mold work is excellent, and the luster is satisfactory. Colors are marigold (often pale), amethyst, green, and rarely white.

BEADED ACANTHUS

It's hard to believe this outstanding pattern was made in this one shape only, but to date I've heard of no other. This milk pitcher, like the Poinsettia, measures 7" high and has a base diameter of 3¾". It is found mostly on marigold glass or smoke, but a very outstanding green exists, and I suspect amethyst is also a possibility. The coloring is usually quite good, and the iridescence is what one might expect from the Imperial Company.

BEADED BAND AND OCTAGON LAMP

Here is a seldom-seen oil lamp that is really very attractive. The coloring is adequate but watery, indicating 1920's production. It was reportedly made in two sizes, 7½" and 9¾", but I can't confirm this. The maker is unknown.

Banded Rib

Basketweave (Northwood)

Banded Grape and Leaf

Basket

Beaded Acanthus

Barbella

**Beaded Band
and
Octagon Lamp**

Basketweave and Cable

Barber Bottle

BEADED BASKET

While the beaded basket is, in many respects, just as attractive as the footed Northwood version and less expensive, it can be found with the upper edge flared or flattened down. It has been seen in several colors including marigold, blue, amethyst, lavender, smoke, vaseline, and white. Green has now been reported, but not confirmed at this time.

BEADED BULL'S EYE

There are several variations of this vase pattern often caused by the "pulling" or "slinging" to obtain height. Nevertheless, the obvious rows of bull's eyes on the upper edge serve to establish identity. Found mostly in marigold, these Imperial vases are not easily found.

BEADED CABLE

The Beaded Cable rose bowl has long been a favorite with collectors for it is a simple yet strong design made with all the famous Northwood quality. Usually about 4" high, these rose bowls stand on three sturdy legs. The prominent cable intertwines around the middle and is, of course, edged by beads. Nearly all pieces are marked and are made in a wide variety of colors. Of course, these pieces are sometimes opened out to become a candy dish, like many Northwood footed items.

BEADED PANELS AND GRAPES

Reportedly made in Czechoslovakia, this 4½" tumbler has beaded panels that remind one of the old Holly Amber design. Three panels feature grapes and leaves that drop from a band of vines, leaves, and grape clusters. Marigold is the only color I'm aware of, but others may exist.

BEADED PANELS COMPOTE

This little beauty was made by the Dugan/Diamond company and can be found in marigold, amethyst, a rare milk glass with a vaseline finish, and the peach opal finish shown. It isn't rare but certainly is a pretty addition to any collection.

BEADED SHELL

Known also in custard glass, Beaded Shell is one of the older Dugan patterns and is found in a variety of shapes, including berry sets, table sets, water sets, and mugs. Colors are purple, blue, green, marigold, and white with blue and purple somewhat more easily found.

BEADED SPEARS

Beaded spears is a scarce water set, made in Czechoslovakia for export and shipped to many areas of the world. The set shown lives in Australia. Marigold is the only reported color, but tumblers are known in two sizes (shown is the flared lemonade version). The design of peaks, prisms and plain circles is unique and very pretty.

BEADED STAR

Most often found on a smallish bowl shape shown, this is a pattern that doesn't receive many raves, nor does it especially deserve them. It is found on rose bowls, and a plate shape also in marigold and amethyst.

Beaded Star

Beaded Panels and Grapes

Beaded Basket

Beaded Bull's Eye

Beaded Cable

Beaded Panels Compote

Beaded Shell

Beaded Spears

BEADED SWIRL

This Scandinavian pattern can be found in a covered butter dish, sugar, and milk pitcher as well as the compote shown. Colors are marigold and blue, much like the Grand Thistle water set that was made in Finland, and this pattern may well be from the same concern.

BEADS

It's really a shame this pattern isn't found more often and is restricted to the exterior of average-size bowls, because it is a well-balanced, attractive item, especially on vivid colors. Combining three motifs – daisy-like flowers, petalish blooms and beads – this pattern, while not rare, is certainly not plentiful and is a desirable Northwood item.

BEARDED BERRY

One of Fenton's primary exterior patterns the Bearded Berry pattern has six branches of berries and leaves. The berries themselves have small whisker-like lines from their ends. Tying all the bunches together is a thin cable-like line above them, circling the bowl.

BEAUTY BUD VASE

This Dugan pattern was a popular one, which was made in large runs and is easily found today, mostly in marigold. You will notice that except for the missing limbs around the base, it is exactly like the Twigs vase from the same maker.

BELL FLOWER

If you will compare this handled compote with the Bells and Beads pattern shown elsewhere in this book you might think they were the same; however, they are not. On the latter the flowers are open while on this compote they are viewed from the side, and their number and placement are different. In addition, the Bell and Beads design swirls outward from the center while this compote has a design rimming its bowl. It is, however, Dugan and the coloring shown is a good cobalt blue.

BEE ORNAMENT

This tiny solid glass ornament is only about 1½" long and reminds me of the famous Butterfly ornaments that were made to attach to flower arrangements. The Bee Ornament has been found in marigold, and I finally got to hold one of the scarce white ones at an ACGA Convention this year. I've been told Westmoreland is the maker.

BEETLE ASHTRAY

Unusual is the word for this rare ashtray. It was made by the Regolleau Christalerias Company of Buenos Aires, Argentina around 1925. As you can see, the mold work is outstanding, and the cobalt blue coloring is excellent. To date only two of these have been reported.

BELLAIRE SOUVENIR

This curious bowl measures 7" in diameter and is roughly 2½" deep. The lettering and little bell are all interior work while the fine ribbing is on the outside. Just when this bowl was given, or why it remains is a mystery to me, but I'm quite sure it would have great appeal to the collector of lettered glass. This was made by Imperial.

BELLS AND BEADS

Shards of this pattern turned up in the Helman digs, so we know this is another Dugan pattern. Found in small bowls, plates, hat shapes, nappies, compotes, and a handled gravy boat, Bells and Beads' colors are marigold, blue, amethyst, green, and peach opalescent.

Beetle Ashtray

Bee Ornament

22

Beaded Swirl

**Beauty
Bud Vase**

Beads

Beaded Berry

Bellaire Souvenirs

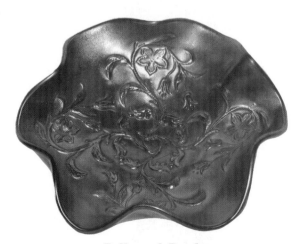

Bells and Beads

Bell Flower

23

BERNHEIMER BOWL

The only difference between this much sought bowl and the famous Millersburg Many Stars pattern is, of course, the advertising center, consisting of a small star and the words: Bernheimer Brothers. This replaces the usual large star and demonstrates how a clever mold designer can capitalize on a good design. While not nearly as plentiful as the Many Stars bowls, the Bernheimer bowls are found in blue only.

BIG BASKETWEAVE

This Dugan pattern is found on the exterior of Fanciful and Round-Up bowls, the base pattern for the Persian Garden two-piece fruit bowls and for vases as shown, as well as a miniature handled basket. Colors are marigold, amethyst, blue, peach opalescent, and white.

BIG FISH

Rarer than the Trout and Fly pieces that were also made by the Millersburg company, the Big Fish has more realistic mold work. It can be found in a host of shapes; round, tri-cornered, square, and tightly ruffled. Colors are the usual Millersburg ones; marigold, amethyst, green, vaseline, and rarely clambroth.

BIG THISTLE PUNCH BOWL

I could spend pages raving about this very superb Millersburg rarity, but let me simply say I consider it the most beautiful of all the Carnival glass punch bowls. Two are known, and both are amethyst. One has a flared top while the other is straight up. Needless to say, the glass is clear, the mold work superior, and the iridescence beyond belief.

BIRD WITH GRAPES

Larger than the Woodpecker wall vase, the Bird with Grapes vase is also called Cockatoo. The coloring tends to be somewhat amberish, and the flat back has a hole to attach it to a wall hook. The maker is unknown, at least to me.

BIRDS AND CHERRIES

Found quite often on bonbons and compotes, this realistic Fenton pattern is sometimes found on rare berry sets and very rare plates. The birds, five in number, remind me of grackles. I've heard of this pattern in marigold, blue, green, amethyst, white, pastel-marigold, and vaseline.

BLACKBERRY (FENTON)

Found often as an interior pattern on the open-edge, basketweave, hat-shape Fenton produced in great numbers, Blackberry is a very realistic pattern, gracefully molded around the walls of the hat. It is known in many colors including marigold, cobalt blue, green, amethyst, ice blue, ice green, vaseline, and red. The example shown is blue with marigold open-edge.

BLACKBERRY (FENTON)

This rare Fenton whimsey is shaped from the two-row open edge basket with Blackberry pattern interior. The vase has been shaped into a 8¼" high beauty. The only color reported is a beautiful cobalt blue, but others may certainly exist.

Bernheimer Bowl

Big Basketweave

Big Fish

Big Thistle Punch Bowl

Bird With Grapes

Birds and Cherries

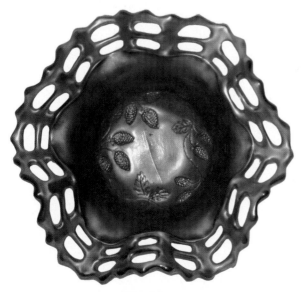

Blackberry

Blackberry Whimsey Vase

BLACKBERRY (NORTHWOOD)

While several companies had a try at a Blackberry pattern, Northwood's is one of the better ones and quite distinctive. The pattern covers most of the allowed space, be it the interior of a 6" compote or an 8½" footed bowl. Combined with the latter is often a pattern called Daisy and Plume. The colors are marigold, purple, green, and white.

BLACKBERRY BANDED

Like many Fenton patterns, Blackberry Banded is limited to the hat shape and without an exterior pattern. These ruffled hats are usually between 3¼" and 3¾" high with a base diameter of 2½". Found mostly in marigold or cobalt blue, they are rarely found in green and milk glass with marigold iridization.

BLACKBERRY BLOCK

This is one of the better Fenton water set patterns and can be found in marigold, blue, amethyst, green, and rarely white. The all-over pattern of wire-like squares with berries and leaves vining over them is very pleasing.

BLACKBERRY BRAMBLE

A very available pattern on bowls and compotes. Blackberry Bramble is a very close cousin to the Fenton Blackberry pattern but has more leaves, berries, and thorny branches. The bowls are rather small with diameters of 6" to 8¼", and the compotes are of average size. Colors are marigold, green, and cobalt blue, but others may certainly exist.

BLACKBERRY SPRAY

I've always felt this a poorly designed pattern, but others may disagree. There isn't too much graceful about the four separate branches, and the fruit isn't spectacular. Nevertheless, it can be found on hat shapes, bonbons, and compotes in marigold, cobalt blue, green, amethyst, aqua, and red. The examples of aqua I have seen do not have opalescence.

BLACKBERRY WREATH

In all the years I've been writing about glass, this pattern along with its sister pattern of Grape Wreath and Strawberry Wreath have provoked the most inquiry. Just remember Blackberry Wreath always has a berry and four leaves in the center of the design. Colors are typical Millersburg ones: marigold, green, amethyst, vaseline, and clambroth, the large bowl in a rare blue.

Blackberry

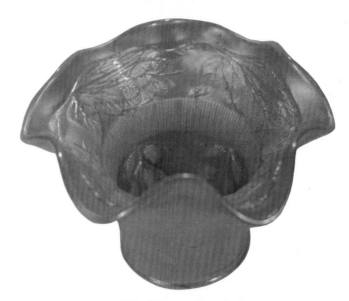

Blackberry Banded

Blackberry Block

Blackberry Bramble

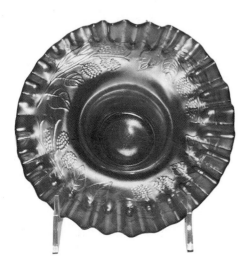

Blackberry Spray

Blackberry Wreath

BLACK BOTTOM (FENTON)

This very Art Deco little candy jar once had a lid but it has long since been separated. These are shown in the old Fenton ads in a host of colors in stretch glass, but this is the first one I've seen in marigold. The base has a spray-painted finish that has been then fired to keep its black color.

BLOCKS AND ARCHES

Often confused with the very similar Ranger pattern, Blocks and Arches is really an Australian design found only on tumblers and pitchers like the one shown. Colors are marigold and amethyst.

Blocks and Arches

BLOSSOMS AND BAND

Blossoms and Band is not a very distinguished pattern, and its origin is questionable. Found primarily on berry sets in marigold, a car vase is also known, as shown. The design is quite simple with a row of blossoms, stems and leaves above a band of thumbprints and prisms. The color has a good deal of pink in the marigold, much like English glass. The mold work is adequate but far from outstanding. Needless to say, this is not the same pattern as that found on the Millersburg Wild Rose lamps that are often called by the same name. This is possibly an Imperial pattern.

BLOSSOMTIME

Even if this outstanding compote was not marked, we'd surely assign it to the Northwood company because it is so typical of their work. The flowers, the thorny branches (twisted into a geometrical overlapping star), and the curling little branchlets are all nicely done and are stippled, except for the branchlets. The background is plain and contrasts nicely. Blossomtime is combined with an exterior pattern called Wild Flower and is found in marigold, purple, green, and pastels. The stem is quite unusual, being twisted with a screw-like pattern. Blossomtime is a scarce pattern and always brings top dollar.

BLOWN CANDLESTICK

Very thin and hollow from the base to the bottom of the candleholder, this European candlestick is quite tall (12¼") and has the even light lustre associated with items from the continent. Other colors may exist, but I haven't heard of them.

BLUEBERRY

May I say in the beginning, I'm quite prejudiced about this Fenton water set for I think it is outstanding in both design and execution. What a shame it wasn't made in other shapes such as a table set. I've heard of Blueberry in marigold, cobalt blue, and white only, but that doesn't mean it wasn't made in other colors.

BOOKER MUG

This cutie is in the collection of Carl and Eunice Booker, so I've named it after them. It is smaller than most, has a beautiful spray of enameled flowers and an amethyst handle! It is probably European.

BO PEEP MUG AND PLATE

While the Bo Peep mug is simply scarce, the plate is a quite rare item, seldom sold or traded from one collection to another. The color is good marigold and reminds us of that found on most of the Fenton Kitten items. Of course, all children's items in glass were subjected to great loss through breakage, but I doubt if large amounts of the Bo Peep pattern were made in the beginning. So, of course, small quantities have survived.

BORDER PLANTS

Typical of many Dugan-Diamond designs this dome-based bowl (also found in a collar base) has a large central flower design bordered by stippling and a series of stemmed flowers that alternate with a series of three-leafed designs. Colors are amethyst, lavender, and the usual peach opalescent.

Black Bottom (Fenton)

Blossomtime

Blossoms and Band

Blueberry

Bo Peep Mug and Plate

Blown Candlestick

Booker Mug

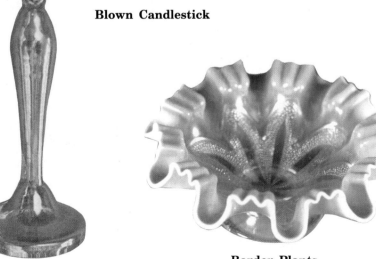

Border Plants

29

BOUQUET

If you look quite closely at this bulbous water set, you'll notice several common devices used by the Fenton company, such as fillers of scales surrounding an embroidery ring. No other shapes exist, and the water set is found in marigold, blue, and white. The mold work is quite good, and the colors are typically Fenton.

BOUTONNIERE

This little beauty is a Millersburg product. It usually has a fine radium finish and is most often seen in amethyst. And although I haven't seen one, I've been told there is a variation sometimes found with a different stem and base. Boutonniere is also found in marigold and green.

HEISEY BREAKFAST SET

While it isn't so marked, I'd guess this very attractive marigold breakfast set was a Heisey product. The coloring is very dark and rich, and the handles are like those on known Heisey products.

BROCADED ACORNS

The lacy effects of all these brocaded patterns by the Fostoria company are a joy to behold. This was achieved by an acid cutback process, and after the iridescence was fired a gold edging was applied. Found in several shapes, Brocaded Acorns was made in pink, white, ice green, ice blue, and vaseline.

BROCADED DAFFODILS

Like the other brocaded patterns, this was made by Fostoria. The shape is a 7½" x 6½" handled bowl in pink. The lovely pattern consists of beautifully realistic daffodils, leaf swirls, and small star fillers.

BROCADED PALMS

Shown is one example of Fostoria's Brocaded series, a large handled cake plate in Brocaded Palms pattern. As you can see, the design is created with an acid cutback effect on the glass before iridization, and the edges are gold trimmed. All the patterns are generally handled in this manner, and colors found include ice green, ice blue, pink, white, and a lovely and rare rose shade, as well as a rare vaseline color.

Brocaded Acorns

Bouquet

Boutonniere

Heisey Breakfast Set

Brocaded Daffodils

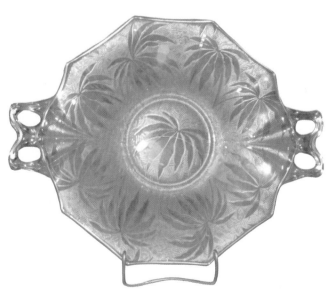

Brocaded Palms

31

BROKEN ARCHES

Broken Arches is a beautiful geometric Imperial pattern found only in punch sets of rather stately size. Not only is the coloring good, but the mold work is outstanding. The colors are marigold and amethyst. Often there is a silver sheen to the latter which detracts from its beauty, but when a set is found without this gunmetal look, the result is breathtaking. The marigold set is more common and sells for much less than amethyst. A green Broken Arches would be a great rarity.

BROOKLYN BOTTLE

I suspect this beautiful 9⅝" cruet may be of European origin. The glass is very thin, and the non-iridized handle and stopper are very attractive amethyst glass.

BROOKLYN BRIDGE

Like the Pony bowl pattern, this beautiful advertising bowl apparently came from the Dugan factory. The only color reported is marigold, and the mold work is outstanding. Brooklyn Bridge is a scarce and desirable pattern. A rare unlettered example is also known.

BULL'S EYE AND LEAVES

Confined to the exterior of bowls and found mostly in green or marigold, this pattern is a trifle too busy to be very effective and is certainly not one of Northwood's better efforts. All in all, there are five motifs, including leaves, beads, circles, fishnet, and a petal grouping. Although each appears on other Northwood products, not in this combination.

BULL'S EYE AND LOOP

This is one of the nicer small Millersburg vases. It has four rows of loops with bull's-eyes appearing on alternating loops in a staggered pattern. It is quite rare and usually brings a premium price. All examples I've seen had a radium finish, and colors known are marigold, amethyst, and green.

BUTTERFLIES

This outstanding Fenton pattern is found only on bonbons often flattened into a card tray shape. The colors are very good with eight butterflies around the edges and one in the center. The exterior carries a typical wide panel pattern and often is found with advertising on the base. Colors are marigold, cobalt blue, green, amethyst, and white. At least these are the ones about which I've heard.

BUTTERFLIES AND WARATAH

Normally seen in the compote shape, this one has been flattened into a very stylish footed cake stand. The beautiful purple is typical of Australian Carnival glass and can stand with the best. It is also found in marigold.

Bull's Eye and Loop

Broken Arches

Brooklyn Bottle

Brooklyn Bridge

Bull's Eye and Leaves

Butterflies

Butterflies and Waratah

BUTTERFLY (NORTHWOOD)

This popular Northwood bonbon pattern shows a well-designed butterfly with rays eminating from the center. The usual exterior is plain but a rare "threaded" exterior can sometimes be found. Colors are marigold, amethyst, blue, purple, green, electric blue, ice blue, lavender and smoke.

BUTTERFLY BOWER

The interior design of a stippled central butterfly flanked by trellis work and flora is hard to see. However, the exterior's S-Band pattern shows quite well. This deep bowl is 6½" across and stands 3" tall. It can be found in marigold and purple. The rim has a bullet edge. Manufactured in Australia.

BUTTERFLY LAMP

Named for the wing-like projections of the metal base, this very unusual lamp stands approximately 13" tall to the burner. The very rich marigold font has a series of stylized designs around the curving that resemble the Art Deco bowl shown elsewhere in this book, and I suspect the lamp may well be from England also.

BUTTERFLY TUMBLER

The tumbler shown is one of the top prizes in tumbler collecting. The color is an unusual amber-marigold and the design, four butterflies, a stippled background and bands of circles at top and bottom is very pretty. It was made by U.S. Glass. In addition to the one marigold example, four smoky-olive ones have been found.

BUTTERFLY AND BERRY

One of Fenton's prime patterns, found on a large array of shapes including footed berry sets, table sets, water sets, a hatpin holder, vase whimseys, spittoon whimsey, nutbowl whimsey and a centerpiece whimsey. Colors are marigold, cobalt blue, green, amethyst, red, white, and a very rare Nile green opalescent shown.

BUTTERFLY AND CORN VASE

This interesting vase is rare for several reasons, and it is a pleasure to show it here. First is the pattern which has been reported only twice in the past few years. Both examples are identical in size (5⅞" tall and 2¾" base diameter). Secondly, the base color of the glass is vaseline with a marigold finish. While this coloring is found rarely on both Millersburg and Northwood items, I believe the Butterfly and Corn vase to be a product of the latter.

BUTTERFLY AND FERN

Made by the Fenton Art Glass Company, this is a very pretty water set. Colors are marigold, amethyst, green, and blue and all are Fenton at its best with outstanding moldwork and rich coloring.

BUTTERFLY AND TULIP

Make no mistake about it, this is a very impressive Dugan pattern. The bowl is large, the glass heavy and the mold work exceptional. Found in either marigold or purple, this footed jewel has the famous Feather Scroll for an exterior pattern. Typically, the shallower the bowl, the more money it brings with the purple bringing many times the price of the underrated marigold.

Butterfly Bower

S-Band Exterior

Butterfly and Berry

Butterfly (Northwood)

Butterfly Lamp

Butterfly Tumbler

Butterfly and Corn Vase

Butterfly and Fern

Butterfly and Tulip

BUTTERFLY ORNAMENT

I'm told this interesting bit of glass was made as a giveaway item and attached to bonbons, baskets, and compotes by a bit of putty when purchasers visited the Fenton factory. This would certainly explain the scarcity of the Butterfly ornament for few are around today. Colors I've heard about are marigold, amethyst, cobalt blue, ice blue, white, and green.

BUTTERFLY PINTRAY

While most of these are seen in marigold, often pale and washed out, this example is the pastel version with pink wings and blue body and is a richly iridized beauty. It measure 8" across and is 7" tall. These were made by the same company that made the Tall Hats.

BUTTERMILK GOBLET

Exactly like the Iris goblet also made by Fenton, the plainer Buttermilk Goblet is a real beauty and rather hard to find, especially in green or amethyst. As you can see, the iridescence is on the interior of the goblet only, and the stem is the same as the Fenton Vintage compotes.

BUTTON AND DAISY HAT

Again, here is an item that has been reproduced in every type of glass known, but the example shown is old and original and has resided in one of the major Carnival glass collections in the country for many years. Like so many of the miniature novelty items, the coloring is a beautiful clambroth with lots of highlights. Manufacturer unknown.

BUZZ SAW CRUET

This eagerly hunted Cambridge novelty always brings top dollar when it comes up for sale. Found in two sizes, the colors seen are green and marigold. The mold work is fantastic as is the iridescence. Oddly, the base shows a pontil mark indicating the cruet was blown into a mold. Again, these were probably designed as container for some liquid, but just what, we can't say.

CACTUS (MILLERSBURG)

This Rays and Ribbons exterior reminds me of the famous Hobstar and Feather pattern with its incised fans, edged with needles and the hobstars above. In addition, there is a small file filler near the base, merging into a diamond where the feathers meet.

CAMBRIDGE #2351

This Cambridge near-cut pattern was made in a host of shapes in crystal, but in iridized glass only the punch set pieces and a bowl have been reported so far. The punch set was advertised in marigold, amethyst, and green, and the one reported bowl is also green.

CANADA DRY BOTTLE

Used in the mid-20's, the bottle shown says "Canada Dry Incorporated — Gingerale #13" on the base. It was used for a product from that company called "Sparkling Orangeade" and has remarkably good iridization for a throw-away bottle.

CANDLE VASE

While I know nothing about this unusually-shaped vase except that it is 9½" tall, I can say with some certainty it was probably shaped in several other ways in many instances. I haven't had any other colors reported, but they may exist.

CANE

One of the older Imperial patterns, Cane is found on wine goblets, bowls of various sizes and pickle dishes. The coloring is nearly always a strong marigold, but the bowl has been seen on smoke, and I'm sure amethyst is a possibility. Cane is not one of the more desirable Imperial patterns and is readily available, especially on bowls; however, a rare color would improve the desirability of this pattern.

Button and Daisy Hat

Butterfly Ornament

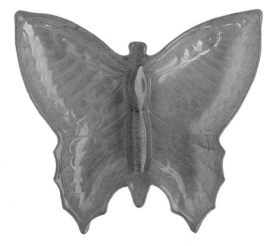

Butterfly Pintray

Cambridge #2351

Cactus (Millersburg)

Candle Vase

Buzz Saw Cruet

Canada Dry Bottle

Buttermilk Goblet

Cane

CANE AND SCROLL (SEA THISTLE)

I'd guess there are other shapes around in this pattern, but the small creamer shown is the only one I've seen so far. As you can see, there are four busy patterns competing with one another but their combination isn't unattractive. The marigold has a reddish hue.

CANNON BALL VARIANT

While the shape of this Fenton water set is the same as the Cherry and Blossom usually found in cobalt, this marigold version has a much different enameled design. The tumblers have an interior wide panel design, and I'm sure this is quite a scarce item.

CAPTIVE ROSE

Captive Rose is a very familiar decorative pattern found in bowls, bonbons, compotes, and occasional plates in colors of marigold, cobalt blue, green, amethyst, amber, and smoke. The design is a combination of embroidery circles, scales, and diamond stitches and is a tribute to the mold maker's art. The roses are like finely stitched quilt work. Manufactured by Fenton.

CARNIVAL BEADS

I have always resisted showing strands of beads before, even though they are very collectible and quite attractive, but when Lee Briix sent this very interesting photo using a Diamond Point Columns vase as a prop, I changed my mind. Most of these beads were made in smaller glass factories or in Europe.

CAROLINA DOGWOOD

This very interesting Westmoreland pattern is rather hard to find and the few examples I've seen have all been on milk glass base with either a marigold luster or a beautiful bright aqua finish. The design is fairly good, featuring a series of six dogwood sprays around the bowl with a single blossom in the center – simple but effective.

CARTWHEEL COMPOTE

Not only is this flash-iridized compote marked, it is marked twice – on the base and on the bowl. The color is pale as are most items from the Heisey Company but quite pretty.

CATHEDRAL (CURVED STAR)

After years of uncertainty and guessing, we've traced this pattern to Sweden and the Eda Glassworks. Several shapes exist including a chalice, pitcher, bowl, flower holder, epergne, compote, butter dish, creamer, open sugar, two-piece fruit bowl, and a rare rose bowl. Colors are marigold and blue.

CENTRAL SHOE STORE

Perhaps this is one of the more scarce Northwood advertising pieces and like most it is a shallow bowl, nearly 6" in diameter. Its lettering reads "Compliments of the Central Shoe Store – Corner of Collinsville and St. Louis Avenues – East St. Louis, Illinois." The floral sprays are much like others used on similar pieces from the Northwood Company.

Central Shoe Store

Carnival Beads

38

Cane and Scroll

Cannon Ball Variant

Captive Rose

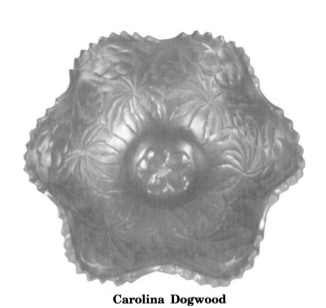

Carolina Dogwood

Cartwheel Compote

Cathedral (Curved Star)

CHATELAINE

Most of the authorities in the field agree this very rare, beautiful water set pattern is an Imperial item. However, I'm listing it as a questionable one because I've seen no proof of its origin. Of course, I can't emphasize too strongly its quality or scarcity, and the selling price on the few examples to be sold publicly verify this. The only color I've heard of is a deep rich purple.

CHECKERBOARD

It has been pretty well established that Checkerboard was a Westmoreland product, which partially explains its rarity today. I've seen about half a dozen tumblers over the years, but the pitcher shown is one of only three known to exist. The color, iridescence, and mold work are outstanding. A rare goblet is occasionally found iridized.

CHECKERBOARD PANELS

Like so many European flat shallow bowls this previously unlisted bowl pattern is really a series of compatible fillers; rows of file alternating with raided bands with borders at top and bottom of file edging. I suspect it may be English but can't be sure. The interior is plain and the color very rich.

CHERRY (DUGAN)

The Dugan-Diamond version of the Cherry pattern can be found in berry set pieces, footed bowls that are often quite deep, a 6" plate, and a very rare cruet in white carnival. Other colors are marigold, amethyst, and peach opalescent. Sometimes the exterior has the Jeweled Heart pattern but not always.

CHERRY (MILLERSBURG)

Sometimes called "Hanging Cherries" this very realistic pattern is simply the best of cherry patterns in all of carnival glass. It can be found in many bowl sizes, a water set, a table set, rare plates, a rare compote, a milk pitcher, and several whimsey shapes. Colors are marigold, amethyst, green, blue, clambroth, and vaseline.

CHERRY AND CABLE

Sometimes called "Cherry and Thumbprint," this is a very difficult Northwood product to locate, and to date I've seen one tumbler, one pitcher, a table set, and a small berry bowl. The pattern is very much a typical Northwood design and reminds one of the famous Northwood Peach, especially in the shape of the butter dish bottom which carries the same exterior base pattern as the Prisms compote. I know of no colors except a good rich marigold, but others may certainly exist.

CHERRY CHAIN

Cherry Chain is a close relative of the Leaf Chain pattern shown elsewhere in this book. Found on bowls, plates, and bonbons, this all-over pattern is well done and effective. The colors are marigold, blue, green, amethyst, and white. There is an extremely rare example of this pattern on a red slag base glass, and it is the only one I've heard about. There is a variant also.

Checkerboard Panels

Chatelaine

Checkerboard Water Set

Cherry (Dugan)

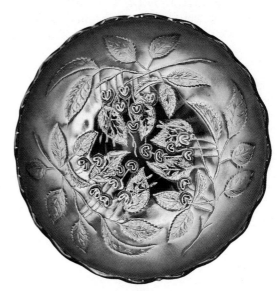

Cherry (Millersburg)

Cherry and Cable

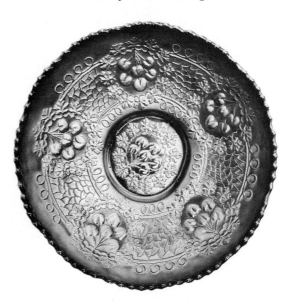

Cherry Chain

CHERRY CIRCLES

This Fenton piece employs a pattern of fruit combined with a scales pattern, the latter being a favorite filler device at the Fenton factory. Cherry Circles is best known in large bonbons, but compotes, bowls, and occasional plates do exist in marigold, cobalt blue, green, amethyst, white, and red.

CHERRY/HOBNAIL (MILLERSBURG)

On comparison, the interior cherry design varies enough from the regular Millersburg Cherry to show its separate example with the hobnail exterior. These bowls are quite rare and are found in marigold, amethyst and blue and measure roughly 9" in diameter. A 5" bowl can also be found, both with and without the hobnail exterior.

CHRISTMAS COMPOTE

What an elegant large compote this is in either purple or marigold. The interior has a fine rib radiating from the center with holly and leaves while the exterior sports the same holly and leaves with four partial poinsettias near the rim. The Christmas Compote measures 9½" across the rim, is 5½" tall, and has a base diameter of 5½". The maker has not yet been confirmed.

CHRYSANTHEMUM

For years I thought this might be an Imperial pattern for it so reminded me of the Windmill pattern, but it really is Fenton. Found on large bowls, either footed or flat, Chrysanthemum is known in marigold, blue, green, ice green, white, and a very beautiful red.

CHRYSANTHEMUM DRAPE LAMP

This beauty would grace any glass collection. As you can see, the font is beautifully iridized and has been found in pink glass as well as white. Strangely, most of these lamps have been found in Australia, but the maker is, thus far, unknown.

CIRCLE SCROLL

Dugan's Circle Scroll is not an easy pattern to find, especially in the water sets, hat shape, and vase whimseys. Other shapes known are berry sets, compotes, creamers, and spooners. The colors I've seen are marigold and purple, but certainly others may exist with cobalt a strong possibility.

CLASSIC ARTS

What an interesting pattern this is. It is available in a covered powder jar, a rose bowl, a 7" celery vase, and a rare 10" vase. The design is very "Greek" in feeling, and the tiny figures quite clear. The green paint gives an antiquing effect which adds greatly to the beauty. It was made in Czechoslovakia.

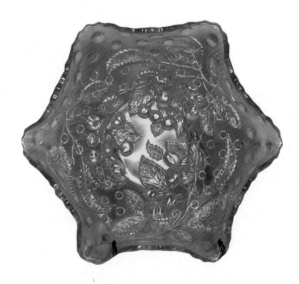

Cherry/Hobnail (Millersburg)

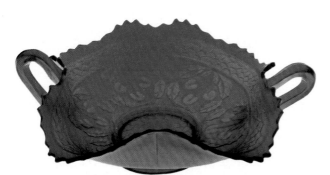

Cherry Circle

Christmas Compote

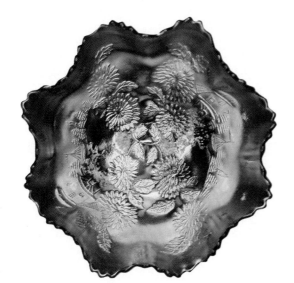

Chrysanthemum

Chrysanthemum Drape Lamp

Classic Arts

Circle Scroll

CLEVELAND MEMORIAL TRAY

Undoubtedly made to celebrate Cleveland's centennial birthday, this cigar ashtray depicts the statue of Garfield, his tomb in Lake View cemetery, the Soldiers and Sailors Monument, the Superior Street viaduct, and the Cleveland Chamber of Commerce building. The coloring and iridescence are typically Millersburg, and the mold work compares favorably with that of the Courthouse bowl. A real treasure for any glass collector. Found also in amethyst.

COAL BUCKET (U.S. GLASS)

These rather rare little match holders can be found in both marigold and green and are a miniature collector's dream come true. Few are around, and they bring high prices when sold.

COBBLESTONES

This simple Imperial pattern is not often seen, but certainly is a nice item when encountered. Found on bowls of various sizes – often with Arcs as an exterior pattern. Cobblestones is also found on handled bonbons where a beautiful radium finish is often present, and the exterior is honeycombed! A curious circumstance to say the least! The colors are marigold, green, blue, amethyst, and amber. There is also a variant, as well as a rare plate.

COIN DOT (FENTON)

This pattern is fairly common on medium size bowls but can sometimes be found on plates and a handled basket whimsey. The colors are marigold, cobalt blue, green, amethyst, and red, but not all shapes are found in all colors. The bowl and rose bowl are the only shapes reported in red.

COIN DOT (WESTMORELAND)

Once these were all thought to be made only by the Fenton company. The variations and some timely research have disclosed that the rose bowl shown, as well as a compote shape and bowl from which the rose bowl was pulled, are from the Westmoreland plant. Colors are marigold, amethyst, green, milk-glass iridized, blue milk-glass iridized, teal, and aqua opalescent.

COIN SPOT

This undistinguished little Dugan compote holds a dear spot in my heart for it was the first piece of Carnival glass we ever owned. Made in opalescent glass also, in Carnival glass it is found in marigold, green, purple, peach, white, and blue. The design is simple, consisting of alternate rows of indented stippled ovals and plain, flat panels. The stem is rather ornate with a finial placed midway down. Often in marigold, the stem remains clear glass.

COLONIAL

Imperial's Colonial pattern is simply one version of wide paneling. The shapes I've heard about are vases, toothpick holders, open sugars, candlesticks and the handled lemonade goblet shown. Colors are marigold, green, and purple, usually of the very rich nature.

COLONIAL LADY

Just look at the color on this rare vase! It certainly rivals Tiffany and only proves Imperial was topped by no one in purple glass. Colonial Lady stands 5¾" tall and has a base diameter of 2¾". I've heard of no other color except marigold, but certainly others may exist. Needless to say, these are not plentiful.

COLONIAL VARIANT

Perhaps this isn't really a variant, but with the lid it looks different. It was made by Imperial and is found in marigold and sometimes clear Carnival.

Coin Spot

Colonial Variant

44

Cleveland Memorial Tray

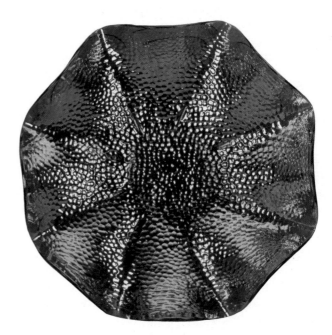

Cobblestone

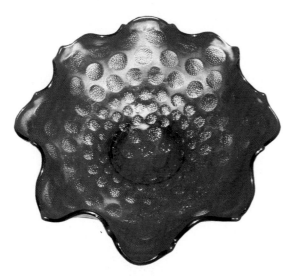

Coin Dot (Fenton)

**Coin Dot Rosebowl
(Westmoreland)**

Colonial Lady

Coal Bucket (U.S. Glass)

Colonial

COLUMBIA

Made first in crystal, Columbia is found in Carnival glass on compotes and vase shapes, all from the same mold. The coloring is usually marigold, but amethyst and green are known. While the simplicity of Columbia may not be appreciated by some collectors, it certainly had its place in the history of the glass field and should be awarded its just dues. Manufactured by Imperial. Shown in a rare rose bowl whimsey.

COMPASS

A Dugan pattern of hobstars, hexagons, and other geometric designs that manages to fill nearly all the allowed space. Compass is found on exteriors of Dugan Heavy Grape bowls, and the example shown demonstrates why peach opalescent is such a collected color.

COMPOTE VASE

Approximately 6" tall, this well done stemmed piece is found in all the standard colors but is mostly seen in amethyst or green. Often, the stem is not iridized, but the luster on the rest of the compote vase more than makes up for it. I believe it to be a Dugan product, since I catalog pieces of it from the Dugan digs.

CONCAVE DIAMOND

Most of us have seen the Concave Diamond water sets in ice blue and tumblers in vaseline, but I hadn't seen another shape until encountering this quite rare pickle caster in a beautiful marigold. That brought back a memory of finding a small fragment of this pattern in the Dugan shards from the 1975 Indiana, PA diggings, so I would speculate this rare item originated at that factory. Also known are "tumble-ups" in aqua, marigold, and aqua opalescent.

CONCAVE FLUTE (WESTMORELAND)

This rather plain pattern is attributed to the Westmoreland company and is found as shown on rose bowls and pulled out into a vase shape. Colors I've heard about are marigold, amethyst, and green, but certainly aqua is a possibility.

CONCORD

Even among all the other grape patterns in iridized glass, I'm sure you won't confuse Concord with the others, for the net-like filler that covers the entire surface of the bowls' interior is unique. Found in both bowls and plates, Concord is a very scarce Fenton pattern and is available in marigold, green, amethyst, blue, and amber. It is a collector's favorite and doesn't sell cheaply.

CONE AND TIE

The simple beauty of this very rare tumbler (no pitcher is known) is very obvious; and while most collectors credit it to Imperial, I cannot verify its maker. The coloring is a very outstanding purple on the few examples known, and the selling price only emphasizes its desirability. Rarely does one of these move from one collection to another.

CONNIE (NORTHWOOD)

This beautiful Northwood water set, shaped much like the Swirl tankard from the same company, is a tribute to the decorator's skill. Floral sprays in whites, pinks, and blues nearly cover both pitcher and tumbler, and the iridization, while light and airy is obvious in the photo, giving the set a frosty whiteness.

CONSTELLATION

One of the smaller compotes, the Constellation is 5" tall and about the same size across the rim. It has an exterior pattern called Seafoam which is much like the S-Repeat pattern. The Constellation pattern consists of a large center star with bubble-like dots over the area and a series of raised bars running out to the rim. Colors are marigold, amethyst, peach opalescent, white, and a frosty pearlized finish over vaseline glass.

COOLEEMEE, N.C.

This 9" advertising Heart and Vine plate is a rare one. Only four or five are known, and all are marigold. The plate was sold to promote the J.N. Ledford textile mill company of Cooleemee, NC and undoubtedly was a giveaway item. Today it is a rare and valuable collector's item. Of course, it was made by Fenton.

Concave Flute (Westmoreland)

Cooleemee, N.C.

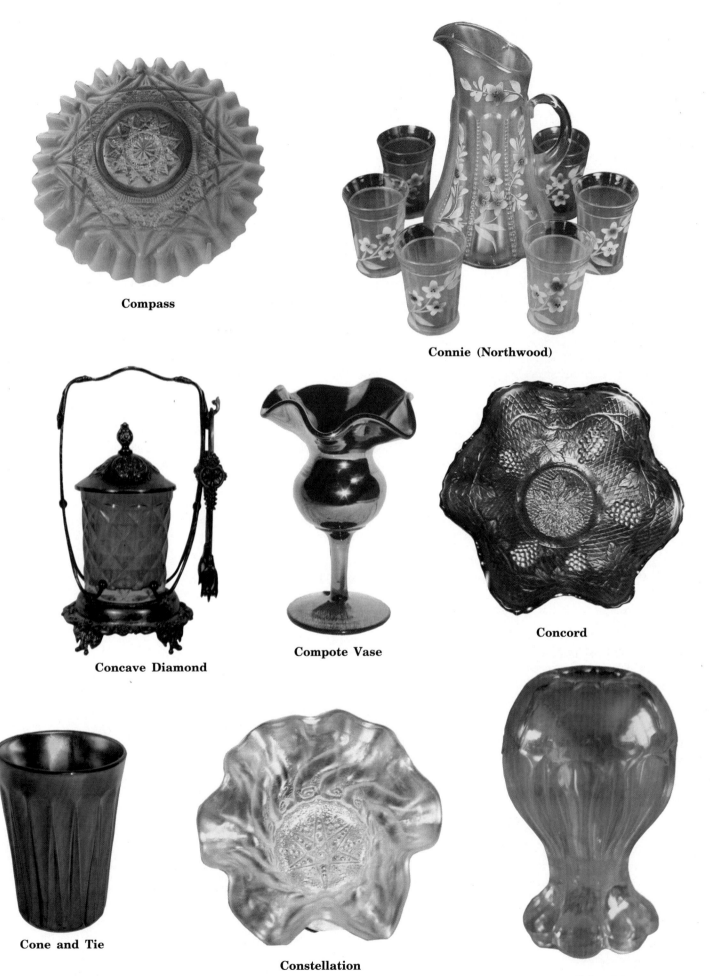

Compass

Connie (Northwood)

Concave Diamond

Compote Vase

Concord

Cone and Tie

Constellation

Columbia

47

CORAL

I'd guess the same designer who gave us the Peter Rabbit and Little Fishes pattern is also responsible for Coral; the bordering device for all three is almost identical. Coral is found in bowls mostly, but a rare plate and rarer compote are known in various colors, including marigold, blue, green, vaseline and white. Manufactured by Fenton.

CORINTH

Long attributed to Northwood, Corinth is another pattern from the Dugan factory. It is found on bowls, vases, and the beautiful banana dish (shown) in marigold, green, amethyst, and peach opalescent. The example shown is 8¼" long and is iridized on the inside only. A variant is credited to Westmoreland.

CORN BOTTLE

Perhaps the Corn Bottle is not an Imperial product, but the beautiful helios green has always made me feel it was. So while I list it as a questionable Imperial product, I stand convinced it is. Colors found are marigold, green, amethyst, and smoke (another indication Imperial made it), all of good quality. The iridescence is usually outstanding as is the mold work. It stands 5" tall and usually has a cork stopper.

CORN CRUET

Since I first saw this years ago, I've been able to learn little about it. The only color reported is the white. Rumor places it in the Dugan line, but I can't be sure.

CORNUCOPIA VASE

Since this vase is pictured in a Jeanette catalog that dates from the 1920's, the maker of this vase is no longer in question. It is 5" tall and 4¼" across the base. It has typical light iridization like most carnival glass of this period. It is similar in design to the Cornucopia candleholder found in white made by Fenton except for the base design and size variation.

CORN VASE

This is one of the better-known Northwood patterns, and that's little wonder because it is such a good one. Usually about 7" tall, there are certain variants known; especially noteworthy is the rare "pulled husk" variant that was made in very limited amounts. The colors are marigold, green, purple, ice blue, ice green, and white. The mold work is outstanding, the color superior, and the glass fine quality – truly a regal vase.

CORNING INSULATOR

While I've never been very excited by insulators, this one has super color and is marked "Corning – Reg. USA Pat." It is only one of several sizes that can be found.

CORONATION (VICTORIAN CROWN)

This bulbous vase shape stands 5" tall and measures 3" across the lip. It has four Victorian crowns around and suspended coronets between. It is, of course, English, but from what company I can't say, nor can I pin down its use except to call it a vase shape.

COSMOS

Green seems to have been the only color in this Millersburg pattern, and small bowls abound; however, an occasional 7" plate can be found. The radium finish is spectacular, and the mold work is outstanding.

COSMOS AND CANE

Made in berry sets, table sets, water sets, a rosebowl, a tall compote, plates, a short compote, and several whimsey shapes, this U.S. Glass pattern is a scarce one. The design, an incised cosmos flower and leaves banded by rows of cane, can be found in marigold, honey-amber, white, and a rare amethyst.

Cornucopia Vase

Corning Insulator

48

Corn Cruet

Coral

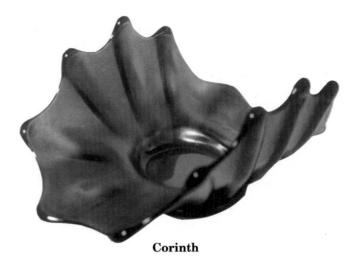

Corinth

Corn Bottle

Coronation (Victorian Crown)

Corn Vase

Cosmos

Cosmos and Cane

COSMOS AND HOBSTAR

There is something special about these fruit bowls on a metal standard, and this is one of the pretty ones. The pattern is one I don't recall seeing before and is a series of diamond panels with hobstars and cosmos blossoms alternating. Above the diamonds are fans and below, half-diamonds filled with a file pattern. The marigold is very rich, but I can't say if other colors were made or just who the maker was.

COSMOS VARIANT

Cosmos Variant is a Fenton pattern found in bowls and occasionally plates (a compote has been reported but I haven't seen it). Amethyst is probably the most available color, but Cosmos Variant can be found in marigold, purple, blue, white, iridized milk glass, and red.

COUNTRY KITCHEN

Used as both a primary and secondary pattern, this hard-to-come-by design is quite artistic. The berry sets are next to impossible to locate, and the four-piece table sets are quite scarce and expensive. These, of course, are all primary uses; however, Country Kitchen is more often seen as an exterior pattern on the lovely Fleur-de-lis bowls where it compliments the latter perfectly. Millersburg seemed to have a flair for creating outstanding near-cut patterns, and this is certainly one of them. A variant is called Potpourri.

COURTHOUSE

The Millersburg Courthouse 7– 7½" bowl is one of the best loved advertising pieces in all of carnival glass. Found only in amethyst, the bowl can be seen in both ruffled and plain shapes, in regular with the lettering: "Millersburg Souvenir – Millersburg Courthouse" or the so-called unlettered bowl with "Millersburg Courthouse," which is much rarer.

COVERED HEN (CHIC)

The Covered Hen is probably the best-recognized piece of English Carnival glass made at the Sowerby Works. Known in a good rich marigold as well as a weak cobalt blue, the Covered Hen is 6⅞" long. The mold work is very good but the color ranges from very good to poor. While reproductions have been reported, my British sources tell me this isn't true, and that no examples have been made since the 1940's.

COVERED FROG

Made by the Co-Operative Flint Glass Company of Beaver Falls, PA this novel covered dish is a stand-out in design and color. It measures 5½" long and 4" tall and has been seen in pastel green, pastel blue, marigold, and rarely amethyst. The eyes are painted black and are very realistic.

COVERED SWAN

This beautiful English pattern is a companion to the Covered Hen and can be found in both marigold and amethyst. It measures 7¾" long, and the neck doesn't touch the back! What a mold maker's achievement! The base is similar to that of the Covered Hen dish. Both are butter dishes.

CRAB CLAW

Crab Claw is indeed a curious near-cut pattern that very seldom enters discussion by collectors but isn't as readily found as many other geometrics from the Imperial Company. Found on bowls of various sizes, a two-piece fruit bowl and base, and scarce water sets, the pattern is most often found in marigold, but amethyst and green are known in the bowl shapes. The design features hobstars, curving file, and diamond devices, and daisy-cut half-flowers, all seemingly interlocking.

Cosmos and Hobstar

Covered Frog

50

Cosmos Variant

Country Kitchen

Courthouse

Covered Hen

Covered Swan

Crab Claw

CRACKLE

Crackle is a very common, very plentiful pattern available in a large variety of shapes, including bowls, covered candy jars, water sets, auto vases, punch sets, plates, spittoons, and a rare window ledge planter. Marigold is certainly the most found color, but green and amethyst do exist on some shapes. And often the color and finish are only adequate. Crackle was mass-produced in great amounts, probably as a premium for promotional giveaways, so I suppose we can't expect it to equal other Carnival items.

CRUCIFIX

Now known to be from the Imperial Glass Company, these rare candlesticks are known in marigold Carnival glass and crystal. The Crucifix candlestick is 9½" tall and is very heavy glass.

CRYSTAL CUT

This beautiful compote comes to us from Australia and as you can see, is a very nice geometric design. Other colors and shapes may exist, but if so, I haven't seen them. It measures 7" in diameter.

CURTAIN OPTIC

Made in the 1920's by the Fenton company, this beautiful pattern is a kissin' cousin to the stretch pieces. It can be found on ice tea sets, guest sets, and possibly other shapes as well. The pastel coloring is a pleasant relief and compliments the opal drapery effect.

CURVED STAR (CATHEDRAL)

Here is another view of this Swedish pattern. Shown is the base of the fruit set which, upended, makes a nifty compote as you can see. It is probably used more often in this capacity than its original purpose.

CUT ARCHES

While I'm fairly confident this is another geometric pattern of English origin, I can't remember even seeing another shape in this pattern. As you can see, it is a banana boat of quite heavy glass. The only color reported is the marigold shown, and it has the typical marigold look of English glass. The deeply cut design would certainly lend itself to a water set.

CUT ARCS

While it is most often found on the exterior of 8"–9" bowls, Fenton's Cut Arcs is occasionally seen on compotes of standard size and a vase whimsey, pulled from the bowl shape. On the example shown the edging is a tight candy-ribbon, and the interior carries no pattern at all.

CUT COSMOS

How I wish I knew who made this beautiful tumbler! The design is top-notch and certainly deserves full recognition, but the maker remains unknown. The only color reported is the marigold shown, and it has the typical marigold look of English glass. The deeply cut design would certainly lend itself to a water set.

CUT FLOWERS

Here is one of the prettiest of all the Jenkins' patterns. Standing 10½" tall, the intaglio work is deep and sharp, and the cut petals show clear glass through the luster, giving a beautiful effect. Most Cut Flowers vases are rather light in color, but the one shown has a rich deep marigold finish. Cut Flowers can also be found in a smoke color.

Cut Arches

Cut Arcs

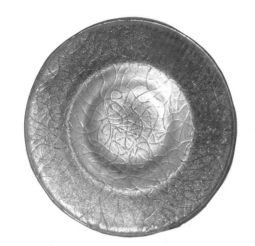

Crackle

Crucifix

Crystal Cut

Curved Star

Cut Cosmos

Cut Flowers

Curtain Optic

CUT OVALS

This Fenton pattern falls into the stretch glass field, but because of the etching it is considered Carnival glass. Known in both candlesticks and bowls, Cut Ovals can be found in marigold, smoke, ice blue, ice green, pink, white, tangerine, lavender, red, and vaseline. The candlesticks are 8½" tall, and the bowls are known in 7", 8", 9", and 10" sizes.

DAHLIA

Make no mistake, Dahlia is an important, often scarce, always expensive, Dugan pattern. The glass is fine quality, the design highly raised and distinct, and the iridescence super. Found only in marigold, purple, and white, Dahlia is made only in berry sets, table sets, and water sets, all useful shapes, which probably explains the scarcity due to breakage in use. The water sets are much sought.

DAISY

Found only in the bonbon shape, Fenton's Daisy pattern is very scarce. The pattern is a simple one of four strands of flowers and leaves around the bowl and one blossom with leaves in the center. While marigold has been reported, blue is the color most found, and although I haven't seen amethyst or green, they may exist.

DAISY AND CANE

Shown is the decanter shape in this scarce pattern. It can also be found in a stemmed wine, a vase, and a spittoon whimsey shape. Colors are mostly marigold, but the spittoon has been found in blue. The pattern of file squares holding alternating daisies and large cane circles is a good one.

DAISY AND DRAPE

This pattern is probably a spin-off of the old U.S. Glass pattern, "Vermont," the main difference being the standing row of daisies around the top edge. Made in most of the Northwood colors, the purple leads the vivid colors, while the aqua opalescent is the most sought of the pastels. White is probably the most available color, but even it brings top dollar.

DAISY AND PLUME

Daisy and Plume is an exterior pattern found on the large Northwood Blackberry compotes as well as the primary pattern of its own compotes and footed rose bowls. It is, of course, a very adaptable pattern and could be used on many shapes. One wonders why it does not appear on table sets or water sets, but unfortunately this is the case. The colors are marigold, white, purple, electric blue, green, peach and aqua.

Dahlia

Cut Ovals

Daisy

Daisy and Cane

Daisy and Drape

Daisy and Plume

DAISY BASKET

Like many other of the Imperial handled baskets in shape and size, the Daisy Basket is a large hat-shaped one with one center handle that is rope patterned. The basket stands 10½" tall to the handle's top and is 6" across the lip. The colors are a good rich marigold and smoke, but be advised this is one of the shapes and patterns Imperial reproduced in the 1960's.

DAISY BLOCK ROWBOAT

Originally used as a pen tray in crystal, this Sowerby product had a matching stand, but I've never seen the stand in Carnival. Daisy Block was made in marigold, amethyst, and aqua in iridized glass. It measures 10½" in length.

DAISY CUT BELL

What a joy this very scarce Fenton pattern is. It was called a "tea bell" in a 1914 catalog, and as you can see, the handle is clear and scored and the Daisy design is all intaglio. The Daisy Cut Bell stands 6" tall and is found in marigold only. It is a four mold design and has a marking inside "PATD APPLD."

DAISY DEAR

I've always called this pattern "Triplets", based on Mrs. Hartung's drawing of it in her book V, but since I am told the pattern should really be identified as "Daisy Dear", I am happy to make that correction. It is a Dugan exterior pattern, found on smallish 7 – 7½" bowls in marigold, amethyst, lavender, peach opalescent, green, and white.

DAISY SQUARES

Found in stemmed rosebowls, compotes, and goblets this very pretty pattern has a simple design of daisies, stems, and leaves arranged to form squares. Around the raised base is a row of raised beads and the inside has honeycombing. Colors are marigold, amethyst, amber, and a soft green, sometimes over an amberish base glass.

DAISY WEB

What a hard-to-find pattern this is. Only the hat shape is known, and the only colors I've seen are amethyst, blue, and marigold. From the exterior design of Beaded Panels we know this pattern came form the Dugan company, so peach is a definite possibility.

DAISY WREATH

Apparently Westmoreland decided this pattern looked best on a milk glass base for I haven't heard of it any other way. The 9" bowl in marigold on milk glass is quite scarce. Equally scarce is the aqua blue on milk glass shown.

DANCE OF THE VEILS

I've heard of three of these beauties by the Fenton Company in iridized glass, and they are truly a glassmaker's dream. Marigold is the only Carnival color although crystal, pink, green, custard, and opalescent ones are made.

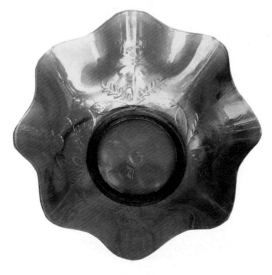

Daisy Dear

Daisy Web

Daisy Basket

Daisy Block Rowboat

Daisy Cut Bell

Daisy Squares

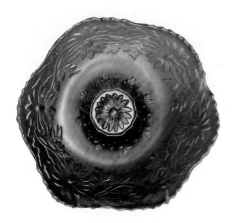

Daisy Wreath

Dance of the Veils

57

DANDELION

I have serious misgivings about labeling both of the pictured items as the same patterns, but since this is how they are best known, I will yield to tradition. Actually, the mug is certainly a dandelion pattern that is quite rare and popular, especially in aqua opalescent. Occasionally a mug bears advertising on the base and is called the "Knight Templar" mug; it brings top dollar! The water set, while known as Dandelion, is not the same design, but nonetheless is an important Northwood pattern. It is found in marigold, purple, green, ice blue, white, and a very rare ice green. The tankard pitcher is regal.

DEEP GRAPE

Millersburg made beautiful compotes, and this is a fine example of their art. It can be found in various shapes including a rare stemmed rosebowl, a squared top compote, and a cone shaped one. The design of grapes, tendrils, and leaves wind around the top and hang down the sides realistically. Colors are marigold, amethyst, green, and blue with vaseline rumored. All colors and shapes are rare.

DIAMOND AND DAISY CUT

This beautiful pattern is found on 10" vases, compotes and rare water sets (which have been mistakenly labeled Mayflower). Found primarily in a good rich marigold, the compote has been in amethyst so perhaps other colors exist.

DIAMOND AND DAISY CUT VARIANT

While not exactly like the water set with the same name, this punch bowl is near enough to be termed a variant, resembling the compote more nearly. It is the only example thus far reported and I know of no base or cups but certainly there must have been.

DIAMOND AND FAN (MILLERSBURG)

This is a beautifully designed exterior pattern, always found with the Nesting Swan bowl in Carnival glass. As you can see, the pattern literally covers all available space but doesn't seem busy.

DIAMOND AND FILE

I'm not at all sure this pattern is Imperial but list it here as a possible one. It hasn't a great deal of imagination, but may have been intended as giveaways or quick sales. The small bowl shown is quite deep, possibly intended as a jelly holder. The color is adequate, and I've heard of these in smoke as well as marigold.

DIAMOND POINT COLUMNS

While this pattern bears the same name as the simple berry sets so often seen, the patterns are really quite different, and one need only examine the ribbed column area to see why. Shown is a beautifully iridized green vase 9½" tall with very strong color. It is found in all the standard colors as well as pastels of white, ice green, and ice blue.

DIAMOND AND RIB

Diamond and Rib is a Fenton pattern that has caused great confusion on the collecting world. This is because the jardiniere shape was long suspected to be a Millersburg product. This size has been found in large vases just like the smaller ones, so that we know there were two sizes of molds used. Colors are marigold, green, amethyst, smoke, and blue.

Diamond And Fan (Millersburg)

Diamond and Daisy Cut Variant

Dandelion

Deep Grape

Diamond and Daisy Cut

Diamond and File

**Diamond Point
Columns**

Diamond and Rib

DIAMOND AND SUNBURST

Found in bowls, decanters, goblets, and a rare oil cruet whimsey, this Imperial pattern is a very nicely done geometric design. Colors are marigold, green, purple, amethyst, and amber.

DIAMOND FLUTES

Besides the 7¼" parfait glass shown, the Diamond Flutes pattern was made in a creamer and sugar. Marigold is the only reported color at this time, and sometimes it tends to be very light on this U.S. Glass pattern.

DIAMOND FOUNTAIN

This beautiful cruet has now been traced to the Higbee company and appears in their 1910 ads as a pattern called Palm Leaf Fan in crystal. As you can see, the mold work is quite good and the color adequate.

DIAMOND LACE

Over the years, I've seen scores of purple water sets in this pattern and not one has been anything but well-iridized and a sight to behold. The pattern is found in berry sets also in marigold and purple, and the water sets are also found rarely in marigold, lavender, and rumored in white.

DIAMOND OVALS

Known in only two shapes thus far, a creamer on a foot and a stemmed compote, Diamond Ovals is a Sowerby product. The creamer is one of the smaller ones, measuring 4¾" tall. The only color reported is marigold, but certainly others may exist.

DIAMOND PINWHEEL

Perhaps there are other shapes in this pattern, but if so, I haven't seen them. As you can see, it is a simple geometric design, but very pleasing. The glass and luster all have good quality and certainly add to any collection.

DIAMOND POINT

While this Northwood pattern is quite typical of most vase patterns, it has a certain distinction of its own. While refraining from "busyness," it manages an interesting overall pattern. It is found in purple, blue, aqua opalescent, green, marigold, peach, and white and is normally of standard height, being 10" to 11" tall.

Diamond and Sunburst

Diamond Flutes

Diamond Fountain

Diamond Lace

Diamond Ovals

Diamond Pinwheel

**Diamond Point
(Northwood)**

DIAMOND POINT COLUMNS

I haven't heard of this Imperial pattern in any other color than a good rich marigold, but that certainly doesn't mean they do not exist. The shapes known are compotes, plates, vases, table sets, and powder jars (which are rare). While the design of alternating rows of plain and checkered panels is quite simple, the overall appearance is quite effective. It is also found in small bowls.

DIAMOND POINTS BASKET

Although the dimensions are nearly the same as Northwood's Basket, the Diamond Points Basket is a much rarer pattern. And while some collectors have credited the Fenton company with this much-sought novelty, I lean toward Northwood as the maker. The colors found are marigold, purple, and a radiant cobalt blue. The mold work is sharp and precise and the iridescence heavy and outstanding. I have heard of less than a dozen of these baskets, so you are lucky if you own one.

DIAMOND PRISMS

I've seen this same compote shaped with the sides squared, and it was also on the same shade of marigold with much amber in the tint.

DIAMOND RING

This typical geometric design of file fillers, diamonds, and scored rings is found on berry sets as well as a fruit bowl of larger dimensions. The usual colors of marigold and smoke are to be found, and in addition, the fruit bowl has been reported in a beautiful deep purple. While Diamond Ring is not an outstanding example of the glass maker's art, it certainly deserves its share of glory. Manufactured by Imperial.

DIAMONDS

Most collectors are familiar with this pattern in the water sets, but it does appear on rare occasions in a punch bowl and base (no cups have yet to come to light). Like its cousin, Banded Diamonds, the design is simple but effective. The glass and iridescence are very good, and all have the "Millersburg look."

DIVING DOLPHINS (ENGLISH)

For many years, this scarce item was credited to the Imperial company, but we know now it was a Sowerby product. The interior carries the Scroll Embossed pattern, and Diving Dolphins is found in marigold, blue, green and amethyst with the latter easiest to find. It measures 7" across the bowl and may be round, ruffled, turned in like a rose bowl, or five-sided.

Diamond Point Columns

Diamond Points Basket

Diamond Prisms

Diamond Ring

Diamonds

Diving Dolphins

DOGWOOD SPRAYS

This is a pattern so very familiar to all Carnival collectors, for there are probably more bowls with various floral sprays than any other design. Dogwood Sprays, while well done, is not extraordinary in any sense of the word. Found on both bowls and compotes, the color most seen is peach, but purple does turn up from time to time. Manufactured by Dugan.

DOLPHINS COMPOTE

Millersburg created many fine glass items but nothing better in design or execution than the Dolphins Compote. From the Rosalind interior to the three detailed dolphins that support the bowl from the plate base, it is a thing of beauty. Colors are amethyst, green, and a rare blue.

DOTTED DIAMONDS AND DAISIES

Here's another of those very plain tumblers whose only mold design is the series of narrow interior ribs. Its main appeal lies in the very nice enamel work of stylized leaves, daisies, and a diamond grid of dots. It is reported in marigold only.

DOUBLE DOLPHIN

Some people will probably question this pattern appearing here for it is rightly considered stretch glass, but the mold work of the dolphins tends to bridge the gap between the stretch and Carnival glass so I've shown it here. This Fenton pattern was made in many shapes, including bowls, compotes, vases, covered candy dishes, candlesticks, and cake plates. Colors are ice blue, ice green, white, pink, red, topaz, tangerine, and amethyst.

DOUBLE DUTCH

While it's difficult to say whether this pattern came before or after Windmill and the NuArt plate, it is quite obvious they were all the work of the same artist. All depict various rural scenes with trees, a pond and bridge. This Imperial pattern is featured on a 9½" footed bowl, usually in marigold but occasionally found in smoke, green, and amethyst. The coloring is superior and the mold work very fine. The exterior bowl shape and pattern is much like the Floral and Optic pattern.

DOUBLE LOOP

This Northwood pattern is found on creamers, as shown, and an open sugar with a stem. Often these are trademarked, but not all are. The colors known are marigold, green, purple, aqua opalescent, and cobalt with the latter most difficult to find.

DOUBLE SCROLL

The Double Scroll pattern was Imperial's try at an Art Deco pattern in iridized glass and can be found on candlesticks, a dome-based console bowl, and a punch cup in marigold, green, amethyst, smoke, and red (not all colors in all shapes). The candlesticks measure 8½" tall, and the oval-shaped console bowl that went with them is 10½" x 8½" in diameter and stands 5" tall. The scrolls are of solid glass. The glass is thick and fine and the coloring is excellent.

Dotted Diamonds and Daisies

Dogwood Sprays

Dolphins Compote

Double Dolphin

Double Dutch

Double Scroll

Double Loop

DOUBLE STAR

In reality, this is the same pattern as the Buzz Saw cruet, but for some reason it has been called by this different name. Found in water sets and a rare spittoon whimsey formed from a tumbler, this Cambridge pattern is seen mostly in green, but marigold and amethyst can be found. I consider Double Star one of the best designed water sets in all of Carnival glass.

DOUBLE STEM ROSE

Like other patterns made at the Dugan plant, this pattern has mistakenly been attributed to the Fenton company. Double Stem Rose is found on dome-footed bowls of average size in marigold, blue, green, lavender, amethyst, and white. The design is interesting and well executed.

DRAGON AND BERRY (STRAWBERRY)

Obviously a companion piece to well-known Dragon and Lotus pattern, Dragon and Berry apparently didn't have the popularity of its cousin for few examples are to be found. Known in both footed and flat based bowls and in colors of marigold, green, and blue, this Fenton pattern is a much-sought item.

DRAGON AND LOTUS

Probably one of the best known of all Carnival glass patterns, Dragon and Lotus was a favorite of all Fenton patterns produced over several years. Shapes are flat or footed bowls and rare plates. Colors are marigold, green, blue, amethyst, peach opalescent, iridized milk glass, aqua opalescent, vaseline opalescent, red, and the pastels.

DRAGON'S TONGUE

Known mostly in light shades in a milk glass with marigold iridescence, Dragon's Tongue is also found on a large footed bowl that has a diameter measurement of 11". The only color reported on the bowl shape is marigold, but certainly other colors are possible, especially Fenton's famous cobalt blue.

DRAGON VASE

Many years ago I saw a large iridized plate with a Dragon motif. When I returned to the shop to buy it someone else had, and until now I haven't seen another item with this pattern until I was sent this photo. As you can see, the vase is six-sided, and all sides have a dragon. The base carries a many-rayed, geometric star. The color is a rich amethyst, and I have no idea who made it.

DRAPERY

Long a favorite of rosebowl and candy dish fanciers, this graceful Northwood design of three ribs and drapery looks good from any angle. Also found in the vase shape, Drapery is known in marigold, blue, purple, green, aqua opalescent, ice blue, ice green, and white.

DRAPERY VARIANT (NORTHWOOD)

This variant is just that because the ribbing, unlike the regular Northwood Drapery, doesn't run over the base to created any footed look. It is marked "Northwood," however, and stands about 8¼" tall. Colors seen by the author are marigold, amethyst, and green but others may certainly exist.

DUGAN'S MANY RIBS

Shown in the hat shape in peach opalescent this seldom discussed Dugan pattern can also be found in small vases. Colors are marigold, peach opalescent, blue, and amethyst. The ribs are slightly wider than either Northwood or Fenton's Fine Rib patters. The hat shape shown is 4½" tall and 6½" across the top and has a base diameter of 2⅝".

Drapery

Dugan's Many Ribs

Dragon Vase

Drapery Variant

Double Star

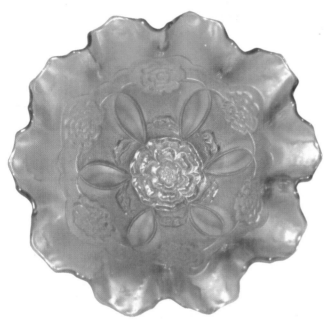

Double Stem Rose

Dragon and Berry

Dragon and Lotus

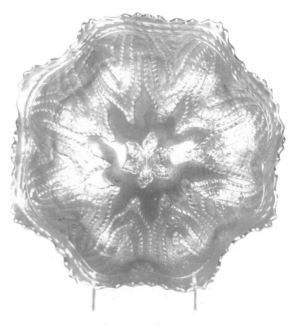

Dragon's Tongue

67

DUGAN'S VINTAGE VARIANT

I certainly wish we could avoid all the variants, but for the life of me, I don't know what else to call this very rare plate. It is one of five or six known. It is much different in arrangement of grape clusters, and the tendrils of the leaf center and the edging is different. It has a 1" collar base and is found in blue and amethyst as well as the marigold shown.

ELEGANCE

What a pretty allover pattern this is! It has a bit of everything: a stippled center blossom, a row of beading, alternating triangles of stippling and flowers, more beads and an edging of flowers. Elegance is a rare pattern, known in the marigold shallow bowl shown, an ice blue bowl, and an ice blue plate.

ELKS (FENTON)

Given or sold as souvenirs at their conventions, the Elk pieces are very collectible today. Fenton's pattern can be found in bowls, plates, and bells, and the design of each is outstanding. Colors are cobalt blue, green, and marigold all with heavy lustre.

ELKS (MILLERSBURG)

Larger than the Fenton Elk bowl the Millersburg example is called "two-eyed elk" and is more detailed. It is found only in amethyst with a radium finish. Millersburg also made a rare Elks paperweight with the same design in amethyst and green.

ELKS NAPPY (DUGAN)

For many years I thought this beautiful nappy (two known) was a Millersburg product, but recent information assures us it came from the Dugan factory. As you can see, it is a real beauty with stunning color and fine mold work. The only color is purple.

ELKS PAPERWEIGHT (MILLERSBURG)

Besides the rare bowls, Millersburg also made these very rare paper weights in both amethyst and green. These are 4" long and 2⅝" wide and except for a rim on the underside are solid glass. A copy-kat weight was made in the 1970's in other colors, but a close look will distinguish the real thing from the copy.

EMBROIDERED MUMS

A close cousin to the Hearts and Flowers pattern, also made by the Northwood company, Embroidered Mums is a busy but attractive pattern. It can be found on bowls, plates, and stemmed bonbons in a wide range of colors including marigold, pastel marigold, ice blue, ice green, purple, teal blue, electric blue, aqua opalescent, lavender, sapphire blue, lime opalescent, and the bonbons in white.

EMU

The Emu bowl is one of the better Australian patterns and is available on 4½" and 10½" bowls as well as large compotes and footed cake stands. The color most found is purple, but marigold and the amber over aqua base glass are found rarely. Some call this pattern Ostrich, but the Ostrich lives in Africa, and the Emu is an Australian bird with a similar appearance.

ENAMELED CARNIVAL GLASS

Toward the latter years of the Carnival glass "craze," patterns become simpler, and in order to give the customer something different, items (especially water sets and bowls) were marketed with hand-painted enamel work on them. Most of these were simple floral sprays, but occasionally an interesting fruit pattern emerged, like the scarce water set shown here. Today, these seem to be gaining in popularity and certainly deserve a place in Carnival glass history. This is a Northwood pattern called Enameled Grape.

Elks Nappy (Dugan)

68

Dugan's Vintage Variant

Elegance

Elks Paperweight

Elks (Fenton)

Elks (Millersburg)

Embroidered Mums

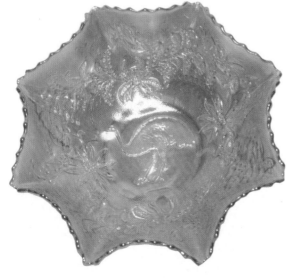

Emu

Enameled Carnival Glass

ENAMELED PANEL

While this very pretty goblet has all sorts of designs, one matched against another such as etching, gold enameling, and mold-work, it is the applied enamel panel with beautifully hand-painted roses that makes it quite elegant. The base is hollow, giving another strange twist to the whole, but the marigold coloring is very rich and the look very much one of quality.

ENAMELED PRISM BAND

This beautiful Fenton tankard water set is a standout in the series of enameled water sets. It can be found in marigold, blue, green (rarely), and a very impressive and scarce white. Also the floral work may vary slightly from one item to another.

ENGLISH HOB AND BUTTON

This pattern has been reproduced in the last few years in this country, especially on tray and bowl shapes in an odd shade of amberish marigold on very poor glass. The English version shown is another thing, however. The glass is clear and sparkling. The shapes are bowls, mostly, in marigold, green, amethyst, and blue.

ENGLISH HOBSTAR

This oddly shaped bowl was made to fit into a fancy silvered holder. The bowl is 6" long and just under 4" wide. The pattern is two hobstars on each side and one on each end, all separated by X-cuts with diamond centers. The metal holder is very ornate with metal maple leaves branching from stems to support the bowl.

ENGRAVED DAISY AND SPEARS

Made by Fenton in their Grecian Cut Gold Assortment, this very interesting small goblet (4½" tall) is very much like the Engraved Daisy tumblers except for the added "spears" to the design. All the Grecian Cut Gold items date from 1916 – 1918 and are color-flashed.

ENGRAVED GRAPE

This lovely etched pattern is from the Fenton factory and has been seen on many shapes including vases, candy jars, tall and squat pitchers, tumblers, juice glasses, and a tumble-up. Colors are marigold and white.

ENGRAVED ZINNIA

While the engraving of tall and short-stemmed flowers is rather difficult to see, the tumbler has good luster, and the shape is quite nice. Has anyone seen the pitcher?

ESTATE

Estate is a Westmoreland pattern found in mugs, perfumes, a creamer and a sugar. The items known are small in size (the mug is only 3" tall) and the design a maze-like wide band around the lower portion of the piece. Colors reported are marigold, aqua, aqua opalescent, and a very rare smoke.

ETCHED DECO

This footed 8" plate is typical in many respects of English and European glass and surely came from one or the other. The only decoration are the five etched bars with cross-hatching around the rim, but the color is good and the iridization adequate.

EVELYN

Since I showed this rare Fostoria pattern, a second one identical in size and color has been found in Washington State. So at least two of the trial run were not destroyed as thought. The design of hobstars and file windmills is a good one, and the rich emerald green top-notch.

FAN

Despite the fact most collectors have credited this pattern to Northwood, I'm really convinced it was a Dugan product. In custard glass it has been found with the well-known Diamond marking. Of course, many more shapes of the Fan pattern were made in custard. In Carnival glass, the availability is limited to the sauce dish and an occasional piece that is footed and has a handle. The colors seen are marigold, peach, and purple. Peach is the most available color.

FAN-STAR (MILLERSBURG)

Except for the base, this very unusual Millersburg exterior is completely plain. The base has a very odd star, bursting into a fan of root-like fingers that match the ones on the Tulip Scroll vase exactly. The interior pattern is Zig-Zag and is found in the usual Millersburg colors.

Engraved Zinnia   **Engraved Grape**

Enameled Prism Band

English Hob and Button

Estate Mug

Fan

Evelyn

Fan-Star (Millersburg)

English
Hobstar

Engraved
Daisy
and
Spear

Enameled
Panel

Etched Deco

71

FAN-TAIL

Fan-Tail is a pattern found on occasion as the interior design of Butterfly and Berry bowls. Actually, the design is made up of a series of peacock's tails swirling out from the center of the bowl, and while it is an interesting pattern, certainly is not a designer's success. This Fenton pattern has been reported in marigold, cobalt blue, green, and white.

FANCIFUL

Probably many collectors will challenge this pattern being attributed to Dugan, but shards from the Dugan factory were identified by this author in both marigold and purple, so here it is. Actually, if a comparison is carefully made with the Embroidered Mums, Heart and Flowers and Fancy patterns, one finds a close similarity that isn't evident on first glance. Fanciful is available on bowls and plates in colors of marigold, peach, purple, and white. The familiar Big Basketweave adorns the exterior.

FANCY CUT

Much like the small creamers in design, Fancy Cut is actually the pitcher from a child's water set (tumblers to match are known in crystal). The color is a good rich marigold and the pitcher measures 4" tall and has a base diameter of 2¼". The design is a bit busy, combining several near-cut themes, but the rarity of the iridized version more than makes up for this.

FANS

This English pattern was made by Davison Glass and can be found in the small pitcher shown (5" tall, 7" across the handle), a matching tumbler, and a cracker jar with metal lid. The pattern is very pretty with an allover design, and the color is usually quite rich. Reported in marigold only.

FARMYARD

The only word for this Dugan-Diamaond pattern is bold. The chickens scratching in a barnyard is pure whimsey but very well done, and the exterior pattern of Jewelled Heart is quite complimentary. Colors are purple, fiery amethyst, green, and peach opalescent; all are scarce and sought. Shapes are many including a square bowl and a near-plate shape.

FASHION

Fashion is probably the most familiar geometric pattern in all of Carnival glass. It was manufactured in huge amounts over a long period of time and was originally called "402½" when first issued. The shapes are creamers, sugars, punch sets, water sets, a bride's basket, and a fruit bowl and stand. While marigold is the most often seen color, smoke, green, and purple are found but are scarce. This pattern was made by Imperial. A rare red punch set was made since cups exist.

FEATHER STITCH

This pattern is a kissing cousin of the well-known Coin Dot design and as such is found on bowl shapes only, although I suspect a plate shape does exist. The colors seen are marigold, blue, green, and amethyst, and the bowls may vary in size from 8½" to 10". Feather Stitch was produced by Fenton.

FEATHER AND HEART

This fine Millersburg water set, found in green, marigold, and amethyst is typical in many ways of all the Millersburg water sets. The pitcher lip is long and pulled; quite low while the rim is scalloped quite like its cousin, the Marilyn set. The glass is quite clear, rather heavy and has excellent iridescence. A little difficult to find, the pattern adds greatly to any collection.

Fanciful

Fancy Cut

Fans

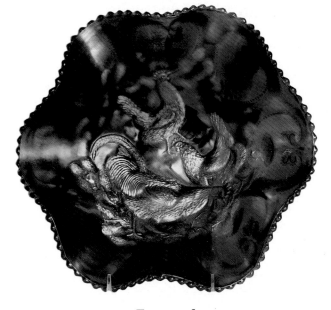

Farmyard

Fashion

Feather Stitch

Feather and Heart

Fan-Tail

FEATHERED FLOWERS
This pretty exterior pattern is found on the Australian Kiwi bowls. It is an intaglio pattern of swirls and stylized blossoms and is quite attractive.

FEATHERED SERPENT
Available on large and small bowls as well as a spittoon whimsey that is rare, this Fenton pattern has an exterior design called "Honeycomb and Clover." Colors are marigold, green, blue, and amethyst. The lustre is usually heavy and the finish a satin look.

FEATHERS
Northwood certainly made its share of vases perhaps, because they were so decorative and useful. The Feathers vase is an average example usually found in marigold, purple, and green and is of average size and quality.

FENTONIA
Known in berry sets, table sets, fruit bowls, and water sets, Fentonia is an interesting all-over pattern of diamonds filled with the usual Fenton fillers of scales and embroidery stitchery. Colors are marigold, blue, green, and occasionally amethyst, but the pattern is scarce in all colors and is seldom found for sale. There is a variant called Fentonia Fruit.

FERN
Again we find a pattern that is sometimes combined with the well-known Northwood pattern, Daisy and Plume. Fern is usually found as an interior pattern on bowls and compotes. It is an attractive pattern but really not an outstanding one.

FERN BRAND CHOCOLATES
Like so may of the small Northwood advertising pieces, this is a treasure for collectors, and a real beauty for advertising buffs. The only color is amethyst, and it measures 6¼" across.

FERN PANELS
Like so many of the Fenton novelty pieces of Carnival glass, Fern Panels is found only on the hat shape. Not too exciting, but then it apparently had an appeal of its own then as now. The colors are the usual ones: marigold, blue, green, and occasionally red.

FIELD FLOWER
Originally called "494½," this much overlooked Imperial pattern is really a little jewel. Found only on a standard size water set and a rare milk pitcher, Field Flowers is found in marigold, purple, green, and a very beautiful clambroth. The design, basically a flower framed by two strands of wheat on a stippled background, is bordered by double arches that edge the stippled area and continue down to divide the area into panels. All in all, this is a beautiful pattern that would grace any collection.

Feathered Flowers

Fern Brand Chocolates

Fern Panels

Feathers

Fentonia

Fern

Feathered Serpent

Field Flower

FIELD THISTLE

Field Thistle is a U.S. Glass Company pattern, scarce in all shapes and colors. Shapes known are berry sets, table sets, water sets, a vase, plate, and small creamer and sugar called a breakfast set. Colors most found are marigold or green, but the breakfast set is known in a beautiful ice blue, so other colors may exist. The pattern is all intaglio, and sometimes the marigold coloring is a bit weak.

FILE

For many years, File was designated as a product of the Columbia Glass Company, but was actually made by the Imperial Glass Company and is shown as such in their old catalogs in many shapes, including bowls, water pitchers, compotes and table sets. The colors are marigold, green, smoke, and amethyst, and usually the luster is quite good with much gold in evidence. The mold work is far above average.

FINE CUT AND ROSES

The real pleasure of this Northwood pattern is the successful combination of a realistic floral pattern with a pleasing geometric one. Of course, rose bowls have a charm all their own. Really well done mold work and super color both add to its attraction, and even though it is slightly smaller than many rose bowl patterns, it is a favorite of collectors.

FINE CUT HEART (MILLERSBURG)

Here is the back pattern of the beautiful Primrose bowl, but the one shown is something special. An experimental piece with a "goofus" finish under iridization. I've seen one other Millersburg example of this on a Peacock and Urn ice cream bowl, and it was also amethyst.

FINE CUT OVALS (MILLERSBURG)

As a companion to the Whirling Leaves pattern, Fine Cut Ovals has eight ovals, each containing two sections of fine cut and two of file. At the edges, a fan flairs from a diamond center, giving interesting contrast.

FINE PRISMS AND DIAMONDS

This large English vase stands some 13½" tall and has a hefty base diameter of nearly 4". Obviously it was intended to be used and not just a decorative item. And while the design qualities aren't impressive, the glass is of good color and luster.

FINE RIB (NORTHWOOD)

Can you imagine anything simpler? Yet the Fine Rib pattern was and is a success to the extent it was used time and time again by the Northwood company as secondary patterns and is the primary one in attractive vases like the one shown. While common in marigold and purple, the green color is a scarce one in Fine Rib.

FINE RIB VASE (FENTON)

While both Northwood and Fenton produced a Fine Rib vase pattern, there are differences in the design. On the Northwood vase, the ribbing extends all the way down on the base, while the Fenton design ends in a distinctive scalloped edge above the base. Of course, Fenton made this shape and pattern in red too.

FISH-SCALES AND BEADS

Most of these bowls I've seen are small – 6" to 7" in diameter. Nevertheless, they are well done, interesting, and add much to any collection. The Fishscale pattern is on the interior while the Beads design is on the exterior. When held to the light, one pattern fits happily into position to complement the whole, giving a pleasant experience.

Fine Cut Heart (Millersburg)

76   **Fine Cut Ovals (Millersburg)**

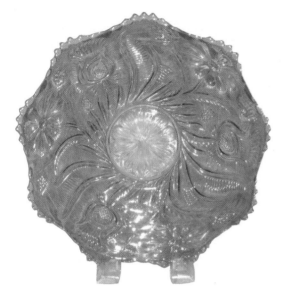

Field Thistle

File

Fine Cut and Roses

**Fine Prisms
and Diamonds**

**Fine Rib Vase
(Fenton)**

Fine Rib (Northwood)

Fishscales and Beads

FINECUT RINGS

From a set of copyright drawings we know this pattern was made by the Guggenheim, Ltd. Company of London in 1925. Shapes shown in the drawing are an oval bowl, vase, footed celery, covered butter dish, creamer, stemmed sugar, round bowl, footed cake plate, and covered jam jar. The only color I've seen is marigold, and as you can see, the coloring, mold work, and luster are outstanding.

FISHNET EPERGNE

Made by the Dugan Glass Company, this classy one-lily epergne can be found in amethyst or peach opalescent. The netting is all on the lily, and the bowl is perfectly plain except for the dome base where a series of scoring lines radiate from top to bottom. Note that the base is sometimes clear.

FISH VASE

This handsome vase has finally been traced to the makers of the Zipper Stitch pattern as well as the Hand Vase and is believed to come from Czechoslovakia. I've seen only marigold, but have had both amethyst and green reported to me by a British collector.

FISHERMAN'S MUG

This very popular mug pattern has the fish and waterlily on one side only with the reverse side plain. The mug is generous in size and heavy. It was made by Dugan-Diamond and is usually seen in amethyst. Other colors known are marigold, lavender, purple, peach opalescent, horehound, and ultra-rare cobalt blue.

FIVE HEARTS

Like so many of the Dugan patterns in peach opalescent, Five Hearts is found only on dome-footed bowls of average size. It has been estimated that 60% to 75% of all peach Carnival was made by this company. Personally, I'd say it would be closer to 90%.

FIVE PANEL

Most companies had a try at these stemmed candy jars (the one shown is missing its lid), but the Five Panel seems to have a different dividing rib than either the Fenton or Northwood versions. The coloring is a good marigold, and most of these were made in several colors, especially pastel shades.

FLARED WIDE PANEL ATOMIZER

I've often wondered just how many iridized patterns in atomizers there really are. Certainly it was a popular item in the days of Carnival, and each of them seem to have a charm of its own. This one, while rather plain, is a real cutie.

FLEUR DE LIS (MILLERSBURG)

Named, of course, for the stylized figures which symbolize the lily of the French royal family, this beautiful Millersburg design is found on bowls of all shapes and as an interior pattern on an occasional Hobstar and Feather punch bowl. The overall pattern is formal though well-balanced, and the quality of workmanship, iridescence, and color rank with the best. Especially beautiful is the dome-footed three-cornered bowl in amethyst.

FLEUR DE LIS VASE (CZECH)

Like other Czech patterns, this heavy vase has a deeply intaglio pattern. It stands a stately 10½" tall and is found on a rich marigold.

FLORABELLE

What a beauty this pastel water set with enameled flowers and gold foliage is. While it is shown in pastel green, I suspect it may have been made in white. The wide rolling of the lip and the reeded handle give it a look of quality.

Fishnet Epergne

Flared Wide Panel Atomizer

Finecut Rings

Fish Vase

Florabelle

Fisherman's Mug

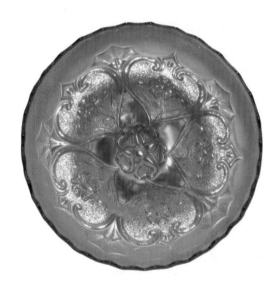

Five Hearts

Fleur De Lis

Fleur De Lis Vase

Five Panel

FLORAL AND GRAPE

Without question, Floral and Grape is one of the most familiar Fenton patterns. The water sets are plentiful, especially in marigold. The only other shape is a hat whimsey pulled from the tumbler and other colors are cobalt blue, amethyst, green, and a scarce white. Also, there are variations due to the wear of molds and creation of new ones. A variant is credited to the Dugan company.

FLORAL AND OPTIC

Most people are familiar with this pattern in rather large footed bowls in marigold or clear Carnival, although it exists on rare cake plates and rose bowls and in smoke, iridized milk glass, red, a stunning aqua, white, and iridized custard glass. The pattern is quite simple, a series of wide panels edged by a border band of vining flower and leaf design. A green or amethyst bowl in Floral and Optic would be a real find in this Imperial pattern.

FLORAL AND WHEAT

Floral and Wheat is an exterior pattern found on compotes and stemmed bonbons. Often it accompanies an interior pattern called Puzzle. Colors are marigold, amethyst, blue, and peach opalescent. It was made by the Dugan-Diamond company.

FLORAL SUNBURST

This very impressive vase is rather large and has an intaglio design of two panels of stylized daisies amid free-form leaves that are separated by large sunbursts that end at the top in stylized blossoms. I suspect this scarce vase is from England, and the flower reminds us of the one found on the Sunflower and Diamond vase. The color is a rich, dark marigold. It is 8½" tall and 5" across the top.

FLORENTINE

Both Fenton and Northwood made these candlesticks, and it is difficult to tell them apart. These shown are the Fenton version, however. They come in many colors including pastels and red as well as the usual Carnival glass colors.

FLOWER BLOCK

This pattern is a spin-off of the Curved Star pattern, and I'm showing it here in its entirety so collectors will be able to see the complete block as designed. Most of the ones around have lost their fancy wire base and wire arranger on the top.

FLOWER MEDALLION

While I can't tell you who made this tumbler, I can say I am impressed with its design. It reminds me of Curved Star in many ways. The Flower Medallion is a pale marigold, stands 4½" tall, and has a flashed look. The design, a series of arches filled with a lily-like flower, is very well balanced.

FLOWER POT (BLUE)

While both Imperial and Fenton made these flower pot and saucer planters, the one shown is from the Fenton Art Glass Company. It is a beautiful ice blue and is 5" tall and 4¾" in diameter. The plate is 6¼" in diameter. It has been seen mostly on pastels including pink but can also be found on marigold.

FLOWERING DILL

Once again we encounter a Fenton pattern that was chosen for the hat shape only, but Flowering Dill has a bit more to offer than some in that the design is graceful, flowing and covers much of the allowed space. Flowering Dill can be found in marigold, cobalt blue, green, and red.

Floral And Wheat

Florentine

Floral and Grape

Floral and Optic

Flower Block

Flower Pot

Flowering Dill

Flower Medallion

Floral Sunburst

FLOWERING VINE

The Flowering Vine compote is indeed a very scarce Millersburg item. To date, I've heard of only two examples, one in green and one in amethyst. The compote is a large one, some 9" high and 6½" across. The interior pattern is one of grape-like leaves and a dahlia-like flower. The finish is a fine radium one on heavy glass.

FLOWERS AND FRAMES

Here is another of Dugan's dome-footed bowls found primarily in peach opalescent, but also available in marigold as well as purple and green. The bowls vary from 8" to 10" depending on the crimping of the rim and usually have very sharp mold detail.

FLUFFY PEACOCK

This is Fenton at its best, and it is a shame it is only found on water sets. The design is very flowing from the stylized peacocks to the tall strands of feathering that run from top to bottom. Colors are marigold, blue, green, and amethyst, and all are desirable.

MILLERSBURG FLUTE

The Millersburg Flute has one or two distinct differences from any of the other Flute patterns. One, of course, is the clarity of the base glass itself but the most pronounced is the ending of the flutes themselves plus the clover leaf base. It is found in punch sets, berry sets, vases, and a rare compote.

FLUTE (NORTHWOOD)

While it is certainly true that all of the major makers of Carnival glass used the Flute pattern one way or another, apparently only Imperial and Northwood thought enough of it to make it a primary pattern. Thus, we find many useful shapes in an array of colors coming from the Northwood factories – including sherbets, water sets, table sets, berry sets, and even individual salt dips (an item seldom encountered in Carnival glass). The green water set is probably the rarest color and shape in this pattern. Shown is a rare plate.

FLUTE #3 (IMPERIAL)

Made in table sets, water sets, a toothpick holder (small), cruet, celery vase, a punch set, berry set, and a two-handled toothpick holder, the Imperial Flute design is quite strong with a flaring edge at the bottom. Colors of marigold, purple, green, clambroth, amber and rarely blue are usually very rich, especially the purple which is highly prized.

FLUTE AND CANE (IMPERIAL)

Found in wines, champagnes, punch cups, a milk pitcher, and the water set pieces shown, this is a very scarce pattern indeed. All shapes are found in marigold, but the water pitcher is reported in white also and is much sought in either color as are the marigold tumblers.

FLUTE AND HONEYCOMB (MILLERSBURG)

Here's a better look at the 5" bowl I showed in *Millersburg, Queen of Carnival Glass*. You can see by the design above the base why I've renamed it rather than simply calling it a Flute variant. Super amethyst is the only color I've seen, and it matches the Big Thistle punch bowl in color and finish.

FLUTE SHERBET (ENGLISH)

This little cutie is signed "British" in script on the underside of the base. In size they are small, measuring 3¼" tall and 3" across the top. The only color reported is a good marigold of deep hue.

Flute and Cane (Imperial)

Flowering Vine

Flute #3 (Imperial)

Flowers and Frames

Millersburg Flute

Flute (Northwood)

Fluffy Peacock

Flute and Honeycomb

Flute Sherbet

FLUTED SCROLLS

Perhaps this should be called a spittoon, but regardless of the name if is a very rare, one-of-a-kind product in Carnival. While often found on opalescent glass, this is the only iridized item in this pattern of which I've heard. Perhaps it was a novelty a Dugan worker produced for himself. The coloring is a good amethyst with average luster.

FOLDING FAN COMPOTE

The only shape I've seen for this Dugan pattern is the stemmed shallow compote shown. Most have the ruffled edge, and the average size is 7½" in diameter and 4" tall. Colors are marigold, amethyst, green, and peach opalescent. The one shown has a clear base, but this isn't always the case.

FOOTED PRISM PANELS

What a nice design this pretty 10" footed vase is! It is a Sowerby product, and the only reported colors are a good rich marigold and a scarce green. The design is a series of six panels filled with star prisms in graduating sizes. The stem base is domed and gently scalloped, giving great space to the appearance.

FOOTED SHELL

Made in two sizes, 5" and 3", this little novelty from the Westmoreland company is a scarce item, especially in the smaller size. The shell rests on three stubby feet, and the iridization is on the inside only. Colors I've seen are amethyst, green, marigold, and blue. Also milk glass iridized.

FORKS

I first showed this rare cracker jar in my *Rarities in Carnival Glass* book as an unlisted pattern but have since learned it was called "Forks" in old Cambridge ads. The only color I've seen is a very rich green, but I wouldn't rule out marigold or amethyst.

FORMAL

I'm a wee bit skeptical about this pattern, but new evidence points to Dugan as the maker. Nevertheless, it is an interesting pattern found only on the vase shaped in a jack-in-the-pulpit manner and a quite scarce hatpin holder. The colors most seen are purple and marigold, but I'm told pastels do exist. The hatpin holder stands 7¼" tall.

FOUR FLOWERS

For many years I've been puzzled by the origin of this beautiful design, but since peach opalescent is a prominent color, I'm satisfied it was also a Dugan product. Known in bowls and plates from 6" to 11", colors are purple, green, marigold, peach, blue, and smoke.

FOUR FLOWERS VARIANT

With all the recent research on this pattern, I seem to grow even more confused, but for argument's sake, I'll say the theory now seems to place this pattern's maker in the Scandinavian orbit of glass making. It is a beauty, whoever made it, much prettier than the regular Four Flowers and is found in bowls, plates, and a stunning salver on a metal base.

FOUR PILLAR

Often credited to Northwood, examples in amber, green, and amethyst have also been seen with the Diamond-D mark. Other colors known are marigold, ice blue, ice green, white, aqua opalescent, and the strange yellow-green shown called citrine. Occasionally, advertising appears on the base, and pieces with gold decoration on the lip are found.

474

Here is a very pretty near-cut pattern that really looks quite good on all shapes. I know of punch sets, table sets, water sets, and a milk pitcher in 474, as well as a nice fluted bowl. The color is usually marigold, but amethyst and green do exist in some shapes and are highly prized. The glass is heavy and clear, the coloring extra fine, and the mold work superior – all making Imperial's 474 a real treat to own. Rare vases are also known.

Folding Fan
Compote

Four Flowers

84

Fluted Scrolls

Footed Prism Panels

474

Footed Shell

Forks

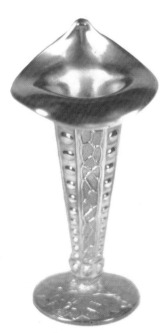

Formal

Four Pillar

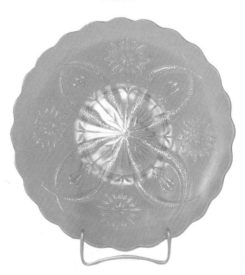

Four Flowers Variant

85

FRENCH GRAPE

While the photo certainly doesn't do justice to the design of this 5" bowl, the pattern is one I hadn't seen before. The design is a simple grape and leaf design and the finish is a watery flashed iridescence of vaseline color. It is marked "Made in France".

FRENCH KNOTS

I suppose most people credit this pattern to Fenton because of the shape – a typical hat with ruffled top. The design is quite nice and gracefully covers most of the space except the base. The exterior is plain but nicely iridized, and the only colors I've heard about are marigold and blue. French Knots is 4" tall and has a base diameter of 2½".

FROLICKING BEARS

Rare is hardly the word for this distinguished pattern, and I certainly wish I could identify the maker positively, but I can't (although I lean toward the U.S. Glass Company). The coloring is an odd gunmetal luster over an olive green glass. The mold work is good but not exceptional. To date the Frolicking Bears tumbler has sold for more money than any other, and the pitchers rank near the top of the market.

FROSTED BLOCK

Frosted Block is a very Imperial pattern found in several shapes including bowls, creamers, sugars, compotes, plates, milk pitchers, pickle dishes, and rose bowls. The color most seen is a good even marigold, but as you can see from the photo, a beautiful fiery clambroth is known in most shapes. In addition, some pieces are marked "Made in USA." These pieces are much scarcer and are well worth looking for.

FRUIT AND FLOWERS

Apparently a very close relative to the Three Fruits pattern, this is another of Northwood's floral groupings so well designed and produced. Also, there are several variations of this pattern, some with more flowers intermingled with the apples, pears, and cherries, often meandering almost to the very outer edge of the glass. Again the Northwood Basketweave is the exterior pattern, and Fruits and Flowers is found on compotes with handles as well as bowls and rare plates.

MILLERSBURG FRUIT BASKET

I couldn't quite believe my eyes when I first saw this Millersburg compote. But there it was with the exterior design and shape exactly like the Roses and Fruit Compote with an interior basketweave design and a pineapple, grapes and fruit! It was a real find, and I've been grateful ever since for the privilege of photographing it. It is my belief that this compote was the original pattern design but had to be modified because of the difficulty in producing the intricate design and remain in a competitive price area. At this time, four have been found. Of course, it must be classified as an extreme rarity.

FRUIT SALAD

Westmoreland seems to be the maker of this beautiful and rare punch set after years of speculating. Found in marigold, amethyst, and peach opal, the design is outstanding and desirable.

GARDEN PATH

Just why there are two nearly identical patterns as this one and the variant shown elsewhere is puzzling. The major difference are the addition of minor embellishments at the outer edge of the design. Not much reason in my opinion to call for a second mold but evidently reason enough for the makers.

GARDEN PATH VARIANT

Essentially the same as the regular Garden Path pattern except for the addition of six winged hearts and an equal number of five-petaled flora, the Garden Path Variant can be found on 9" bowls, 10" fruit bowls, 6 – 7" plates, and a rare 11" plate. The exterior pattern is Soda Gold and colors found are amethyst and peach opalescent.

Fruit Salad

French Knots

Garden Path

Garden Path Variant

Frolicking Bears

Frosted Block

Millersburg Fruit Basket

Fruits and Flowers

French Grape

GARDEN MUMS

Here is the Northwood design used on so many of their advertising pieces. The flat plate is 6" across, and the coloring is a typical amethyst. Just why these few examples were left unlettered is a mystery, but they certainly add much to any collection.

GARLAND

Quite often you'll spot one of these nicely done footed rose bowls in cobalt blue or marigold, but the green is quite rare. I haven't heard of an amethyst one, but I suspect it was made in that color. Made around 1911, these are shown in Fenton ads well up into the later dates of iridized glass and must have been quite popular. There are three sets of wreaths and drapery around the heavily stippled bowl.

GAY 90'S

Not only because of its extreme rarity but because the design is so very well suited for a water set is this pattern recognized as one of two or three top water sets in all of Carnival glass. In every regard excellence of workmanship is obvious. Even the solid glass handle shows leaf veining at the top and intricate petal sliping at the base. Add to this the beautiful Millersburg finish and the clarity of superior glass, and you have a real winner – the Gay 90's water set.

GEORGE W. GETTS PLATE

Here is still another of the Northwood advertising small plates with the Garden Mums design. As you can see, this one's claim to fame is the backward "S" in "Grand Rapids." Whether intentional or not, it catches the eye. Amethyst is the only reported color.

GIBSON GIRL

What a cute little toothpick holder this is despite having no pattern whatsoever! It stands 2⅜" tall. Who made it and in what other colors I haven't a clue.

GOD AND HOME (DUGAN)

For many years little was known about this unusual water set, except that it was found only in cobalt blue. It has a laurel wreath, a sun, and rays. On one side it reads "In God We Trust" and on the other side "God Bless Our Home." This rare set is now thought to have been made at the Dugan/Diamond factory, and it is a real pleasure to show it here, thanks to the Yohes of Stuttgart.

GODDESS OF HARVEST

Goddess of Harvest is the rarest of all Fenton bowl patterns and certainly deserves all the attention it gets. I've heard of six or seven of these beauties in colors of marigold, blue, and amethyst, and each is highly treasured by its owner. The bowl measures about 9" in diameter and is usually found with a candy ribbon edge.

GOLDEN CUPID

This very scarce Australian beauty is something to behold. In size it is only 5¼" in diameter and quite shallow. The glass is clear with the cupid in guilt and a strong iridescence over the surface. It may be an ashtray, but I can't be sure. Large bowls are reported also.

GOLDEN FLOWERS

Made by Jenkins just as the Stork vase, the Golden Flowers is much harder to find and usually has a richer finish. It is 7½" tall with a top opening of 3" and a base measuring 2⅞". The background has a heavy stippling, and the flowers are two types, large and small.

George W. Getts Plate

Garden Mums

God and Home (Dugan)

Golden Flowers

Garland

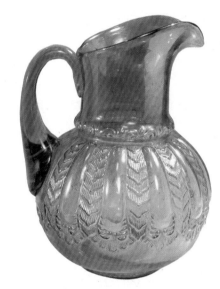

Gay 90's

Gibson Girl

Goddess of Harvest

Golden Cupid

GOLDEN GRAPE

Known only in bowls or rose bowls on a collar base, this is a neatly molded item without much elaboration. The exterior is completely plain, and the only colors found are green, marigold, or pastel marigold, usually with a satin finish. Golden Grape was manufactured by Dugan.

GOLDEN HARVEST

Here is another U.S. Glass pattern found mostly in marigold but occasionally seen in amethyst and reported in white. As you will notice, the wines are different from the decanter but are the proper ones. The stopper is solid glass.

GOLDEN HONEYCOMB

This interesting Imperial pattern provides an all-over design without being busy. The small bowls have odd little solid glass handles that are like the ones on the breakfast set while the plate and compote do not. The only color I've heard of is a good deep marigold with very rich iridescence. While this certainly isn't in the same class as the Dugan Honeycomb rose bowl, it is a better than average item to own.

GOLDEN OXEN

While this mug has never been one of by favorites like the Heron, it is hard enough to find so that many people want one. Taller than most mugs, the only color I've seen is marigold.

GOLDEN WEDDING

I am very pleased to show the complete item, just as sold. Notice that the cap is still sealed, the whiskey is still inside, the labels are intact, and the beautiful box, dated December 31, 1924, gives us a time frame for the bottle. Several sizes exist from a full quart down to the tiny 1/10 pint size.

GOOD LUCK

Harry Northwood must have loved this pattern for the color range available is staggering. The design is simple — floral sprays around the inside of the bowl with a horseshoe and riding crop centered and the words, "Good Luck" above. There are minor mold variations and some pieces have stippling and others do not. Both bowls and plates with various edge treatments are known.

GOTHIC ARCHES

Unlisted up until now, this beautiful vase stands 10" tall. The flared or morning glory style top adds to the interest as does the fine smoke coloring. The maker is unknown, but I suspect Imperial. To date other colors have not been reported but probably exist.

GRACEFUL

Once again we find a very simple pattern, so very different from most Northwood offerings in the Carnival glass field. Found mostly in marigold, occasionally a rich purple or deep emerald green vase in this pattern will surface, and when one of these is found, the simple beauty of the Graceful pattern becomes obvious.

GRACEFUL TUMBLER

While there is a well-known Northwood vase pattern by this same name, most collectors will not confuse the two. The tumbler name honors Grace Rinehart (and it's about time) and is from Europe. It stands 4" tall and can be found in cobalt blue and amber. Its main design features are the series of scrolls and rococo fillers.

Gothic Arches

Golden Oxen

90

Golden Grape

Graceful Tumbler

Golden Harvest

Golden Honeycomb

Golden Wedding

Good Luck

Graceful

GRAND THISTLE (WIDE PANELED THISTLE)

Regardless of which of the three names you choose to call this pattern (the third is Alexander Floral), the beautiful intaglio pattern and the rich lustre are quality. Colors are marigold and cobalt blue with the marigold a bit on the amber side on at least one of the tumblers.

GRAPE (IMPERIAL)

Perhaps reproductions have detracted too much from this beautiful Imperial pattern for most of us, but regardless of that, it remains a beautifully designed, nicely done pattern. In fact, for sheer realism, it doesn't take a back seat to any Grape pattern! The shapes are almost endless, and the colors range from marigold to amethyst, green, smoke, clambroth, and amber, all usually with a very fine luster.

GRAPE AND CABLE (FENTON)

Yes, Fenton made a Grape and Cable pattern, and it is often hard to distinguish it from Northwood's. Fenton's contribution is found in bowls (both flat and footed), plates and large orange bowls usually with the Persian Medallion interior. Colors are marigold, green, amethyst, blue, and rarely red.

GRAPE AND CABLE (NORTHWOOD)

Without question this is the all-time favorite Northwood pattern. It led the field when made, and it is still very popular. The shapes available are staggering, and the color range is almost as large. I've heard of entire collections built around this one pattern and hardly a collection would be complete without one example.

GRAPE AND CHERRY

Known only on large bowls, this Sowerby pattern is a real beauty. The design is exterior and all intaglio and is a series of grapes and cherries separated by an unusual torch and scroll design. The base has a grape and leaf design, also intaglio. The only colors I've heard about are marigold and cobalt blue, but others may certainly exist.

GRAPE AND GOTHIC ARCHES

Made in a variety of kinds of glass including crystal, custard, gold decorated, and Carnival glass, this pattern is certainly one of the earlier grape patterns. The arches are very effective, reminding one of a lacy arbor framing the grapes and leaves. While the berry sets often go unnoticed, the water sets are very desirable and are a must for all Northwood collectors.

GRAPE ARBOR

This is an underrated pattern, especially in the large footed bowl shape which carries the same exterior pattern as the Butterfly and Tulip. Of course, the tankard water set is popular, especially in the pastel colors of ice blue, ice green, and white. The marigold set seldom brings top dollar, and this is a shame since it is quite nice. The only other shape in Grape Arbor is a scarce hat shape.

GRAPE DELIGHT

Here is a pattern I'm sure will bring on a few outcries, because I've often heard it declared to be a Fenton product. I'm very sure, however, that it came from the Dugan family. On close comparison with several Dugan products, the mold work is certainly compatible. Not only does it come in the scarce nut bowl shape shown but in the more often seen rose bowl. The colors are both vivid and pastel and the most unusual feature, the six stuffy feet.

Grape Delight

Grand Thistle

92

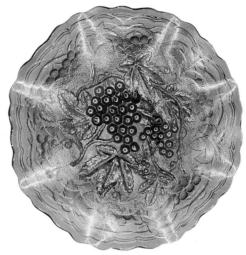

Grape (Imperial)

Grape and Cable (Fenton)

Grape and Cable, (Northwood)

Grape and Cherry

Grape and Gothic Arches

Grape Arbor

GRAPE LEAVES (DUGAN?)

Yes, this bowl is marked "Northwood" but in over twenty years of research, I haven't seen another Northwood bowl with this edging used so often by Fenton and Dugan! Add to that the unusual coloring of this bowl, described by the owner as "sea green" (it has also been seen in cobalt blue) and one has to wonder if this mold was left at Indiana, PA when Northwood left and was put into limited production by Dugan!

GRAPE LEAVES (MILLERSBURG)

Seldom found and always costly, this rare Millersburg pattern is quite like the Blackberry, Grape and Strawberry Wreath patterns except for its rarity. The major design difference lies in the center leaf and grapes, and it is found in marigold, amethyst, green, and vaseline.

GRAPE LEAVES (NORTHWOOD)

Personally, I like this grape pattern better than the famous Grape and Cable one. The four grape-leaf stems and four bunches of grapes are a very strong, balanced design. The exterior has the famous Wild Rose pattern and a wide range of colors including purple, green, cobalt blue, amethyst, ice blue, amber, and smoke exist.

GRAPE WREATH

This bowl might be called the "missing link" for it stands squarely between the Blackberry Wreath and the Millersburg Strawberry and seems to be a part of the series – perhaps from the same designer. Besides the various sizes of bowls, a rare spittoon whimsey, 6" and 10" plates are known.

GRAPE WREATH MULTI-STAR VARIANT

Here is the third example of a Millersburg variant in this pattern and as you can see, the difference lies in the center design of concentric stars. Some collectors call this the "Spider Web Center," and I can certainly see why. It can be found on the same sizes the other Grape Wreath bowls were made and in the same colors.

GRAPE WREATH VARIANT (MILLERSBURG)

Actually, only the center design has been changed on these, and as you can see, it is a stylized sunburst. I've seen several sizes of bowls with this center, but it looks best on the large 10" ice cream bowls. Colors are marigold, green, amethyst, and a beautiful clambroth with much fire in the luster.

GRAPEVINE LATTICE

I personally doubt the plate is really the same pattern as the water set known by the same name, but I will give in to tradition and list them as one and the same. The plate and bowl could be called "Twigs," since they closely resemble the Apple Blossom Twigs pattern minus the flowers and leaves. The colors are both vivid and pastels, usually with very good iridescence. This pattern was manufactured by Dugan.

GREEK KEY

This simple continuous Northwood pattern, called Roman Key in pressed glass, is really very attractive when iridized. Actually, there are three motifs used: the Ray center pattern, the Greek Key, and the Beads (in the much sought water set a fourth motif of prisms is added). Besides the water set, there are flat and footed bowls as well as plates. The colors are both vivid and pastels.

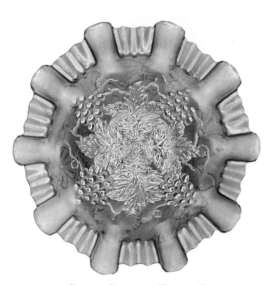

Grape Leaves (Dugan?)

Grape Wreath Variant

Grape Wreath Multi-Star Variant

Grape Leaves (Millersburg)

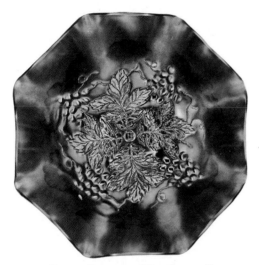

Grape Leaves (Northwood)

Grape Wreath

Grapevine Lattice

Greek Key

GREEK KEY AND SCALES (NORTHWOOD)

Here's a rather nice Northwood secondary pattern usually found on dome-based bowls with the Stippled Rays variant interior. The design is crisp and does a nice job.

HALLOWEEN

This is a very appropriately named pattern since the bright rich marigold is contrasted nicely with narrow black banding at top and bottom. There are two sizes in both tumblers, and the matching pitchers and the pitchers have black handles.

HAMMERED BELL

Whoever made this scarce and attractive light shade should be proud for it is an imaginative work of art. Found only on a frosty white, the pattern is clear and distinct. The metal handle may vary in design, but all were used to suspend the bell **above** or **below** the bulb.

HANDLED VASE (IMPERIAL)

Mrs. Hartung shows this neat vase with the lip turned down, and Rose Presznick drew it cupped in like a rose bowl. But here it is in the original shape, and it is very pretty indeed. It stands about 9" tall, and the coloring is a deep rich marigold well down before paling to a lighter shade.

HARVEST FLOWER

Here is a seldom-seen pattern, found only on a pitcher and tumbler in marigold, amethyst, and green on the latter and only in marigold in the pitcher. The tumblers have been reproduced in a dingy purple as well as white, so beware.

HARVEST POPPY

Seldom found or discussed this very well designed compote has been seen in marigold, amethyst, peach opalescent, and white, and I strongly suspect it may have been made in other colors as well. The design is very strong with poppies, stems of wheat, leaves, and stippling between the flowers.

HATTIE

While there is little to be called outstanding about Hattie, it nonetheless has its own charm and has the distinction of having the same pattern on both the exterior and interior. Most often found on 8" bowls with a collar base, it is also found in a scarce rose bowl and two sizes of plates, both of which are rare. The color most seen on this Imperial product is marigold, but green and amethyst do exist, and I've heard of both amber and smoke bowls.

HAWAIIAN MOON

Like the Late Waterlilly tumbler shown elsewhere, this is a machine-enameled item with a flashed finish. It has been seen in marigold and a scarce cranberry and came along in the depression era.

HEADDRESS

Here is a pattern found in two varieties because it was made both in America and in Sweden. It is found in 9" bowls and on compotes in marigold, green, and blue.

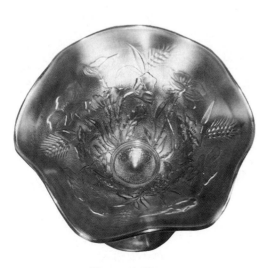

Harvest Poppy

Greek Key and Scales

96

Hammered Bell

Harvest Flower

Hattie

Handled Vase

Headdress

Halloween

Hawaiian Moon

HEART AND HORSESHOE

Yes, Fenton had a version of the Good Luck pattern, and it is much harder to find than the one Northwood produced. Note that it is simply the familiar Heart and Vine pattern with the horseshoe and lettering added. Colors are marigold and green with the marigold most prevalent and the green very hard to find.

HEART AND TREES

Found as an interior pattern on some of the footed Butterfly and Berry bowls, Heart and Trees is a combination of three well-known Fenton standards. Colors known are marigold, green, and blue, but certainly others may exist.

HEART AND VINE

Apparently this was one of Mr. Fenton's favorite designs for he used several variations of it combined with the Butterfly and Berry pattern as Stream of Hearts or on the Heart and Horseshoe pattern. The Heart and Vine pattern can be found on both bowls and plates and occasionally with advertising on the latter (the Spector plate). Colors are marigold, green, amethyst, blue, and white.

HEARTS AND FLOWERS

Intricate though it is, the Hearts and Flowers pattern is one of Northwood's best and much resembles the Embroidered Mums design in that respect. It can be found in bowls (mostly with Fine Rib exterior but rarely with a basketweave), plates, and stemmed compotes. The color range is very broad including marigold, amethyst, blue, green, ice blue, purple, white, ice green, aqua opalescent, clambroth, blue opalescent, and a rare marigold on custard (ivory).

HEAVY BANDED DIAMONDS

Perhaps designed as a companion to the Banded Diamonds water set, this beautiful Australian berry set, available in both marigold and purple, is a joy to behold. The diamonds are heavily molded and stand out below the narrow thread lines, and the iridescence is very rich.

HEAVY DIAMOND

I'd always thought this pattern to be a Dugan product until this vase shape in smoke appeared, so apparently it is an Imperial product. Previously reported only in marigold, shapes known besides the vases are large bowls, creamers and sugars, but others probably are around.

HEAVY GRAPE (DUGAN)

So similar in many ways to the Millersburg Vintage bowls, this Dugan pattern does have several distinctive qualities of its own. The most obvious one is, of course, the grape leaf center with grapes around its edge. Also missing are the usual tendrils and the small leaflets, and the exterior doesn't carry a hobnail pattern but a typical near-cut design.

HEAVY GRAPE (IMPERIAL)

Once called a Fenton product, this beautiful Grape design is now known to be an Imperial pattern and is available on berry sets, nappies, custard sets and plates in three sizes. The colors on most pieces are simply spectacular and include marigold, green, purple, smoke, amber, pastel green, smoky blue and clambroth. The 11" chop plate is highly sought and always brings top dollar when sold.

Heart and Horseshoe

98

Heavy Grape (Imperial)

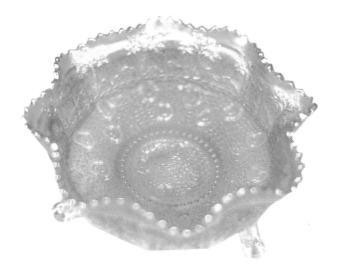

Heart and Trees

Heart and Vine

Heart and Flowers

Heavy Banded Diamonds

Heavy Diamond

Heavy Grape (Dugan)

HEAVY HOBNAIL

I first showed this unusual item in *Rarities in Carnival Glass*. At that time, only the white version was known, but since then a spectacular purple example has been seen. These were the Fenton Rustic vases that weren't pulled or slung into the vase shape and very few are known.

HEAVY IRIS

Just why Dugan-Diamond didn't use this very spectacular pattern on shapes other than the water set has always puzzled me for it is a first-class design. It is bold and heavy and certainly uses its space to the best advantage. Colors are marigold, amethyst, purple, white, pastel marigold, peach opalescent, amber, and ice blue, but beware, this pattern was reproduced by Wright in 1978.

HEAVY PINEAPPLE

Made by the Fenton company, Heavy Pineapple is a very scarce pattern, found on large footed bowls in marigold, cobalt blue, and white. The pattern is all exterior and highly raised.

HEAVY PRISMS

This beautiful celery vase stands 6" tall and shows the quality English Carnival glass makers attained. The maker is Davisons, and the colors reported are marigold, amethyst, and blue. The glass is very thick and heavy, and the luster top notch.

HEAVY SHELL

Found only on white Carnival, this Dugan pattern is rather scarce. The shapes are oval bowls and matching candlesticks. The glass is quite heavy, and the luster very rich.

HEAVY WEB

Found primarily on large, thick bowls in peach opalescent, Heavy Web is a very interesting Dugan pattern. It has been found with two distinct exterior patterns – a beautifully realistic grape and leaf design covering most of the surface and an equally attractive morning glory pattern. I've seen various shapes including round, ruffled, square, and elongated ones. A vivid purple or green bowl in this pattern would certainly be a treasure.

HERON MUG

Like the Fisherman's mug this pattern came from Dugan-Diamond company also but is harder to find and in my opinion, better designed. The Heron is on one side of the mug only, but does fill more space in a graceful rendering of the bird, and its marshy domain. The Heron mug has been reported in marigold, purple, and amethyst only.

HERRINGBONE AND BEADED OVAL

This very hard to find compote was listed in Imperial advertising as #B-54½, and the pattern was shown on a light shade. The compote has superb marigold color on the bowl, and the stem and base is clear. No other color has been reported and only three or four are known.

Heavy Web

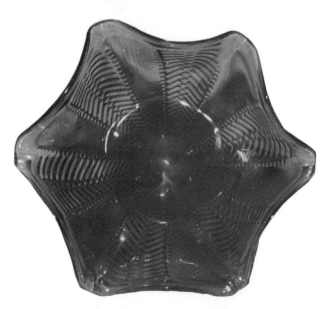

Herringbone and Beaded Oval

100

Heavy Hobnail

Heavy Iris

Heavy Pineapple

Heavy Prisms

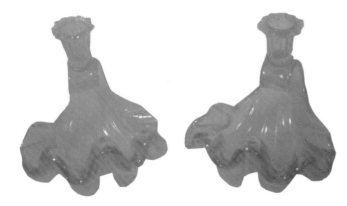

Heavy Shell

Heron

HERRINGBONE AND MUMS

Made by the Jeanette Glass company in the late 1920's, this rare depression era tumbler is a close relative to the Iris and Herringbone pattern by the same company. Both are found only in marigold, but the Herringbone and Mums is shorter and has the novel six-sided block base.

HEX BASE CANDLESTICK

Nearly every glass maker had a try at candlesticks shaped like this one, especially in Stretch glass. The one shown is reported to be from the Imperial company and has a very rich dark marigold coloring. Most of these candlesticks were sold in pairs with a console bowl and in a wide range of colors including green, purple, and even red.

HEX OPTIC

Produced in the late days of Carnival glass, the Hex Optic pattern like the Treebark Variant came from the Jeanette company. The line consisted of water sets, various table pieces including large and small bowls, saucers, and jelly and relish dishes. Sometimes light in iridization, the mold work is less complicated than early glass, even from the same company.

HOBNAIL

While plentiful in many other types of glass, Hobnail is quite a rare item in Carnival and one of real beauty. The very pattern seems perfectly suited for iridescence. The base carries a many-rayed design, and all the pieces I've seen are top-notch. The pitchers and tumblers are very rare and extremely hard to locate, but even the rose bowl is a prize, and the lady's spittoon is a little darling. Hobnail was made by Millersburg.

HOBNAIL VARIANT

This rare and exciting Millersburg pattern is quite different from the regular Hobnail made by the same company, because it has 11 rows of dots with 18 in each row around. The top row has only nine hobs, however. I suspect this was a copycat item from Fenton's Heavy Hobnail, but it is definitely Millersburg since mold drawings from there exist. Shapes known are vases, rose bowls, and a jardiniere. Colors reported are marigold, amethyst, and green.

HOBNAIL SODA GOLD

While most spittoons found in Carnival glass are of a daintier size, Imperial's Hobnail Soda Gold spittoon is a larger, more practical size. It measures 7" across the top and stands 5" high. I've seen examples in marigold and green as well a peculiar dark shade of amber. Many of these have a great deal of wear on the bottom indicating they were actually used!

HOBSTAR

Apparently this was one of the early near-cut patterns from Imperial. I'd guess it experienced great popularity from the first for it was carried over from crystal to Carnival glass in many shapes, including berry sets, cookie jars, table sets, bride's baskets and a very rare pickle caster in an ornate holder. Marigold is the common color with purple and green quite scarce.

HOBSTAR AND ARCHES

Found mostly in bowls, this well-done Imperial geometric pattern was also sold with the same base as the Long Hobstar fruit set (most companies got double mileage whenever possible with patterns) giving them a footed fruit bowl in this pattern also. Colors are marigold, green, amethyst, and smoke.

Hex Optic

Hobnail Variant

**Hex Base
Candlestick**

Hobnail

Hobnail Soda Gold

Hobstar

Hobstar and Arches

**Herringbone
and Mums**

HOBSTAR AND CUT TRIANGLES

This very unusual pattern is typically English in design, with strong contrast between geometrically patterned areas against very plain areas. Rose Presznick lists bowls, plate, and a rose bowl in this pattern in both green and amethyst, but the only shapes I've seen are bowls, rose bowls, and compotes in marigold or amethyst.

HOBSTAR AND FEATHER

This Millersburg pattern is simply the best geometric pattern in Carnival glass. Bold, deeply cut, and impressive, it is massive in concept. Found in punch sets, table set pieces, a giant footed rosebowl, small bowls of various shapes, a compote, a dessert, and several whimseys. Colors are marigold, amethyst, purple, green, and rare examples of blue and vaseline.

HOBSTAR AND FILE

What a pleasure it is to be able to list this very rare water pitcher (the only one known). Besides the pitcher, two tumblers have been reported. The coloring is a good marigold, and the mold work excellent. It is probably Imperial, but I have no confirmation at this time. (Photograph not available)

HOBSTAR AND FRUIT

Made by Westmoreland, this seldom found, seldom discussed pattern is found mostly on small bowls but is known on a larger 10" bowl and a 10½" plate. Colors are mostly peach opalescent, but we are happy to show a banana bowl whimsey in marigold and a 6½" shallow bowl in blue opalescent.

HOBSTAR BAND

This scarce Imperial pattern is found only on handled celery vases and water sets of two varieties. The usual pitcher is flat based, but as you can see a quite rare pedestal variant is known. The only color reported is a good rich marigold.

HOBSTAR DIAMONDS

Another rare tumbler, this very pretty geometric pattern has eight small hobstars around the base, eight larger ones at the top of the design, and long panels of plain diamonds between. The coloring is a pretty honey-marigold.

HOBSTAR FLOWER

This beautiful little Northwood compote is seldom seen and usually comes as a surprise to most collectors. I've heard it called "Octagon" or "Fashion" at one time or another, and most people say they've never seen it before. It is a rather hard-to-find item. It is known in marigold, but is mostly found in amethyst.

HOBSTAR PANELS

Apparently the English glassmakers like the creamer shape, for they certainly made their share of them. Here is a well-conceived geometric design with hobstars, sunbursts, and panels integrated into a very nice whole. The only color I've seen is the deep marigold shown, but certainly there may be others.

HOBSTAR REVERSED

Shown is what was called a "sideboard set" in the advertising by Davisons of Gateshead. It consists of a flower frog and holder that is footed and two side vases which were also used as spooners. Also known is a covered butter dish. The colors listed are marigold, amethyst, and blue, but not all colors are found in all shapes.

Hobstar
and Feather

Hobstar Diamonds

104

Hobstar and Fruit

Hobstar and Cut Triangles

Hobstar Band

Hobstar Flower

Hobstar Panels

Hobstar Reversed

HOBSTAR WHIRL (WHIRLIGIG)

While I can't be certain who made this very nice compote, I wouldn't rule out Dugan or Northwood. The design is simple but effective, and the luster very good. The coloring is cobalt blue.

HOLIDAY

Holiday is a Northwood pattern that so far has turned up only on this 11" tray. It is shown here in marigold and has the Northwood mark. It is also known in crystal but seems to have no accompanying pieces.

HOLLY

Most collectors are familiar with this Fenton pattern, found on bowls, plates, compotes, goblets, and hat shapes. The design is simple: tendrils of holly and leaf vining from the center out to the rim of the piece. Colors are marigold, green, amethyst, fiery amethyst, lavender, blue, aqua opalescent, white, vaseline, red, celeste blue, lime green opalescent, and cobalt opalescent.

HOLLY AND BERRY

This Dugan pattern, found mostly in rather deep bowls and nappies (one-handled bonbons) as well as an occasional sauce boat, is so similar to the Millersburg Holly pattern that most people simply accept it as a product of that company. The one distinguishing difference is the leaf and berry medallion in the center of the Holly and Berry pattern while the Millersburg design has no such center motif. Holly and Berry is found in purple, green, marigold, blue, and most often peach opalescent. A large piece of this pattern was discovered in the Dugan diggings.

HOLLY SPRIG (or WHIRL)

I have combined these two Millersburg patterns under one title, because, frankly, I can distinguish no discernible difference in them. Either can be found with or without a wide panel or the near-cut wreath pattern. The holly leaves and berries do vary somewhat from shape to shape, but certainly not enough to warrant separate titles. At any rate, it is a simple, well-executed pattern, especially nice on a one-handled nappy. The colors are usually green, marigold, and a fine amethyst.

HOLLY WREATH VARIANT (MILLERSBURG)

Besides the Grape Wreath variants, Millersburg's Holly patterns were often given the three same center patterns of feathers, stylized clovers and multi-ringed stars. Here is a very pretty example of the feather center on a bowl with a candy-ribbon edge. All of these are found on 7" – 8" bowls in the usual Millersburg colors.

HOLLY WREATH VARIANT WITH MULTI-RINGED STARS

A close comparison with the two other Millersburg variants in this pattern shown elsewhere will exhibit the only differences are in the center design. Just like the Grape Wreath pattern, three different center designs are found.

HONEYBEE POT

Shown in a Jeanette catalog as late as 1959, this cute honey container stands 4¼" tall. Besides the lightly iridized one that has a yellowish color, it was made in shell pink milk glass as well as clear and amber glass that was not iridized.

HONEYCOMB AND CLOVER

While this Fenton pattern is best known as the exterior design of Feathered Serpent pieces, it is also used as the primary pattern for bonbons and the scarce compote. Colors I've heard about include marigold, green, blue, amethyst, amber, and white, but others may exist!

Honeybee Pot

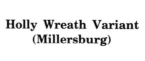

Holly Wreath Variant (Millersburg)

Hobstar Whirl

Holly Sprig

Holly and Berry

Holiday

Holly Wreath Variant with Multi-Ringed Stars

Holly

Honeycomb and Clover

HONEYCOMB AND HOBSTAR

This very rare vase is from the Millersburg company and has never been out of the Ohio area. As you can see, it is a very rich blue with heavy even luster. The base design is the same as the Hobstar and Feather rose bowl. The vase stands 8¼" tall. This example was found years ago on a shelf in a defunct Millersburg business and has remained in its present home for many years. Another blue and one amethyst are reported.

HONEYCOMB PANELS TUMBLER

I have been assured this tall tumbler is old, and I must admit it appears so to me. It is rather tall with excellent color and iridization in a rich purple. Three rows of honeycombing above a series of eight panels make the design simple yet effective. I suspect it came from one of the European glass companies but can't be sure at this time.

HONEYCOMB ROSE BOWL

Found only in marigold or peach opalescent glass, this well-designed novelty rosebowl from the Dugan-Diamond glass company is a very popular item with collectors, especially of rosebowls. They stand 4½" tall.

HORN OF PLENTY

What can I say about this bottle that isn't obvious from the photo? It isn't rare or even good Carnival, but it certainly has a place in the history of our glass.

HORSES' HEADS

Sometimes called Horse Medallion, this well-known Fenton pattern can be found in flat or footed bowls, a scarce plate shape and the rare rose bowl. The edges often are varied in ruffling and can resemble a jack-in-the-pulpit shape. Colors are marigold, blue, green, white, vaseline, aqua, and red.

HORSESHOE SHOT GLASS

If it weren't for the pretty horseshoe design in the bottom of this shot glass, it would be just another piece of glass. But with the design, it is very collectible, highly sought, and not cheap. Marigold is the only color so far reported.

HOT SPRINGS VASE

This very interesting vase is a beauty. It measures 9⅞" tall and 4½" wide across the top. The coloring is a pale amber and the iridescence is quite good. It is lettered: "To Lena from Uncle, Hot Spring, Arkansas, Superior Bath House, May 20, 1903" Who says Carnival glass was first made in 1907?

IDYLL (FENTON)

While I apologize for the poor quality of the picture, I have only praise for this very rare vase. It is one of only two ever reported and is a design jewel. The coloring is amethyst, and it stands 7" tall. The pattern of water lilies and butterflies is just right.

ILLINOIS DAISY

How strange the name of this pattern sounds on a British pattern, but Illinois Daisy was a product of Davisons of Gateshead. Shapes known are the familiar covered jar and an 8" bowl. The only color I've heard about is marigold, often very weak, but perhaps time will turn up another color.

ILLUSION

It is rather difficult to describe this seldom-discussed Fenton pattern. It is found on bowls occasionally, but mainly on bonbons and is a combination of flowers, leaves, and odd geometric shadow-like blotches. Colors seen are marigold and blue, but I certainly wouldn't rule out green amethyst. A red Illusion bonbon would be a real treasure, but so far I haven't heard of one.

IMPERIAL BASKET

This Imperial handled basket is identical in size and shape to the Daisy basket and, as you can see, the handle patterns are the same. The coloring is unusual in that it is mostly smoke Carnival with just a touch of marigold around the top.

Idyll (Fenton)

Honeycomb and Hobstar

Honeycomb Rose Bowl

Horseshoe Shot Glass

Horses' Heads

Horn of Plenty

Imperial Basket

Hot Springs Vase

Illinois Daisy

Honeycomb Panels

Illusion

IMPERIAL GRAPE SHADE

Apparently these shades are not in great supply for I've seen very few of them over the years. They are a standard 5½" tall and 5" across, are marked "Nuart" and are very attractive with good color. The pattern is well raised, and the scalloped edging very nice.

IMPERIAL JEWELS CANDLE HOLDERS

These beautiful Imperial Jewels Candle Holders are 7¼" tall. As you can see, they have a bold red iridized finish, and there is no stretch effect. Some are marked with the "Iron Cross" mark, but these are not.

IMPERIAL PAPERWEIGHT

This very rare advertising paperweight was shown in my book on Carnival glass rarities for very few of these are known. The paperweight is roughly rectangular, 5½" long, 3⅛" wide, and 1" thick. A depressed oval is in the center of the weight, and it is inscribed: "Imperial Glass Company, Bellaire, Ohio, USA," "Imperial Art Glass," "Nucut," "NuArt," and "IM | PE." These are all trademarks of the company, of course. The glass is a fine amethyst
RI | AL
with good, rich luster.

INCA BOTTLE

I can't recall ever hearing about the unusual 9½" bottle shown here. A paper label on the back says: "Huaco de oro Peruano". And while the color isn't all that dark the iridization is quite good and the charm of the design is outstanding.

INCA VASE

Like its sister design, the Sea Gulls vase, this is a foreign pattern also. It's probably Scandinavian. The feeling is Art Deco and very well done. The only color reported is a rich marigold.

INDIAN CANOE

This small novelty is really very heavy glass for its 6½" length. The coloring is touched with a bit of amber, but the iridization is quite good. Other measurements are 1½" tall and 2¼" wide. The maker is a mystery to me.

INDIANA SOLDIERS AND SAILORS PLATE

For more years than I care to remember, I've wanted to show this very rare Fenton plate, but was never able to photograph one of the three known. All are cobalt blue with a design of the monument that dominates the Circle in downtown Indianapolis. The exterior pattern is a typical Fenton one, Berry and Leaf Circle (Horse Chestnut). The iridization is superb!

INDIANA STATEHOUSE

Besides the two versions of the Soldiers and Sailors plates, Fenton also made this very rare plate shown in blue. The size is identical to the other two, and the exterior carries the same Berry and Leaf Circle design. This was made in marigold also.

INTAGLIO DAISY

Again, the English have designed a neat, useful near-cut pattern. The bowl stands 4" tall and has a 7½" width. The design is all intaglio, and the only color I've seen is marigold. Sowerby is the maker.

INTAGLIO STARS

What a pretty tumbler this is! It stands 4" tall, has 12 panels that are ¾" wide around the upper portion and a band of three stars and three sunbursts, all intaglio. The marigold coloring is very rich and has a radium-like finish. The maker is unknown at this time.

Imperial Grape Shade

Intaglio Stars

Inca Bottle

Indiana Soldiers and Sailors Plate

Imperial Jewels Candle Holders

Imperial Paperweight

Indian Canoe

Inca Vase

Indiana Statehouse

Intaglio Daisy

INTERIOR FLUTE

Here's another one of the many flute patterns so popular in their day. There was probably a matching sugar, and I haven't seen any other colors, but they probably exist.

INTERIOR RAYS

Since I first showed this table set pattern, we've learned that it may be a U.S. Glass product closely resembling a Depression Glass pattern called Aunt Polly. Here are the covered sugar and the creamer which show the design to the best advantage. There is also a covered butter dish as well as a covered jam jar which casts a shadow on an American origin in my mind.

INTERIOR RIB (IMPERIAL)

This very classy 7½" vase is tissue paper thin, and the only design is the inside ribbing that runs the length of the glass. The color is a strong smoke with high luster, and I've seen only two of these over the years.

INTERIOR SWIRL AND WIDE PANEL

Despite its long name, this squat pitcher is a real cute one with good coloring and lots of character. Other colors and shapes may exist, but I haven't seen them and don't know who the maker is.

INVERTED COIN DOT

The tumbler shown is part of a scarce water set made by the Fenton company, and to the best of my knowledge is not found in other shapes. As you can see, the pattern is all interior. Colors known are marigold, amethyst, and green, but blue may exist.

INVERTED FEATHER

This is probably the best known of all Cambridge Carnival glass patterns and is found in a variety of shapes including a cracker jar, table set, water set, compote, sherbet, wine, milk pitcher, and punch set. All shapes are rare except the cracker jar, and colors known are marigold, green, and amethyst.

INVERTED STRAWBERRY

Like its cousin, Inverted Thistle, this beautiful Cambridge pattern is all intaglio and can be found on several shapes including berry sets, water sets, candlesticks, large compotes, sherbets, milk pitchers, creamers, spooners, a stemmed celery, powder jars, and a lady's spittoon. All shapes are rare, and colors known are marigold, green, amethyst and blue.

INVERTED THISTLE

Cambridge was responsible for very original patterns and superior workmanship and here is a prime example. Known in water sets, a spittoon, a covered box, a pickle dish, and a breakfast set, this is an intaglio pattern. Colors are marigold, amethyst, green, and a rare blue.

IRIS

Along with the plain Buttermilk Goblet, this pattern found in both compotes and goblets, is Fenton. Colors seen are marigold, green, amethyst, and a very rare white.

IRIS AND HERRINGBONE

Made late in Carnival history, this Jeanette pattern can be found in a host of shapes, all useful. Its coloring runs from good to awful, and many pieces are found in crystal, also.

Iris and Herringbone   112   **Interior Swirl and Wide Panel**

Interior Rays

Inverted Coin Dot

Interior Flute

Inverted Feather

Inverted Strawberry

Inverted Thistle (Late)

Interior Rib

Iris

ISAAC BENESCH BOWL

This cute 6¼" advertising bowl is quite easily identified, because of its distinct design. It bears the labeling "The Great House of Isaac Benesch and Sons, Wilksbarre, Pa., Baltimore, Md., Annapolis, MD." The center theme is bracketed by springs of daisy-like blossoms and leaves. The exterior carries the familiar wide panel design and a rayed base. The predominant color is amethyst.

IVY

This cute little souvenir wine has the same stem and base design as Fenton's small Orange Tree compote so we are sure it came from that factory. It is found in both the wine and claret size with various advertisements. Marigold is the only color I've seen, but certainly others may have been made.

J.R. MILLER CO., LYNCHBURG, VA TUMBLER

Shown is the rare J.R. Miller advertising tumbler in a beautiful honey amber coloring. As you can readily see, the exterior pattern is Cosmos and Cane. This is a U.S. Glass pattern and while plain tumblers (no advertising) can be found in true marigold and white, the Lynchburg one is only in this beautiful amber. My thanks to Mike Carwaile for sharing this beauty.

JACK-IN-THE-PULPIT (DUGAN)

Besides the Northwood version of this vase, Dugan had a try at it too, and here is their version. It's a bit plainer and isn't nearly as pretty without the footing, but it does come in several colors and adds a pleasant touch of color and artistry.

JACK-IN-THE-PULPIT (NORTHWOOD)

While both Dugan and Fenton made Jack-in-the-Pulpit vases, the one shown is a Northwood pattern and is so marked. It stands 8¼" tall and has an exterior ribbing. Colors known are marigold, purple, green, aqua opalescent, and white, but others may exist

JACKMAN WHISKEY

Much like its cousin, the Golden Wedding bottle, this was designed to hold whiskey for commercial sale. It is scarcer than the former and generally has better iridescence. The maker is unknown.

JACOBEAN RANGER

Found in several shapes including pitchers, tumblers in three sizes, bowls of various sizes, a stemmed wine, and decanter, this very attractive pattern has been reported first to have come from England and then from Czechoslovakia. The examples I've seen have all been an outstanding marigold with excellent mold work.

JACOB'S LADDER VARIANT (U.S. GLASS)

Besides the Jacob's Ladder perfume, I've heard of this rose bowl shape in the variant and nothing else. Just why more shapes haven't surfaced, I don't know, for the pattern is interesting and well done. The only color is a good marigold.

JELLY JAR

For years I found the lids to these Imperial Jelly Jars in shops and thought they were late Carnival glass "coasters," but a few years back, I saw the two parts put together and was really quite surprised at what I saw. The jar itself is 3" wide and 2¾" tall and of deep, well iridized marigold. All the pattern is interior, so when the jar was upended onto the lid, a design was formed in the jelly. The lid itself also carries an interior design of spokes and an exterior one of a many-rayed star. Again, here is a true rarity, well within any collector's range.

JESTER'S CAP

Called "Northwood's Jester's Cap" by Marian Hartung, this interesting pattern is actually a product of Westmoreland. The design is much like the Corinth pattern and features twelve ribs running the length of the vase. The top is flared and pulled up on one side, giving the pattern its name. Colors are amethyst, marigold, green, blue, white, peach opalescent, and a very pretty aqua blue over milk glass.

Jacob's Ladder Variant (U.S. Glass)

Jacobean Ranger

Isaac Benesch Bowl

Jack-in-the-Pulpit (Northwood)

Jackman Whiskey

Ivy (Wine)

Jelly Jar

Jester's Cap

**J.R. Miller Co.
Lynchburg, VA
Tumbler**

**Jack-in-the-Pulpit
(Dugan)**

JEWELED HEART

Carried over from the pressed glass era, Jeweled Heart is, of course, the famous exterior pattern of the Farmyard bowl. However, Dugan used it as a primary pattern on very scarce water sets when the pitcher is footed – an uncommon shape for water pitchers in Carnival glass. I have seen Jeweled Heart in purple, peach, and marigold, but other colors may exist. If so, they would be considered ultra-rare. A tumbler is reported in white, but I haven't seen it.

JEWELS

This was the name given to a line of unpatterned iridized glass made by both Imperial and Dugan at the same time they were making their wonderful Carnival. Whether you consider it Carnival glass is your business, but I do, so I'm showing it here. It was made in a multitude of shapes.

JOCKEY CLUB

Although very much akin to the Good Luck pattern, Northwood's Jockey Club is certainly a separate pattern and a quick once-over will establish this fact. The floral arrangements are entirely different, even the horseshoe and riding crop are not the same. Jockey Club is found on trademarked bowls which carry the Northwood Basketweave as an exterior pattern. The ones I'm familiar with have been on a good amethyst glass, well iridized.

KANGAROO

This beautiful Australian pattern typifies the quality of the Crystal Glass Factory. Known in large and small bowls, in marigold and purple, Kangaroo has the Wild Fern pattern as its exterior. There is a variant.

KEYHOLE (DUGAN)

Used as the exterior pattern on Raindrop bowls, this Dugan secondary pattern is much more interesting than the one it complements. Colors are marigold, amethyst, and peach opalescent.

KEYSTONE COLONIAL (WESTMORELAND)

At least three of these have been reported, all with the keystone trademark containing a "W." They stand 6¼" tall and are very much like the Chippendale pattern compotes credited to Jefferson Glass. The only color I've seen is a very dark purple.

KINGFISHER

Like many of the other "bird patterns" from down under, this nice Australian bowl has both the animal and flora shown. Kingfisher has a stippled aura, a registration number, and comes in large and small bowls.

KINGFISHER VARIANT

The primary difference between this and the regular Australian Kingfisher pattern is the addition of a wreath of wattle. Both marigold and purple are found.

KING'S CROWN (U.S. GLASS)

In crystal and ruby flashed glass, this pattern can be found in many shapes, but this is the only piece in Carnival glass I've ever heard about. It is a dainty wine goblet in good marigold and very, very rare indeed.

KITTEN PAPERWEIGHT

This slight bit of glass is a rare miniature heretofore unreported in any of the pattern books on Carnival glass. Its coloring, as you can see, is a good even marigold, and the iridization is well applied. In size, it is much like the 3" long Bulldog paperweight. The Kitten paperweight is truly a rare little item.

KITTENS

For many years this Fenton pattern has been a favorite of collectors and the Kittens pieces rise steadily in price and popularity. This is a child's pattern and is known in bowls, cup and saucer, banana bowl, spooner, plate, vase, and a very are spittoon whimsey. Colors are marigold, vaseline, and cobalt blue.

King's Crown
(U.S. Glass)

Jewels

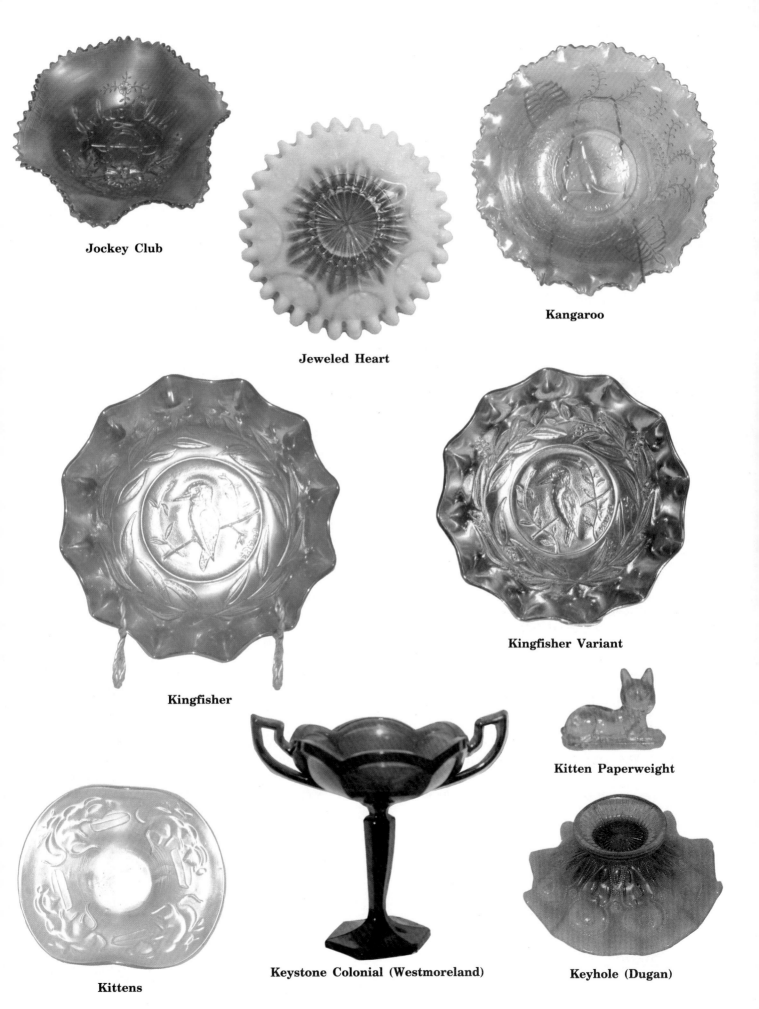

Jockey Club

Jeweled Heart

Kangaroo

Kingfisher

Kingfisher Variant

Kitten Paperweight

Kittens

Keystone Colonial (Westmoreland)

Keyhole (Dugan)

KIWI

This very odd bird is a native of New Zealand. This Australian bowl shows two of them with a mountain range in the background and a border of fine fern branches. Colors are a fine purple and marigold.

KNIFE AND FORK SHADE

While the name is a strange one, the design of two fork tines separating the wide panel of the knife is an old one. On the shade shown the bottom bells out in a stylish ballooning, and the rich coloring and iridization are fantastic.

KNOTTED BEADS

In many ways this is a combination of the April Showers vase pattern and the Diamond and Rib vase pattern for the tiny grouping are gathered into pulled ovals. I know of examples of Knotted Beads in marigold, blue, green, white, and vaseline, and sizes range from 4" to 12" in height. A Fenton product.

KOOKABURRA

Similar to the Kingfisher pattern, the Australian Kookaburra has an upper edging of Flannel Flower, wattle, and two large groups of Waratah flowers flanking a Flannel Flower blossom.

KOOKABURA VARIANT

In this Australian variant the obvious differences are the fine large Waratah flowers around the stippled circle, and, of course, the edging is a bullet rim pattern.

LBJ HAT

This late Carnival ashtray has been called this for the last few years. It has a diameter of 6¼" and stands 3" tall. While not in the class of a Cleveland Memorial Ashtray, it is an attractive specimen of iridized glass.

LACY DEWDROP

There seems to be some very disturbing questions about the origins of this pattern, but currently most collectors believe the iridized pearl pieces were made by Phoenix Glass in the 1930's rather than Westmoreland. So, I'll accept that until more information is available. It was made in water sets, covered compotes, covered bowls, and a banana bowl as well as a table set.

LATE ENAMELED BLEEDING HEARTS

Again we show a tall tumbler that many call a vase. It has a light airy iridization and delicate white and colored enameled flowers. Like most items with this finish, the Enameled Bleeding Hearts tumbler came along fairly late.

LATE ENAMELED GRAPE

Like so many items made near the end of Carnival glass popularity this cute goblet has a light airy lustre, and the bold white enameling of leaves and grapes are the real attraction. The goblet stands only 4½" tall and I have seen a very similar tall tumbler called "Late Strawberry" in the Whitley book.

LATE ENAMELED STRAWBERRY

Very similar to the same pattern shown in the Whitley book, this example, a lemonade glass, has only one roll of glass above the bulging base while the Whitley example has three rolls. The coloring is light, and the enamel work is all white.

LATE WATERLILY

For one of the later patterns in Carnival glass, this certainly is a good one. The coloring is superior, the shape symmetrical, and the design of cattails and waterlilies attractive.

Late Enameled Grape

Late Enameled Bleeding Hearts

Late Enameled Stawberry

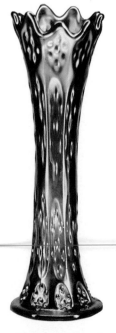

Knotted Beads

118

Kiwi

Late Waterlily

Knife and Fork Shade

Kookaburra

Kookaburra Variant

LBJ Hat

Lacy Dewdrop

LATTICE AND DAISY

Most often seen on marigold water sets, Dugan's Lattice and Daisy was also made on very scarce berry sets. The other colors known are cobalt blue and white, but I certainly would not rule out green or amethyst, especially on the water sets.

LATTICE AND GRAPE

If you examine the shape of this Fenton water set, you'll find it is almost identical to that of the Grapevine Lattice water set, but Lattice and Grape is distinctive in its own right. The mold work is very good, and the design appealing. Available in a rare spittoon whimsey pulled from a tumbler in addition to water sets, Lattice and Grape is found in marigold, cobalt blue, green, amethyst, peach opalescent, and white.

LATTICE AND LEAVES

Much like the Footed Prism Panels vase, the Lattice and Leaves vase stands 9½" tall from a dome foot. It has been found in both deep blue and the stunning marigold shown, both with superior iridization. I suspect it to be a Sowerby product from England.

LATTICE AND POINTS

Distinctive for its latticework as well as the flame design above the base and the distinct cable separating the two, this Dugan pattern is one known in marigold, amethyst, and white. Pressed into the bottom is the daisy design often found on the Vining Twigs bowl and indeed the Lattice and Points vase was pulled from the same mold.

LAUREL AND GRAPE

I know very little about this previously unreported pattern except that it is a vase shape and stands 7" tall. The design, a cluster of grapes inside a laurel wreath is a nice one and reminds me of the English Grape and Cherry pattern. Marigold is the only reported color.

LAUREL BAND

While the dome-base tumblers are seen frequently in this late pattern, the pitcher shown is a find and seldom finds its way out of collections. The pitcher measures 8" tall and has a 4" dome base while the tumbler stands 4⅞" tall. The only color reported is a strong marigold.

LAUREL LEAVES

While Mrs. Hartung showed this pattern in a round plate, here is an eight-sided one. The pattern is one the exterior, and while the design will never win any awards, the color is rich, and the iridization is good. It is well known in marigold, green, and amethyst.

LEA

Found in a handled pickle dish, a footed creamer, and a footed bowl that can be in various shapes, Lea and the Lea variants are patterns produced by the Sowerby company. Most examples are marigold, but I have heard of an amethyst creamer.

LEAF AND BEADS

Here is another very well-known Northwood pattern found not only in Carnival glass, but clear and opalescent glass as well. Available on bowls as well as rose bowls, the twig feet are used by more than one Carnival glass maker. However, the trademark is usually present. Leaf and Beads is found in a wide range of color including marigold, green, purple, ice green, ice blue, and white.

LEAF AND BEADS VARIANT

Here is the variant bowl on a dome base, and as you can see, the design is not so strong as the regular Leaf and Beads. These seem to be found mostly in green, as shown, but marigold and amethyst are known. It is marked Northwood. The shape is considered a nut bowl by many collectors.

Lea

Laurel and Grape

Lattice and Grape

Lattice and Leaves

Lattice and Daisy

Leaf and Beads Variant

Leaf and Beads

Laurel Band

Lattice and Points

Laurel Leaves

LEAF AND LITTLE FLOWERS

This little Millersburg cutie is rather unique, not only in size but also in design. The four free-floating blooms are similar to those on the Little Stars design, but the four large prickly-edged leaves with a center cross blossom is unique. It seems cactus-like. Just 3" tall, the Leaf and Little Flowers compote, has an octagon-shaped base and has been seen in amethyst, green, and rarely marigold.

LEAF CHAIN

Very close to Cherry Chain in design, Fenton's Leaf Chain is more commonly found, indicating it was made in larger amounts. Known in bowls, plates, and bonbons. Leaf Chain was made in a wide variety of colors including marigold, cobalt blue, green, amethyst, white, vaseline, lavender, smoke, aqua, and red. The mold work is quite good and the finish above average.

LEAF COLUMN

While not a spectacular pattern, here is a Northwood vase that takes on new importance on second glance. It is a well-balanced all-over pattern that does the job nicely. The iridescence, especially on the dark colors, is quite nice. The shape is attractive, and the vase is, of course, a very useful item. Certainly any collection of Carnival glass would benefit by adding one of these.

LEAF RAYS

Found mostly on a one-handled, spade-shaped nappy, this Dugan pattern was also made in the ruffled version shown. Colors are marigold, peach opalescent, amethyst, green, blue, white, and clear.

LEAF SWIRL

I've always liked this Westmoreland compote, because it has such a good design and is so well balanced. The lines and leaves swirl upward from the base in six strong panels. Colors are marigold, deep purple, amethyst, lavender, amber and a pretty teal blue. The compote is 5" tall and can be either opened widely or almost goblet shaped.

LEAF SWIRL AND FLOWER

What a beautifully graceful vase this is. It appears to be a Fenton product, stands 8" tall, and has a trail of etched leaves and flowers around the body. I'd guess it was made in marigold and pastels, too but can't be sure.

LEAF TIERS

For some reason, this pattern is difficult to locate. Apparently it wasn't made in large quantities, although it was made in usable shapes, including berry sets, table sets, and water sets. The twig feet were used by both Fenton and Northwood to some degree, and while Leaf Tiers is mostly seen in marigold, very scarce water sets in purple, green, and blue are known. A Fenton product.

LIGHTNING FLOWER

This very rare Northwood pattern, shown on a handled nappy, was shared by Fred and Cathy Roque. The pattern is exterior with an inside design of poppies that reminds me of the Imperial Pansy bowl. There are several narrow rings around the scalloped rim, and the color is good. Rose Presznick reports the Lightning Flower pattern on compotes and plates as well, but neither have been confirmed.

LIGHTOLIER LUSTRE AND CLEAR SHADE

This very collectible shade is 5½" tall and measures 5" across. The panels are on the interior and the outside is smooth. It was a product of Lightolier Company and has, as you can see, very strong iridization.

Leaf Swirl

Leaf and Little Flowers

Leaf Column

Leaf Rays

Leaf Chain

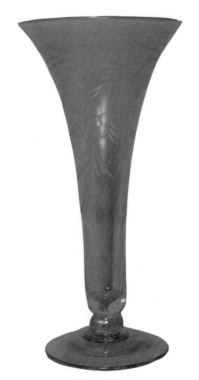

Leaf Swirl and Flower

Leaf Tiers

**Lightolier Lustre and
Clear Shade**

**Lightning
Flower**

LILY OF THE VALLEY

Personally, I feel this is the very best of all Fenton water sets, and the price this rare pattern commands bears me out. Aside from being beautiful, Lily of the Valley is an imaginative pattern. Found only in cobalt blue and marigold, Lily of the Valley would have made a beautiful table set pattern.

LINED LATTICE

Most often seen in a vase shape with odd feet-like projections, the same design is used on a shade frequently associated with the Princess lamp base. The vase, we know, was made by Dugan and can be found in marigold, amethyst, blue, green, peach opalescent, and white.

LION

Someone at the Fenton factory had to be an animal lover for more animal patterns were born there than at any other Carnival glass factory in America. The Lion pattern is a nice one, rather scarce and available in bowls and plates. The colors are marigold and blue in the bowls, but I've seen only marigold in the rare plates.

LITTLE BARREL

Most collectors acknowledge these small containers as being Imperial glass products. They are rumored to have held liquid samples of some sort, and some have been found with paper labels attached. Colors are marigold, amber, green, and smoke and all are desirable. They stand just under 4" tall.

LITTLE BEADS

Made by the Westmoreland company, this odd little pattern is seen mostly on peach opal, but the example shown has an aqua base glass. It measures 2" tall and 5½" across and has a 2½" base.

LITTLE DAISIES

Apparently Fenton made very small amounts of this pattern for few examples are to be found. Marigold is the only color reported, and the only bowl shape found. The exterior is plain.

LITTLE FISHES

A close comparison with the Coral pattern will reveal many similarities to this pattern. Little Fishes can be found in large or small bowls, both flat based and footed, and in rare plates that measure about 9". Colors are marigold, blue, green, amethyst, aqua, vaseline, amber, ice green, and white, which is rather rare.

Lily of the Valley

Lined Lattice

Lion

Little Barrel

Little Beads

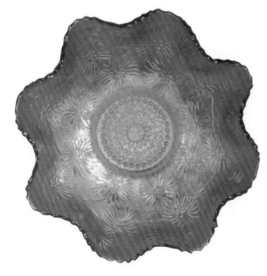

Little Daisies

Little Fishes

LITTLE FLOWERS

Here's another pattern once felt to be Millersburg but now known to be a Fenton product. Little Flowers is found in berry sets and two sizes of rare plates in marigold, green, blue amethyst, amber, aqua, vaseline, and red.

LITTLE STARS

I've found this Millersburg pattern a bit difficult to locate and don't believe many of these bowls are around. The amethyst ones are especially nice, but green and marigold exist. Also a larger size is known as is the plate shape in green. Shown is a rare blue bowl.

LOGANBERRY

Despite the reproduction of this impressive vase in the 1960's, Imperial's Loganberry has remained one of the collector's favorites. The vase is 10" tall and has a base diameter of 3¾". There are four mold marks. The colors found are green, marigold, amber, smoke, and purple with the latter hardest to find. Of course, the quality of design and the beautiful luster make this a real treasure.

LONG HOBSTAR

Imperial was famous for near-cut designs, and Long Hobstar is a prime example of their skills. Shown in a very rare punch bowl and base (no cups known), Long Hobstar can also be found in bowls, and a beautiful Bride's Basket. The colors are marigold, smoke, green, and occasionally purple.

LONG THUMBPRINT

Found in bowls, compotes, creamers, sugars, and vases, this Dugan pattern has little going for it design-wise, but sometimes it is quite nice when the coloring is as good as on the vase shown. Colors are mostly marigold, but amethyst, blue and green are occasionally found, and I've seen the breakfast pieces in a smoky marigold and the vase in peach opalescent.

LOTUS AND GRAPE

Please note the similarities between this pattern and Fenton's Water Lily and Two Flowers. All have a feeling of the small ponds once so much a part of backyard garden displays. Lotus and Grape is found on bonbons, flat or footed bowls, and rare plates in colors of marigold, green, blue, amethyst, white, and red.

LOTUS LAND

What a privilege to show this very rare bonbon, generous in size (8¼" across) and rich in design. From its stippled center flower to the whimsical outer flowers, the pattern is one you won't soon forget. Amethyst is the only reported color on the few examples.

Lotus Land

Little Flowers

Little Stars

Loganberry

Long Hobstar

Long Thumbprint

Lotus and Grape

LOUISA

Louisa is a very pretty, well designed floral pattern that seems perfectly suited for the rose bowl shape shown. Also known on footed candy dishes and a rare footed plate (all from the same mold), Louisa is found in marigold, green, blue, amethyst, and the rare deep amber called "horehound." This is by Westmoreland.

LOVELY

Northwood's Lovely is a seldom-seen interior pattern found on footed bowls with Leaf and Beads as an exterior pattern. While we can't be certain, it is possible this motif was added at the Dugan factory, since shards of Leaf and Beads were found there. The colors seen, thus far, are marigold and purple with very good iridescence.

LUCILLE

Seldom seen, I've long believed this set to be new glass, but after learning what John Britt had to say about it, I have become a believer. The water set shown is a beautiful cobalt blue and tumblers are known in marigold. Brochwitz Glass of Germany is reputed to be the maker, but I can't confirm this.

LUSTRE AND CLEAR

Shown is the handled creamer in this pattern, and I've seen the matching sugar also. Other shapes reported are a berry set, covered butterdish, a water set, and table shakers. Found mostly in marigold, the creamer and sugar are known in purple. The pattern is all interior and the outside plain.

LUSTRE FLUTE

Again we have a very familiar pattern to most collectors, but one that is not really too distinguished. I suppose not every pattern should be expected to be spectacular. The shape I've seen most often is the hat shape in both green and marigold, but punch sets, berry sets, breakfast sets, bonbons, nappies, and compotes do exist in marigold, green, and purple. The base is many-rayed and usually the Northwood trademark is present.

LUSTRE ROSE

Aside from Imperial's Grape or Pansy patterns, this is probably their biggest seller in the early years and was made in berry sets, table sets, water sets, plates, fruit bowls, and a beautiful fernery in colors of marigold, green, purple, cobalt, amber, smoke, and clambroth. Reproduction has devalued this beautiful pattern, but the old pieces are still outstanding examples of glass making with superb craftsmanship and color.

MADAY AND CO.

This quite rare advertising bowl is found as the exterior of Fenton's Wild Blackberry 8½" bowl. The only color known to date is amethyst, while the normal bowls are primarily found in green and marigold. The advertising reads "H. Maday and Co. 1910."

MAGPIE

The Magpie is a different bird altogether, and the one shown on this Australian bowl is probably a New Zealand Parson bird. The flowers are typical Flannel Flowers and wattle.

MAJESTIC

This is a well-designed tumbler made by the McKee Glass company and is very rare. It is 3⅞" tall and has a 24 point star on the base. The design features double fans that enclose a four-section block. Majestic items can also be found in crystal and ruby stained glass.

Majestic

Maday and Co.

Lustre and Clear

Louisa

Lovely

Lucille

Lustre Rose

Lustre Flute

Magpie

MALAGA

Malaga is rather difficult pattern to find, indicating production must have been small on this Dugan design. What a pity for the all-over grape pattern is a good one with imaginative detail throughout. Found only on large bowls and plates, I've heard of marigold, amber, and purple only, but green is a strong possibility.

MALLARD DUCK

I certainly wish I knew more about this rare item, but it's the only true Carnival one I've seen. I believe these were made by Tiffin (mostly in milk glass), and I once saw an example with applied ruby luster. However, I can say with assurance the one shown is old, has been in one of the country's major collections for years, and is a prized rarity of the owner. The coloring is a beautiful clambroth with fiery blue and pink highlights.

MANY FRUITS

This is a truly lovely fruit pattern, something that any company would be proud to claim. The mold work is heavy and distinct, the design is interesting and quite realistic, and the coloration flawless. I personally prefer the ruffled base, but that is a small matter. This Dugan pattern would have made a beautiful water set. The colors are marigold, blue, white, purple, and green.

MANY STARS

Which came first – the chicken or the egg? Or in this case, the Many Stars or the Bernheimer bowl? For they are exactly the same except for the center design where in the former a large star replaces the advertising. These bowls are generous in size and can be found in amethyst, green, marigold, and blue. The green is often a light, airy shade just a bit darker than an ice green and is very attractive when found with a gold iridescence. Millersburg manufactured this pattern.

MAPLE LEAF

Maple Leaf is a carry-over pattern from the custard glass line, but in Carnival glass is limited to stemmed berry sets, table sets, and water sets. I examined shards of this pattern from the Dugan dumpsite, so items in Carnival glass were obviously turned out at that factory. The background is the same Soda Gold pattern as that found on the exterior of Garden Path bowls and plates. Maple Leaf was made in marigold, purple, cobalt blue, and green.

MARILYN

This water set pattern is probably one of the most unusual and outstanding in the field of Carnival glass. First look at the pitcher's shape. Notice the unusual upper edging, so different than those of other companies. Then there is the drooping pouring lip so favored by the Millersburg company. The finish is, of course, the fine radium look, and the glass is heavy. All in all, a real prize for any collector.

MARTEC

Another McKee pattern in the Tec series like Aztec, this nice pattern has only been found in the tumbler in Carnival glass. It stands 4" tall and is marked "Prescut". The design is geometric with two major hobstar variations.

MARY ANN

I don't believe I've heard of another one of these loving cups in collections I'm familiar with, and yet I've always known these existed. As you can see, they are much different from the vase shape, having three handles and no scalloping around the top edge or base. Of course, it is quite rare, and it is a real pleasure to show it here. The Mary Ann vase is Dugan.

MASSACHUSETTS (U.S. GLASS)

While the vase shape shown is the only shape I've heard about in this very attractive pattern, I'd bet it was made in a creamer and sugar as well. It is found only in marigold and brings a good price when sold, for it is a scarce and desirable item.

Mary Ann

Martec

Malaga

Mallard Duck

Many Fruits

Many Stars

Maple Leaf

Massachusetts

Marilyn

131

MAY BASKET

This beautiful basket is called Diamond and Fleur de lis by Mrs. Presznick. It was made by Davisons of Gateshead and has a diameter of 7½" and is 6" tall. Can you imagine how difficult it was to remove this beautiful novelty from the mold? May Basket was made in marigold and has been reported in smoke.

MAYAN

Always one of my favorites this Millersburg bowl pattern is usually found in ice-cream shapes in green that tends toward olive, but a recent find has been a very rare marigold bowl that is ruffled. The design of six feather-plumes that radiate from a large beaded center is quite distinctive.

MAYFLOWER (MILLERSBURG)

Found with the rare Millersburg Grape Leaves bowl, Mayflower is a series of flower-like designs, separated by eight diamond and near-cut sections. Held to the light, the effect is a real surprise through the Grape design. Colors are marigold, green, amethyst, and vaseline, and every one is rare.

MEANDER (NORTHWOOD)

Here's the exterior of the gorgeous Three Fruits Medallion bowl shown elsewhere, and as you can see, the glass is truly black amethyst and has no iridizing on the exterior. The pattern of Meander, however, is a good design and very complimentary.

MELON RIB

Another pattern credited to Imperial, Melon Rib can be found on water sets, candy jars, salt and pepper shakers, and a covered powder jar, all in marigold. As you can see, the pitcher is tall, stately, and very pretty.

MEMPHIS

While an interesting geometrical pattern, Northwood's Memphis has never been one of my favorites – possibly because of its limited shapes. I can imagine how much my interest would increase if a water set were to appear! I have seen an enormous banquet punch set in crystal, but the size was not made in Carnival glass. The shapes are a berry set, punch set, fruit bowl on separate stand, and a compote. The colors found are both vivid and pastel.

MIKADO

Called giant compotes, these beautiful 8½" tall fruit stands have two outstanding patterns – cherries on the exterior and the beautiful Mikado on the inside of the bowl. This design consists of a center Medallion of stippled rays around which are three large chrysanthemums and three oriental scroll devices. The colors are marigold, blue, a rare green, and a very rare red. Mikado was made by Fenton.

MILADY

Again, we show one of the better water sets by the Fenton company. The pitcher is a tankard size, and the design is paneled with very artistic blossoms and stems with graceful leaves. Colors most seen are marigold and blue, but scarce green and a rare amethyst do exist.

Mayflower (Millersburg)

Meander (Northwood)

Melon Rib

May Basket

Mayan

Memphis

Mikado

Milady

MINIATURE BLACKBERRY COMPOTE

This little Fenton cutie is most often seen on blue or marigold and is quite scarce in either color. The white one shown is very rare. Standing only 2½" high with a bowl diameter of 4⅛", this miniature or jelly compote would be a treasure in any collection and certainly would highlight a compote grouping.

MINIATURE HOBNAIL CORDIAL SET

What a nice little set this is! Probably from Europe, it is the only one about which I've heard. The decanter stands 8" tall to the top of its stopper, and, needless to say, the set is quite a rare item.

MIRRORED LOTUS

Here is a Fenton pattern that is quite scarce, especially in some colors. Found mostly on 7" ruffled bowls in blue, green, marigold, or white, it is also known on the rare ice cream shaped 7" bowl in celeste blue, a rare plate in the same color and a rare white rosebowl.

MIRRORED PEACOCKS

For some reason, I'm very excited by the design of this tall tumbler. It is reputed to have come from either Finland or Czechoslovakia and has a very whimsical touch. The design, two large, stylized peacocks stand over several ram-like figures!

MITERED DIAMONDS AND PLEATS

This British pattern is most often seen as shown, a 4½" handled sauce dish, but I've seen 8½" bowls. Mrs. Presznick reports a tray in 10" size as well. The coloring is top notch marigold, but a smoky blue shade has been reported.

MITERED OVALS

This beautiful vase is a Millersburg product. It is a rare item seldom found for sale. The colors seen are amethyst, green and very rarely marigold. In size it is outstanding, being some 10½" tall. The mold work is superior.

MODERNE

I've named this cute cup and saucer the very first name that entered my head, but it seems to fit. I'd guess it is fairly late Carnival, but it still has good coloring and a nice luster.

MOONPRINT

Here is one of the prettiest of all English Carnival patterns. The shapes are a banana bowl, covered jar, vase, covered butter, covered cheesekeeper, compote, milk pitcher, creamer, and bowls that range in size from 8" to 15". Marigold is the basic color with a super finish. I've heard of a peach opalescent covered jar but cannot confirm its existence. I'd guess Sowerby made this pattern.

MORNING GLORY

If there is one water set that stands above all others in sheer beauty, this Millersburg pattern is surely it. Almost 14" tall, the pitcher is stately. It has heavily raised morning glory vines around its center and the applied handle has been shaped to resemble a leaf where it joins the pitcher. The matching tumbler is 3¾" tall and has a rayed base. The glass is sparkling clear, the radium finish is excellent, and the mold work impressive. Along with the Gay 90's, the Morning Glory water set has to be near the top of anyone's list.

Mirrored Peacocks

Miniature Hobnail Cordial Set

134

Miniature Blackberry Compote

Moderne

Mirrored Lotus

Mitered Diamonds and Pleats

Mitered Ovals

Moonprint

Morning Glory

MORNING GLORY VASE

Several companies made similar vases with the flaring top resembling morning glories, but the one shown happens to come from Imperial and is a whopping 17" tall. The color is fabulous! I've seen these as small as 8" and every size between, in several colors including marigold, smoke, green, blue amethyst, white, ice green, teal, and aqua and even one in a strange pale blue and marigold combination.

MT. GAMBIER MUG

I can't be sure this mug is Australian, but this one comes from there. It is etched "Greetings from Mt. Gambier." The color is a good rich marigold.

MOXIE BOTTLE

I normally avoid the bottle cycle unless they are attractive as this well-designed scarcity. The coloring is obviously a very frosty white with heavy luster, and the design of plain and stippled diamonds is a good one. Moxie was a soft drink that went out of favor in the mid 1920's.

MULTI-FRUITS AND FLOWERS

Grape clusters, leaves, blossoms, cherries, peaches, and pears! What an imaginative collection to grace beautiful lustered glass! This fantastic Millersburg pattern is seen mostly on punch sets of medium size, but here is a very scarce water set and a stemmed fruit goblet or compote. The base of the punch set can double a a compote when up-ended and is iridized inside and out.

MUSCADINE

Almost a twin to the Beaded Panels and Grapes tumbler, the Muscadine has a band of geometric squares-within-squares and diamonds-within-diamonds instead of a band of grapes and leaves. Again we have a pattern made in Czechoslovakia for export. The color is marigold, and the tumbler stands 5⅛" tall.

MY LADY'S POWDER BOX

Here is a favorite with collectors and a good price is always assured when one of these sell. Found only in marigold of a good rich quality, the powder jar stands 5½" tall and has a base diameter of 3¼". The figure on the lid is of solid glass. I suspect Davisons is the manufacturer but have no proof.

MYSTIC

I named this 7" vase. So if anyone knows it by another name, I'd be happy to hear from them. The design of elongated shields separated by a hobstar and file filler is interesting. The very mellow coloring reminds me of other Cambridge products, and that is just who made it, according to a 1908 advertisement.

NAUTILUS

It is a shame there aren't more shapes of this pattern in Carnival glass, because every piece of the custard shapes are a joy. In Carnival we find only the small novelty piece described as a boat shape (actually one large footed berry bowl has been seen in marigold – a very, very rare piece of Carnival glass! It appears with either both ends turned up or one end turned down, and the colors are peach and purple. A Dugan product from old Northwood molds.

NEAR-CUT

This attractive Northwood pattern is quite similar to the Hobstar Flower shown elsewhere in this book. In addition to the compote and goblet made from the same mold, there is a very rare water pitcher. I have heard of no tumblers, but they may exist. The colors are marigold and purple with the latter most seen. A rare green compote is known also.

Muscadine

Mystic

136

Mt. Gambier Mug

Moxie Bottle

Multi-Fruits and Flowers

My Lady's Powder Box

Nautilus

Morning Glory Vases

Near-Cut

NEAR-CUT DECANTER

What a triumph of near-cut design this rare Cambridge pattern is! Standing 11" tall, this beauty is found in a sparkling green, but I wouldn't rule out amethyst or marigold as possibilities. The mold work is some of the best, and the finish is equal to any from the Millersburg plant.

NESTING SWAN

This pattern has become one of the most sought Millersburg bowl patterns, and it is certainly easy to see why. The graceful swan, nesting on a bed of reeds, surrounded by leaves, blossoms, and cattails is a very interesting design. The detail is quite good, and the color and finish exceptional. The beautiful Diamond and Fan exterior contrasts nicely and echoes the fine workmanship throughout. In addition to the beautiful green, marigold, and amethyst, Nesting Swan can be found in a beautiful honey-amber shade and a very rare blue.

NEW ORLEANS CHAMPAGNE

Like the other champagnes from U.S. Glass, this version is on clear iridized glass with the design areas hand painted. The alligators along the sides are quite unique in Carnival glass, and the crowned and bearded man represents Rex, King of the Mardi Gras. I really can't think of anything more fitting for a piece of Carnival glass.

NIGHT STARS

What a rare little beauty this Millersburg pattern is! Found on the bonbon shape shown in an unusual olive green, marigold, and amethyst, it has also been seen in a very rare card tray in amethyst and vaseline and an equally rare spade-shaped nappy in amethyst only. All shapes and colors are rare and desirable, so never pass one up.

NIPPON

Certainly Nippon must have been a popular pattern in its heyday, for it is readily found today. The pattern is simple but effective; it is a central stylized blossom with panels of drapery extending toward the outer edges of the bowl. Found in a wide variety of colors, including marigold, green, blue, purple, ice green, ice blue, and white. This Northwood is a nice pattern to own.

NORTHERN STAR

I have some misgivings about this being a Fenton pattern, but since it is listed as such by a noted glass author, I will consider it one. Shown is the 6" card tray, but Northern Star can also be found on a ruffled mint dish, small bowls, and plates, all in marigold. The design is all on the exterior, and both outside and inside are iridized.

Near Cut Decanter

Nesting Swan

New Orleans Champagne

Night Stars

Nippon

Northern Star

NU-ART CHRYSANTHEMUM

Apparently the popularity of the regular Nu-Art plate prompted this, a sister design of striking beauty. Also 10½" in diameter, the Chrysanthemum plate has the same Greek key border device. The flowers are very graceful and heavily raised, and, of course, the iridescence is outstanding. I've seen this plate in marigold, smoke, amber, green, clambroth, and purple, but other colors may exist. Again, this pattern was reproduced in the 1960's. This was produced by Imperial.

NU-ART (HOMESTEAD)

If you will take a few moments to compare this Imperial pattern with the Double Dutch found elsewhere in this book, you will find very similar designs, probably done by the same artist. The Nu-Art plate, however, is a rarer more important design that sells for many times the amount of a Double Dutch bowl. Found is many colors including marigold, green, purple, smoke, amber, white, ice green, and the rare cobalt blue, the Nu-Art plate is sometimes signed. It measures 10½" across and has been reproduced.

NUGGATE

Besides the 4½" handled bottle I showed in the last edition of this book, there is a taller 8" pitcher shape. Both have the threaded marigold handle and the same drooping lip. Iridescence is very good, and I'm sure they are from Europe, but the age is questionable!

NUGGET BEADS

Here is another string of Carnival beads, but much more impressive than the set shown elsewhere in this book. The stringing includes gold spacers, regular iridized beads, and graduated nugget-shaped chunks. The coloring is a very rich amethyst.

#5

This pattern dates from the early days of the Imperial company and was first issued in crystal. The shapes known are a celery holder, 6" tall, and the beautiful dome-footed bowl shown, where the pattern is exterior. The color most encountered is marigold, but, as you can see, the bowl is a rich amber.

#4

Made first in crystal, like so many Imperial patterns, this is a rather simple, not too impressive pattern, found on compotes as well as small footed bowls. The colors are usually marigold or smoke, but I've seen it in clear Carnival as well as green.

#9

This little Imperial cutie is very nice, especially when found on a rich smoky color with golden highlights. Of course, it is also known on marigold, and I suspect green is a possibility. While the pattern is relatively simple – a series of arches filled with small hexagonal buttons – it is quite effective. Sometimes called Tulip and Cane, #9 is also found in wine, claret, and goblet shapes.

#270

Made by the Westmoreland company, this little open-stemmed bowl is found in peach opalescent milk glass, as well as, the aqua color shown. It is a simple but effective pattern well worth collecting.

Nuggate

Nugget Beads

140

Nu-Art (Homestead)

Nu-Art Chrysanthemum

#5

#4

#9

#270

OCTAGON

Next to the Fashion pattern, this is probably Imperial's most common near-cut design, especially when found in marigold. But dark colors show up now and then, and the shape shown is rare in marigold. In the beautiful purple, the toothpick is extremely rare. Octagon is found in table sets, water sets, wine sets, footed vases, milk pitchers, goblets, and rare toothpicks. It is a pleasing all-over pattern.

OCTET

Even if this pattern were not marked, we would attribute it to the Northwood company, because the exterior pattern is the Northwood vintage found on the Star of David and Bows bowl. Octet is also a dome-footed bowl, usually about 8½" in diameter. It is a simple but effective pattern – one that wouldn't be easily confused with others. The colors are marigold, purple, green, white, and ice green. The purple is the most common.

OHIO STAR

This beautiful near-cut vase is almost 10" tall and certainly is a standout in the Carnival vase field. While the majority of vases are of simple design, this one flaunts its multi-cut pattern even to the star in the high domed base. The coloring is excellent and not only is Ohio Star found in the usual marigold, green, and purple but is reported in a beautiful blue! Certainly Millersburg blues are not easily found, and one of these would enhance any collection. A rare compote is known, and a super-rare white vase also.

OLYMPIC COMPOTE

The Millersburg Olympic miniature compote is **extremely** rare. Its measurements are the same as the Leaf and Little Flowers compote made by the same company, and the exterior and base are identical also. If ever the old adage "Great things come in small packages" could apply, certainly it would be to the Olympic compote.

OMNIBUS

This interesting tumbler has been credited to the U.S. Glass company and is rather rare (six known) and little recognized. The primary design is a sunburst teamed with two diamonds of file and a pulled diamond of bubble-like filler along with fanning. The sunburst moves from top to bottom in a series around the tumbler. The design is quite good; the color is super. A rare find.

OPEN EDGE BASKETWEAVE

This Fenton well-known pattern seems to grow in popularity, especially in the large pastel pieces which are scarce to rare. Found in hat shapes, bowls, J.I.P. shapes, banana bowls, vase whimseys, and plates. Colors are marigold, blue, green, amethyst, pink, ice blue, ice green, white, celeste blue, and red.

Omnibus

Octagon

Octet

Ohio Star

Olympic Compote

Open Edge Basketweave

OPEN ROSE

This pattern is very similar to the Lustre Rose pattern but is not found on the wide range of shapes as the latter. The plate shown is the most sought shape, but there are also footed and flat bowls of many sizes available. Colors of marigold, smoke, green, purple, clambroth, and amber are known, and each is usually outstanding. The amber plate shown typifies the Imperial quality.

OPTIC VARIANT

If you examine the Optic Flute that follows, you will recognize the base of this Imperial bowl but will notice the fluting is missing. These have been found on berry sets, but I'm sure other shapes were made. The interior of the 6" bowl shown was highly iridized and had a stretch appearance, and the exterior had only slight luster.

OPTIC (IMPERIAL)

Each panel in this pattern is curved, thus the name and an interesting design above the ordinary. Besides bowls and small compotes, a creamer and sugar are known in marigold and smoke.

OPTIC AND BUTTONS

In crystal this pattern is found in many shapes including table sets, plates, oil bottles, decanters, shakers, and sherbets, but in Carnival glass Optic and Buttons is limited to berry sets, a goblet, a large handled bowl, a small pitcher, tumblers in two shapes, and a rare cup and saucer. Many of the items in Carnival are marked with the Imperial "iron cross" mark including the milk pitcher and the cup. All shapes I've seen are in marigold only.

OPTIC FLUTE

This Imperial pattern is seldom mentioned but can be found on berry sets as well as compotes. Colors I've seen are marigold and smoke, but others may have been made.

ORANGE PEEL

This is a sister design to the Fruit Salad pattern and both are made by Westmoreland. Orange Peel, while not as rare, is made in a punch set, custard set, and a stemmed dessert in marigold, amethyst, and teal, all Westmoreland prime colors.

ORANGE TREE

No other Fenton pattern had more popularity or was made in more shapes than the Orange Tree and all its variants. Known in berry sets, table sets, water sets, ice cream sets, breakfast sets, compotes, mugs, plates, powder jars, hatpin holders, rose bowls, a loving cup, wines, punch sets, and goblets. Orange Tree is found in marigold, blue, green, amethyst, peach opalescent, lustered milk glass, aqua opalescent, white, amber, vaseline, aqua, red, and amberina.

ORANGE TREE AND SCROLL

What a beauty this hard-to-find tankard set is. The Orange Trees are like those on the regular pieces and the Orange Tree Orchard set, but below the trees are panels of scroll work much like the design on the Milady pattern. Colors are marigold, blue, and green, but I wouldn't rule out amethyst or white on this Fenton product.

Optic Variant

Optic (Imperial)

Open Rose

Optic and Buttons

Optic Flute

Orange Peel

Orange Tree

Orange Tree and Scroll

ORANGE TREE ORCHARD

Obviously a spin-off pattern of the Orange Tree, this rather scarce Fenton water set has a nicely shaped, bulbous pitcher. The design is a series of Orange Trees separated by fancy scroll work and has been reported in marigold, blue, green, amethyst, and white.

ORIENTAL POPPY

Here is a very impressive, realistic pattern, especially effective on the chosen shape – a tankard water set. The mold work on this Northwood product is clear and clean, and the glass is quality all the way. Colors are marigold, green, purple, white, ice green, ice blue, and blue.

OSTRICH CAKE PLATE

This Australian pattern is actually the Emu on a footed cake stand but has been misnamed. The exterior is a beautiful Rib and Cane pattern. Colors are marigold and purple, but these are rare.

OVAL AND ROUND

While Imperial's Oval and Round may certainly be thought of as a very ordinary pattern, it does have its own charm on a bowl as nicely ruffled as the one shown. Simple in execution, the pattern is found on plates of large size and bowls of various sizes only. The colors are marigold, green, smoke or purple and are usually very richly lustered.

PACIFICA

Made by the U.S. Glass company, the Pacifica tumbler is quite rare. Originally catalogued as #6425 by the maker, Pacifica has a rather complex pattern of hobstars, file sections, and small daisy-like flowers. Lustre is light, and the coloring has a bit of amber in the marigold.

PACIFIC COAST MAIL ORDER HOUSE

Shown are two colors in a very rare advertising item. The exterior is, of course, Grape and Cable. Three examples are known in each color of marigold and blue. The bowls are footed. They were made by Fenton.

PALM BEACH

Apparently this U.S. Glass pattern was carried over from the pressed glass days. It is scarce in all shapes but can be found in a variety of useful pieces, including berry sets, table set, a cider set, rose bowls, vase whimseys, a plate, and a miniature banana bowl whimsey. The color is often rather weak and marigold, purple, and white are known. The example shown is a bowl whimsey with an iridized "goofus" finish.

PANELED DANDELION

Fenton's Paneled Dandelion is another of those spectacular tankard water sets that are so eye-catching. The panels of serrated leaves and cottony blossoms are very realistic and fill the space allowed nicely. Colors are marigold, blue, green, and amethyst.

PANELED DIAMOND AND BOWS

For some reason this Fenton vase pattern isn't often found, despite not being rare. It ranges in size from the small 6½" version shown to the standard 11" vases and in colors of marigold, blue, green, amethyst, white, and an unusual peach opalescent. The design, a panel of geometric hobstars in diamonds separated by rayed bows, appears on alternating panels (three of six).

Pacifica

Oval and Round

Paneled Diamonds and Bows

146

Orange Tree Orchard

Oriental Poppy

Ostrich Cake Plate

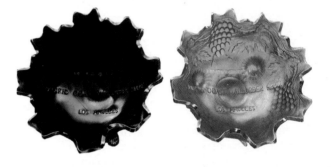

Pacific Coast Mail Order House

Palm Beach

Paneled Dandelion

PANELED HOLLY

This Northwood pattern is found in crystal, gilt glass, and Carnival glass. However, the range of shapes is much less in the latter, limited to the exteriors of bowls, footed bonbons, a rare breakfast set, and an extremely rare water pitcher. While fairly attractive, Paneled Holly is really not a great pattern. It appears a trifle busy and a bit confused. The most often seen color is green, but purple and marigold do exist. I've seen a combination of green glass with marigold iridescence.

PANELED SMOCKING

I've always felt this pattern was from either England or Australia, but I may be wrong on both counts. Marigold is the only color I've seen, and there are no other shapes reported.

PANELED TREETRUNK

While similar to the Northwood Treetrunk vase, this scarce and interesting vase has an appeal all its own. The example shown is 7½" tall and has a base diameter of 4⅞". It has eight panels, and the coloring is a fine amethyst. I suspect it was made by Dugan but can't be positive.

PANSY

The Pansy bowl shown typifies the Imperial quality so often found in iridized glass. The luster is outstanding with a gleaming finish equal to the best Millersburg we all treasure so much. The mold work is super, enhanced by the very rich gold finish. While the Pansy pattern doesn't bring top dollar, it is a pleasure to own such a beautiful item.

PANTHER

Fenton made some of the best animal patterns, and this one is at the top of the heap. Found in footed berry sets with a Butterfly and Berry exterior, the Panther bowl can be found in marigold, blue, green, amethyst, red (small bowls only), white, and the very rare Nile green opalescent bowl shown.

PARLOR PANELS

If you haven't had a chance to see one of these beautiful 4" vases, especially the Imperial purple shown, you've certainly missed a real experience, for these are a glass collector's dream. Parlor Panels was shown in old Imperial catalogs and has not been reproduced to date. I've heard of marigold ones, and I'm sure smoke and green are possibilities. Some examples are swung to 12" lengths.

PASTEL SWAN

Made by Northwood, Dugan, and Fenton, these master salt holders were very popular indeed. They can be found in opalescent glass as well as the iridized versions, and the colors are marigold, purple, ice blue, ice green, peach opalescent, celeste blue, amethyst opalescent, and pink. The example shown is Fenton's and is an experimental piece of amber, cobalt, and aqua glass mixed at the end of day production.

PEACH

Once more we show a Northwood pattern that was also produced in other types of glass. This was more than likely one of the earlier Northwood Carnival glass patterns and is found in a very fine cobalt blue as well as white, the latter often with gilting. What a shame more shapes were not made in Peach, for only berry sets, table sets, and water sets are known. The pattern is scarce and always brings top dollar.

PEACH AND PEAR

While no shards of this pattern were catalogued from the Dugan digs, I'm convinced it was their product. It is available mostly in marigold with an occasional amethyst one turning up. The mold work is excellent, and only the one shape and size are known.

Paneled Treetrunk

Pastel Swan

Paneled Holly

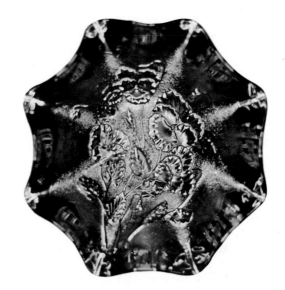

Pansy

Panther

Paneled Smocking

Parlor Panels

Peach

Peach and Pear

PEACOCK (MILLERSBURG)

While both Fenton and Northwood had similar patterns, the Millersburg Peacock is most noted and by far the best example of this design. The detailing is considerably greater, the bird more realistic and the quality of glass and finish superior. There are slight differences between the large bowl and the individual berry bowls in the Peacock pattern, but most of these are in the detail permitted on the allowed space, and a complete berry set is worth searching for. The color most often seen is a fine fiery amethyst, but green, marigold, and clambroth exist as well as blue.

PEACOCK AND DAHLIA

While this Fenton pattern is related in design to the Peacock and Grape, it is a better design and much scarcer. Known only in bowls and plates, Peacock and Dahlia carries the Berry and Leaf Circles pattern on the exterior. Colors known are marigold, blue, green, amethyst, vaseline, white, and aqua.

PEACOCK AND GRAPES

Obviously, this Fenton design and Peacock Dahlia were from the same artist. This too, is found on bowls, flat or footed, and scarce plates. Colors are marigold, blue, green, amethyst, aqua, vaseline, white, red, and peach opalescent.

PEACOCK AND URN (FENTON)

The Fenton version of this pattern (both Northwood and Millersburg had their own) is most often seen on stemmed compotes in marigold or aqua. Other shapes are bowls, plates, and a scarce goblet from the compote mold. Colors known are marigold, blue, green, amethyst, white, aqua, lavender, and red.

PEACOCK AND URN (MILLERSBURG)

Millersburg Peacock and Urn differs from the regular Peacock pattern in that it has a bee by the bird's beak. The shapes known are large bowls or small 6½" bowl, a chop plate, and a giant compote in the usual colors of marigold, green, and amethyst.

PEACOCK AND URN (NORTHWOOD)

Similar to the Millersburg version of Peacock and Urn, the Northwood design has three rows of beading on the urn and has more open area outside the design itself. It is found on ice cream sets, berry sets, a chop plate, and a very rare 6½" plate. Color range is wide from vivid to pastel, including aqua opalescent.

PEACOCK AND URN "MYSTERY" BOWL (MILLERSBURG)

There is little mysterious about this bowl any longer. It is indeed from Millersburg, has a bee and two rows of beading on the urn, and is found in both the ruffled and ice cream shape in 8" and 8½" diameters. Colors are the usual marigold, amethyst, and green and all are rare.

PEACOCK AND URN VARIANT (MILLERSBURG)

Over the years, so much controversy has arisen over all the Millersburg Peacock designs, I'm showing all of them including this 6⅛" very shallow bowl. Note that there is a bee, and the urn has three rows of beads! The only color reported on this piece is amethyst. So far, four are known, so it is rather rare.

Peacock and Urn "Mystery" Bowl

Peacock and Urn Variant

Peacock

Peacock and Dahlia

Peacock and Grapes

Peacock and Urn (Fenton)

Peacock and Urn (Millersburg)

Peacock and Urn (Northwood)

PEACOCK AT THE FOUNTAIN

Peacock at the Fountain probably rates as Northwood's second most popular pattern, right on the heels of the famous Northwood Grape, and it's so easy to see why. It is an impressive, well done pattern with an intriguing design. Available in berry sets, table sets, punch sets, water sets, compotes, and a large footed orange bowl, Peacock at the Fountain was made in a host of colors, including the much-prized ice green and aqua opalescent. Shards of this pattern were found at Dugan, leading us to believe Harry Northwood "farmed out" work to the Dugan Glass Company to keep up with demand on his best-selling patterns. Dugan made a copy cat water set to be sure.

PEACOCK GARDEN VASE

This beautiful, well iridized vase was an early product of Northwood Carnival Glass, and when the Northwood factory closed, many of the molds were purchased by the Fenton company – thus, the reason this vase was re-issued by the Fenton company a few years back in the other types of glass. At any rate, the Northwood Peacock Garden vase is truly a rare and beautiful sight to behold and a real treasure for the owners. The coloring is exceptional.

PEACOCK LAMP

Made on a crystal base, this beautiful lamp base has an enameled interior and an iridized exterior. Colors are red, marigold, amethyst, smoke, and white, and all are rare. It's 10¼" tall, and sometimes has no hole indicating these were sold as both lamps and vases.

PEACOCK TAIL

Very reminiscent of the Northwood Nippon pattern, Fenton's Peacock Tail is known on bowls of all sizes, bon-bons, compotes, hat shapes (some with advertising), and vase interiors. Colors I've seen are marigold, blue, green, amethyst, amber, and red.

PEACOCK TAIL AND DAISY

I am very thrilled to finally show this very rare Westmoreland bowl pattern. Besides the marigold, there is an amethyst and a blue opal milk glass that isn't iridized, but I've heard of no other shapes or colors. As you can see, the pattern is graceful as can be, and the design is very well balanced.

PEACOCK TAIL VARIANT

One look at the iridescence of this little compote, and it becomes quite obvious it is a Millersburg product, culled from three common motifs used by most glass companies of the day – the peacock tail rings, the stippled rays, and the feather. At any rate, it is a nice little item and quite enjoyable to own. Amethyst seems to be the most often seen color, but marigold and green are known.

PEACOCK VARIANT (MILLERSBURG)

This extremely rare 7½" (same size as the Courthouse bowls) variant is an outstanding example of Millersburg craftsmanship. The mold work is very sharp with great detail, and there is a bee, but no beading. Also the urn is quite different than the other peacocks. Colors are marigold, green, and amethyst, but blue may exist.

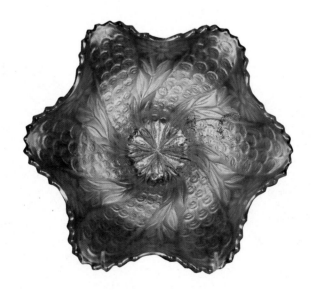

Peacock Tail and Daisy

Peacock at the Fountain

Peacock Garden Vase

Peacock Lamp

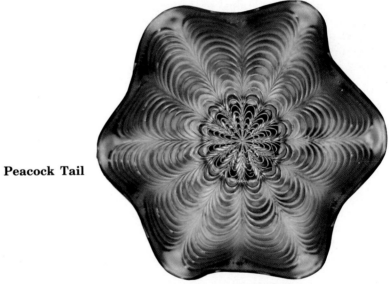

Peacock Tail

Peacock Tail Variant

Peacock Variant (Millersburg)

PEACOCKS

Often called "Peacocks on the Fence," this Northwood pattern typifies what Carnival glass is really all about. An interesting pattern, well molded, and turned out in a variety of appealing colors, Peacocks is a delight. Only average size bowls and plates are known, but the color range is wide, including vivid colors, pastels, and a really beautiful aqua opalescent. The exterior usually carries a wide rib pattern.

PEBBLE AND FAN

This very attractive vase is 11½" tall with a base diameter of 4½" and is truly a triumph. The mold work as well as the basic design is quite good. Colors I've heard about are cobalt blue, marigold, and a rather unusual amber with vaseline finish.

PEBBLES (DUGAN)

Here is the Dugan version of Coin Dot, and as you can see, it has no stippling. Found on open bowls and plates, colors are amethyst, marigold, and green.

PENNY MATCH HOLDER

Once again we picture a rare but useful novelty that is seldom found. The octagonal base is 3⅜" across and the entire Match Holder is 3½" tall. Purple is the only color about which I've heard, and the iridescence is very rich and heavy, very much like the better Northwood products in this color. However, the maker remains unknown.

PEOPLE'S VASE

We are told this masterwork of art glass was produced by the Millersburg company to show appreciation for the help of the Amish people of the area in getting the factory started. The dancing figures represent Amish children, hands clutching, prancing happily in thanks for a successful harvest – the only time their religion permitted such merriment. In the background Grandfather looks on with pleasure. But regardless of the circumstances surrounding the vase's conception, there is no doubt that this is at the very top of Millersburg's best and surely deserves a place in the history of American glass. The only pattern variation occurs in the lip which is usually straight but very occasionally appears in scallops. The vase is 11½" high and 5½" in diameter and weighs 5 lbs. The colors are marigold, amethyst, green, and cobalt blue.

PEPPER PLANT

On first glance this appears to be a Fenton Holly hat in cobalt blue, but examine it closely. You will find that while the stems and leaves are the same, the berries are really pulled into peppers, and each stem ends in a flower design at the top of the hat. The piece shown is 6½" across the top and stands 3" tall with 2" octagonal base.

PERFECTION

This beautiful water set is a fitting companion to its sister design, the Gay 90's. Outstanding mold work, color and iridescence are the hallmark of Millersburg, and the Perfection pattern certainly fits this description. The pitcher is 9½" tall and quite bulbous. It has four mold marks. The tumblers are 4" tall and taper from 2⅞" diameter at the top to 2⅛" at the base which has a 24-point rayed star.

PERSIAN GARDEN

Found in berry sets, ice cream sets, and two sizes of plates, this very well designed pattern came from the Dugan factory. It is available in marigold, amethyst, green, blue, white, ice blue, and ice green.

PERSIAN MEDALLION

Very oriental in flavor, Persian Medallion is one of those well-known Fenton patterns that was extremely popular when it was made and is available on bowls of all shapes and sizes, plates both large and small, compotes, rose bowls, and even a hair receiver (not to mention interiors on punch sets). Colors are marigold, blue, green, amethyst, white, amber, and red.

Pebbles (Dugan)   154   **Persian Medallion**

Peacocks

Pebble and Fan

Penny Match Holder

People's Vase

Pepper Plant

Perfection

Persian Garden

PETAL AND FAN

Found only in bowls of various sizes, this Dugan pattern also has the Jeweled Heart as an exterior design. The motif itself is simple but attractive – a series of alternating stippled and plain petals on a plain ribbed background with a fan-like design growing from each plain petal. The feeling is almost one of ancient Egypt where such fans were made of feathers. Petals and Fans is available in many colors including peach opalescent.

PETALS

This Dugan pattern is primarily a bowl pattern but is occasionally seen in a compote as well as a super banana bowl shape. Colors are the usual Dugan ones and the exterior seems to be found with a wide panel design.

PETER RABBIT

Peter Rabbit is one of Fenton's rare treasures, much sought by collectors and always priced for top dollar when sold. The shapes are 9" bowls and 10" plates in marigold, honey amber, green, blue, and amethyst. The design is closely related to both Little Fishes and Coral patterns.

PICKLE PAPERWEIGHT

Of all the oddities I've come across in Carnival glass, this is probably the oddball of all time. It measures 4½" in length and is hollow. As you can see, it has a super color and finish. I assume it to be a paperweight for I can think of little else it could be used for. The maker is unknown, and the only color reported is amethyst.

PILLAR AND FLUTE

Shown is the compote piece of this appealing Imperial pattern. Found in many shapes including a breakfast set, wall vase, 8" celery tray, berry set and rose bowl which often has the Imperial "Iron Cross" marking, the colors are nearly always marigold or clambroth. The design is a simple flute convex on both inside and out.

PILLOW AND SUNBURST

This pattern is credited to the Westmoreland company, and while it has been seen on several shapes in crystal, the only reported iridized shape is the bowl shape. The pattern is exterior and can be found in marigold or purple. The example shown is an 8½" bowl.

PIN-UPS

This scarce Australian pattern, simple but distinctive, is found mostly on 8½" bowls in a rich purple, but here we show a very scarce marigold. The exterior carries a slender thread border.

PINCHED RIB

Just why the glassmakers collapsed the sides of these vases remains a mystery to me, but certainly they thought there was a reason for several sizes exist. Most are found in marigold or peach opalescent glass, and they range in size from 4" tall to over a foot. The one shown has a pretty crimped lip. Some are Dugan products, but I'm sure other makers had a try at them.

PINCHED SWIRL

We seldom hear much about this attractive design, but it is known in both rose bowls and a rare spittoon, both in peach opalescent. I don't believe the maker has been confirmed, but Dugan or Westmoreland seem likely candidates.

PINE CONE

What a little beauty this design is! Known only on small bowls and scarce plates. Fenton's Pine Cone is seen mostly on marigold, blue or green, but an occasional amber plate has been seen. The design is well molded, geometrically sound, the iridescence is usually quite good.

Pillar and Flute (Imperial)

Pickle Paperweight

Petals

Pinched Rib

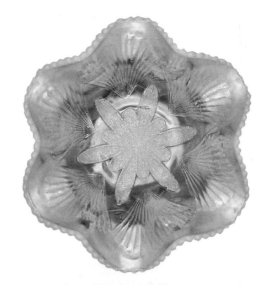

Petal and Fan

Peter Rabbit

Pillow and Sunburst

Pinched Swirl

Pine Cone

Pin-Ups

PINEAPPLE

Sometimes called Pineapple and Bows, this Sowerby pattern is available in 7½" dome-footed bowls, a compote, and a creamer. The mold work is quite good with much attention paid to detail. The luster is very good on the items I've seen, and colors of marigold, purple and blue are known.

PINWHEEL VASES

Now known to be of English origin, these pretty vases are found in three sizes in colors of marigold, blue, and amethyst. The mold work and coloring are very good, and so is the design. Originally, this pattern was called Derby.

PIPE HUMIDOR

Here is a fantastic Millersburg pattern many collectors haven't even seen, because it is just that rare. And what a pity so few of these are around since it is lovely enough to grace any collection. The coloring and iridescence are exceptional and the design flawless. Imagine how difficult to remove the lid from the mold without damage to the pipe and stem. The humidor is just over 8" tall and measures 5" across the lid. A three-pronged sponge holder is inside the lid, intended, of course, to keep the tobacco moist. Around the base is a wreath of acorns and leaves above another leaf-like pattern that runs down the base.

PLAID

On the few occasions this Fenton pattern is found, the coloring is usually cobalt blue with heavy luster or a rare red. As you can see, the coloring is very bright with rich iridescence. Needless to say, these 8½" bowls are a collector's dream and certainly would compliment any collection of red Carnival glass.

PLAIN JANE (IMPERIAL)

The only design whatsoever is the many-pointed star in the base of the bowl. It is found in berry sets in smoke, marigold, green, and purple; it is a close relative to the Plain Jane handled basket shown elsewhere.

PLAIN JANE BASKET

Long credited to the Imperial company, this large basket, while rather plain, has great appeal. It has been seen in smoke as well as marigold and measures 9¼" to the top of the handle.

PLAIN PETALS

Here is a pattern seldom discussed, yet it is found as the interior design of some pieces of Leaf and Beads. It is my opinion the latter was made by both Northwood and Dugan, and these pieces with the Plain Petals interior as well as the famous rose bowl are Northwood. The example shown is on a very interesting leaf-shaped nappy.

PLUME PANELS

For years I felt this rather stately vase was a Northwood product, but as you can see, it has been found in a beautiful red so I'm rather sure it came from the Fenton factory. Other colors known are marigold, blue, green, amethyst, and white.

PLUMS AND CHERRIES

Also known as Northwood's Two Fruits, this very rare pattern is known on a spooner, a lidless sugar, and tumblers. On one side we have three cherries, and the other features two plums. The table pieces have a series of small bands near the top and bubble-like lumps around the base, while the tumblers have only the bands. All are found in cobalt blue, and the tumbler in a rare marigold.

Plain Jane (Imperial)

Plain Petals

Pineapple

Pinwheel Vases

Pipe Humidor

Plaid

Plain Jane Basket

Plume Panels

Plums and Cherries

POINSETTIA (IMPERIAL)

Found only on one shape (the beautiful milk pitcher shown), Poinsettia is an outstanding Imperial pattern. Standing 6½" tall, the Poinsettia is usually found in marigold or smoke color, but as you can see, a rare and beautiful purple does exist as does an equally rare green. What a shame more shapes do not exist in this beautiful design!

POINSETTIA (NORTHWOOD)

For some reason, in years past someone attributed this very stylish pattern to the Fenton Glass Company. Just why, I can't guess, for Poinsettia was made by Northwood in custard glass and was illustrated in their advertising of the day. At any rate, this mistake has been corrected, and we now recognize this well done bowl as a Harry Northwood design. Poinsettia is found either as a flat based or footed bowl with the Fine Rib as an exterior pattern. The finish is nearly always superior. The colors are marigold, green, purple, fiery amethyst, white, and ice green.

POINSETTIA (INTERIOR)

Here is something unusual – a tumbler with all the pattern on the inside. Of course, we've all seen the Northwood Swirl pattern which is also an interior one, but that was a simple geometrical design, while the Interior Poinsettia is an offering of a large flower. Apparently these were never very popular for they are very scarce. Also, to the best of my knowledge, no pitcher has been found. The iridescence is on both the inside and outside and is a good rich marigold. Only some of these Northwood tumblers are marked.

POND LILY

Much like other Fenton patterns such as Two Flowers and Water Lily, Pond Lily has both scale filler and the Lotus-like flower. The only shape I've seen is the bonbon, and colors reported are in marigold, blue, green, and white. Of course, other colors may exist, and certainly red is a possibility.

PONY

For years the origin of this attractive bowl has been questioned, and only recently has it been attributed to the Dugan company. Colors seen are marigold, amethyst, and ice green. The mold work is quite good.

POOL OF PEARLS

Found only on the exterior of Persian Garden plates, this very attractive pattern is not easy to find and often goes unnoticed by collectors. It is a kissin' cousin to the opalescent pattern called Jewell and Flower and also resembles the Garden Path design.

POPPY (MILLERSBURG)

Large open compotes seem to have a fascination all their own, and this one from Millersburg is certainly no exception. It is quality all the way, whether found in green, purple, or marigold. Standing 7" tall and being 8" across, Poppy has four mold marks. It has the Potpourri as a secondary pattern. The poppy flowers and leaves are well done and are stippled.

POPPPY (NORTHWOOD)

This Northwood pattern is most often found on small oval bowls, described as trays or with the sides crimped as pickle dishes. However, it is also found as an exterior pattern on larger bowls, some with plain exteriors, others with a large Daisy in the center of the bowl. The colors are electric blue, marigold, peach, purple, aqua, opal, and white. Others may exist, but these are the ones I've seen.

Poppy

Pool of Pearls

160

**Poinsettia
(Imperial)**

**Poinsettia
(Northwood)**

Poinsettia (Interior)

Pond Lily

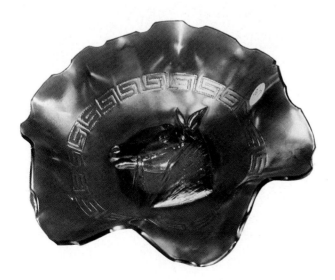

Pony

Poppy

161

POPPY SHOW (NORTHWOOD)

Let me state from the beginning this is not the same pattern as the Poppy Show Vase. It is a beautiful well-made item, very much akin to the Rose Show pattern in concept and design. It is found only on large bowls and plates in a wide range of colors, including marigold, green, blue, purple, white, ice blue and ice green. This Northwood pattern brings top dollar whenever offered for sale.

POPPY SHOW VASE (IMPERIAL)

What a shame this beauty was chosen to be reproduced by Imperial in the 1960's. The old Poppy Show Vase is a real show stopper, standing about 12" tall with a lip diameter of 6¾"! The mold work is very fine with the graceful poppy in a series of four panels around the vase. I've seen this artistic gem in marigold, clambroth, pastel marigold, amber, green, and purple. Naturally, the darker colors are quite scarce and are priced accordingly.

PORTLAND

Made in many shapes in crystal by U.S. Glass, Portland can be found in iridized glass with both tumblers and a water pitcher as well as large and small berry bowls. The bowl I saw was clear glass with very frosty iridization, while the pitcher and tumblers are marigold. This pattern is also called Buttress by some.

PORTLAND ELKS BELL (FENTON)

Like the other Fenton Elk's bells, this rare, previously unreported, Portland bell has the usual Elk's head within a clock face and the ribbed handle. The coloring is a fine cobalt blue with heavy lustre.

POTPOURRI (MILLERSBURG)

I certainly welcome the chance to show this very rare pitcher in the Potpourri pattern, a kissin' cousin to Millersburg's Country Kitchen pattern. Only two of these pitchers have been reported and both are marigold, are smaller than a water pitcher, and were used for milk.

PRAYER RUG

Known only in the finish shown, beautiful custard glass with a marigold iridescence, Fenton's Prayer Rug is a seldom-seen item. The only shape is a handled bonbon, but I suspect time will bring to light additional ones, since uniridized pieces are known in small bowls, vases, and hat shapes.

PREMIUM

Not only found in the well-known candlesticks shown, but also in 8½" bowls, 12" bowls, and 14" plates. Imperial's Premium pattern is shown in old catalogs in marigold, clambroth, purple, green, and smoke. The candlesticks are 8½" tall, heavy and beautifully iridized! While not in the class with the Grape and Cable candlesticks, they are still quite nice. Used with the medium size bowl, they make a nice console set.

PRETTY PANELS

This is a marked Northwood tumbler and as such is quite a sight for tumbler collectors. The color is a very bold frosty green, and the enameled cherry design is above average. It is found in marigold also.

Portland

Potpourri (Millersburg)

**Portland Elks
Bell (Fenton)**

Poppy Show

Poppy Show Vase

Prayer Rug

Premium

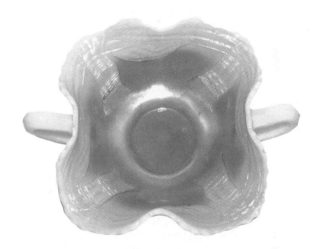

Pretty Panels

PRIMROSE

This well-conceived Millersburg pattern is much neglected and certainly shouldn't be. It is found only on fair-sized bowls in marigold, clambroth, amethyst, green, and a very rare blue. The exterior pattern is always Fine Cut Hearts, and the two are very compatible.

PRIMROSE AND FISHNET (#2475)

This unusual Imperial pattern has two kissin' cousins, also in red Carnival; one showing grapes, the other roses. The floral design is on one side only, and the fishnet covers the remainder of the glass. While red is the only reported color in iridized glass, all three patterns are known in crystal. The Primrose and Fishnet vase stands 6" tall. Needless to say, they are quite scarce.

PRIMROSE RIBBON SHADE

Except for the small panel lines that run from top to bottom, and the very subtle ribbon of flowers around the edge, this very pretty shade relies on rich color for its show. The bell shape turns in at the edge. It measures 5½" tall and is nearly 5" wide.

PRISM AND CANE

This very scarce product of Sowerby has an interior pattern of Embossed Scroll variant, and, as you can see, the base is ground. Apparently it is a sauce dish or jam dish as it measures 5" across the rim and stands 2¼" tall.

PRISM AND DAISY BAND

Apparently one of Imperial's late designs in Carnival glass and intended for a cheap mass sale, Prism and Daisy Band can be found only in marigold in berry sets, breakfast sets, a stemmed compote, and a vase shape. The coloring is adequate but not superior.

PRISMS

We now have evidence to support a Westmoreland origin for this unusual little compote. For quite awhile, amethyst was the only color seen, but here is a marigold of which I've seen some four or five, and green also exists. Prisms measure 7¼" across the handles and is 2½" tall. The pattern is all exterior and is intaglio with an ornate star under the base like the one on the Cherry and Cable butter dish.

PROPELLER

Besides the usual small compote found in this Imperial pattern, I'm very happy to show the rare 7½" stemmed vase in the Propeller pattern. The coloring is a good rich marigold, but others may exist since the compote is seen in marigold, green, and amethyst.

PULLED HUSK CORN VASE

Apparently Harry Northwood wasn't quite satisfied with this very rare example of a corn vase, for few of these are around in comparison with the regular corn vase. Known in two sizes, the Pulled Husk vase has been seen in green and purple, and some are pulled more grotesquely than others.

PULLED LOOP

This rather simple Fenton vase design is found quite often, mostly in marigold, blue, or amethyst, but it is known in a beautiful green, as well as an occasional peach opalescent finish. The size may vary from 8" to 12", but the finish is usually very heavily lustered.

**Primrose Ribbon
Shade**

164

Pulled Husk Corn Vase

Primrose

Primrose and Fishnet

Pulled Loop

Prism and Cane

Prism and Daisy Band

Prisms

Propeller

PUZZLE

Found in stemmed bonbons and compotes, Dugan's Puzzle is an appealing pattern. The all-over design is well balanced, and the stippling adds interest. Colors known are marigold, purple, green, blue, white, and peach opalescent.

QUARTER BLOCK

After seeing a jelly dish complete with a wire frame and spoon attached, I'm convinced this pattern is English. It is found primarily in table set pieces, and I've seen the open sugar, creamer, covered butter, and the jelly piece. Color is usually a good marigold, and the creamer stands 3½" tall and measures 5" across from lip to handle.

QUEEN'S JEWEL

I know very little about this interesting stemmed goblet except that the coloring is light flashing and the design, while busy, gives an interesting cover to the entire bowl area as well as the flared base. I suspect it is from Europe.

QUEEN'S LAMP

While only a handful of these kerosene lamps exist in carnival glass and all in a deep green, sometimes with light iridescence, they are also found in crystal with a matching shade. They are large with a base diameter of 7" and stand 9" to the top of the font.

QUESTION MARKS

Here is a simple Dugan pattern found on the interiors of bonbons and occasionally compotes like the one shown. Again the exterior is usually plain, and the colors are peach opalescent, marigold, purple, and white. Both the compote and the bonbon are footed; the compote is one of the small size, measuring 4½" tall and 4" across the highly ruffled edge. The exterior occasionally has a pattern called Georgia Belle.

QUILL

Once again we show a pattern of which shards were found in the Dugan diggings, and I truly believe Quill was indeed a Dugan Glass Company pattern. The pitcher is some 10" tall and has a base diameter of 4½". The colors are marigold and amethyst, and the iridescence is usually above average. Quill is a scarce pattern and apparently small quantities were made, again pointing toward the Dugan company as the manufacturer. The water set is the only shape.

QUILTED DIAMOND

Certainly one of Imperial's best exterior designs, this pattern is found as a companion to the Pansy pattern on one-handled nappies, dresser trays and pickle dishes. Just why Imperial didn't use it more is a mystery for it is beautifully done and very pleasing to the eye.

RADIANCE

The very name says it all on this rare and attractive enameled water set. Both the tumblers and the pitcher have six creased panels around the perimeter with the latter having a flaring base while the tumbler's base is flat and heavy. Coloring is light and extends only to the neck on the pitcher.

RAGGED ROBIN

Just why more of these Fenton bowls weren't produced is a mystery, but the fact remains these are quite hard to find today. Found only on average size bowls often with a ribbon candy edge. Colors reported are amethyst, marigold, blue, green, and white with blue most available.

Quarter Block

Quilted Diamond

Radiance

Queen's Lamp

Queen's Jewel

Puzzle

Question Marks

Quill

Ragged Robin

RAINBOW (NORTHWOOD)

Similar to the Northwood Raspberry compote or the one with only a Basketweave exterior, this one is completely plain with iridescence on the inside only. The luster swirls around the glass in layers, just like a rainbow, thus the name.

RAINDROPS

Here is another of the dome-footed bowls available in peach opalescent like so many offered by the Dugan company. Remember, I said earlier that I felt Dugan was responsible for at least 90% of the peach Carnival, and a close study of these bowls will support this belief. Raindrops is found without stippling. It has the Keyhole pattern as an exterior companion and has four mold marks. All in all, it is a nice pattern to own, especially if you like the peach opalescent glass. Also found in amethyst.

RAMBLER ROSE

Until quite recently, I'd always felt Rambler Rose was a Fenton product, but upon examining a large shard of this pattern from the Dugan dump site, I'm compelled to admit my mistake. This water set has a bulbous pitcher with a ruffled top. The flowers are well designed and clearly molded. The colors are marigold, purple, blue, and green. Perhaps research in the years ahead will add more information about this pattern.

RANGER

Known in breakfast sets, water sets, a milk pitcher, and table sets, this pattern, often confused with the Australian Blocks and Arches pattern, is found only in marigold. It is an Imperial product, but one version of the tumbler is known to have been produced by Christales de Mexico and is so marked.

RASPBERRY

Even without the famous trademark, this pattern would be recognized as a Northwood product, for it includes the basketweave so often found on that company's designs. Available in water sets, table sets, berry sets, and a milk pitcher. Raspberry has long been a favorite with collectors. The colors are marigold, green, purple, ice blue, and ice green with the richly lustered purple most prevalent.

RAYS

If you look closely at this Dugan pattern you will detect an inner ring of pointed rays before the veins fan out toward the outer edges, distinguishing the simple design from similar ones. It was made in all the Dugan colors, and this one has a Jeweled Heart exterior.

RAYS AND RIBBON

Each of the makers of Carnival glass seems to have had a try at a pattern using stippled rays. The Millersburg version is quite distinctive because of the bordering of ribbon-like design, resembling a fleur-de-lis design. Most of the bowls are not radium finish and usually carry the Cactus pattern on the exterior. Occasionally a plate is found in Rays and Ribbons, but one wonders if this were not produced as a shallow bowl. Amethyst is the usual color, followed by green, marigold, and vaseline in that order.

RIBBED HOLLY

Just like the unusual Fenton Holly items, these small, stemmed pieces had the interior ribbing added for some reason. Most are seen in cobalt blue but here is a brilliant cherry red one! These stemmed pieces can be shaped like compotes, deep unruffled compotes, or goblets.

RIBBON TIE

Sometimes called Comet, this well-known Fenton pattern is found chiefly on all sorts of bowls as well as ruffled plates. The colors range from very good to poor in marigold, blue, amethyst, red, and green, and often the luster is only so-so.

Rays

**Rainbow
(Northwood)**

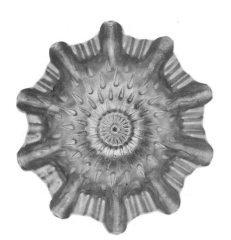

Raindrops

Ribbed Holly

Rambler Rose

Ranger

Raspberry

Rays and Ribbons

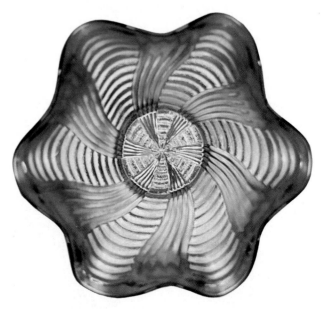

Ribbon Tie

RIBS (SMALL BASKET)

Marian Hartung called this pattern Small Basket, because she had only seen the soap dish, but it is actually a complete dresser set with mirrored tray, ringtree, puffbox, pinbox, three perfumes, cologne, and the soap dish. The color isn't great, but to find the complete set is a minor miracle. It was made in Czechoslovakia and has paper labels saying so. I have renamed it Ribs.

RINGS

Besides the large, 8" vase shown, I've recently seen this pattern on a 6½" covered cookie jar in a pale marigold. This pattern is shown in old Jeanette company ads, and the pattern was still being made in the 1958-59 period in pink milk glass, so it must have been a popular pattern.

RIPPLE

Ranging in height from 8" to 18", this Imperial glass vase, while easy to find, is always a very attractive item. The pattern of rings around the glass that has been swung or pulled out makes for appeal. Colors are marigold, purple, green, blue, teal, clambroth, smoke, and amber.

RISING SUN

Made by U.S. Glass, this very distinctive geometric pattern is seldom mistaken for any other. It can be found in water sets with two different pitcher shapes, a rare table set, and a lemonade tray. Colors are mostly cobalt blue with rare examples of marigold known.

ROBIN

Despite the reproductions of this fine old Imperial pattern, the prices have held up rather well on the old pieces. The water sets, found only in marigold, and the mug found in smoke are especially desirable. Apparently the appeal lies in the handsome presentation of the nicely done bird, the flower and branch dividers, and the flowering leaf pattern, so pleasing to the eye.

ROCOCO

This beautiful little Imperial vase was the first item in smoke I'd ever seen, and I must admit I loved it at first sight! While it may be found on a small bowl shape with a dome base and in marigold as well as smoke, it is the vase most think of whenever Rococo is mentioned. The vase is 5½" tall and shows four mold marks. I have had a green one reported but haven't seen it yet.

ROLLED RIBS

This very pretty bowl is a real mystery and the only example of this treatment I've ever seen. The marigold iridescence rings the out edges for about ½ the depth of the bowl. Then a series of ribs roll out on the exterior, and these are a milky opalescent finish. The owner says the bowl has a metallic ring when tapped.

ROMAN ROSETTE GOBLET (UNLISTED)

While this pattern is not difficult to find in pressed glass, this is the only reported item in iridized glass to the best of my knowledge. As you can see, it is slightly crooked, but the iridization on the clear glass is unmistakable with beautiful blue and pink coloring. It measures 6" tall and has a base diameter of 2¾".

ROSALIND (MILLERSBURG)

Often called Drape and Tie, this classic Millersburg design is found as the interior pattern on Dolphin compotes, on rare 9" compotes and large and small bowls. The colors are marigold, amethyst, and green, but I've seen a 9" bowl in a stunning aqua, and a plate is known in green.

**Ribs
(Small Basket)**

Rings

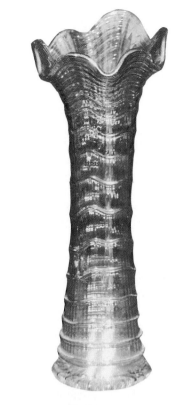

Ripple

Rising Sun

Robin

Rolled Ribs

Rococo

Roman Rosette Goblet

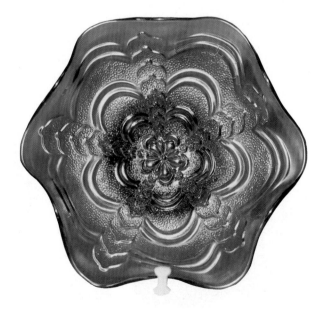

Rosalind

ROSALIND VARIANT (MILLERSBURG)

If you look closely at this design and the regular Rosalind shown elsewhere, you will see a good deal of difference, especially in concentric peacock tail sections. For this reason, I'm listing the compote shown as a variant (and expect letters about it). Colors reported in this compote are amethyst and green, but marigold was probably made also.

ROSE AND GREEK KEY PLATE

This very beautiful square plate is a sight to behold. Not only is it quite unique, but it is so very well designed that I simply cannot understand why there aren't more of these. But alas, there's only the one known. The coloring is a smoky amber. The plate measures 8½" across, and the roses are deep and hollow on the underside, much like the well-known Rose Show bowls.

ROSE BAND

While the name is somewhat confusing with a similar tumbler pattern called Band of Roses, the name certainly does describe the design. The pattern is typically European, and the tumbler is short at 3¾" tall. The color is good, and the pattern rare.

ROSE COLUMN

This stately Millersburg vase is a real beauty and like several Carnival patterns such as the Imperial Grape carafe or the Grape Arbor pitcher, the rows of roses are hollow. This requires great skill by the worker when removing it from the mold, and many must have been broken in doing so. This lovely vase is 10" tall and 5" across the diameter. There are six columns of roses, each topped by a spring of leaves. The iridescence is top quality, and the colors are marigold, blue, green and amethyst. The Rose Column vase would make a lovely companion to the People's Vase.

ROSE GARDEN

Once again we finally have a true maker for a much-disputed pattern, and Rose Garden is now in the list of glass from the Eda Glassworks of Sweden. It is found in many shapes including bowls, round and oblong vases, a pitcher that is rare, a beautiful rose bowl, and a covered butter dish. Colors are marigold and blue only.

ROSE SHOW

What a handsome piece of glass this is! The design of this Northwood is flawless, heavy and covering every inch of available space. Yet it isn't in the least bit busy looking. One has the distinct feeling he is looking into a reeded basket of fresh-cut roses and can almost smell the perfume. Found only on bowls and a plate, the beautiful pattern was produced in small amounts in marigold, purple, blue, green, white, ice blue, ice green, peach opalescent, amber, aqua opalescent, and a rare ice green opalescent.

ROSE SHOW VARIANT

Over the years, very little has been learned about this plate variant of the Rose Show pattern, but as you can see, it is quite different in both flower and leaf arrangement and number. It is found in a host of colors including marigold, amethyst, green, blue, peach opalescent, aqua opalescent, ice blue, and white.

ROSE SPRAY COMPOTE

Standing only 4½" at its tallest point, this beautiful compote is a real treasure. The only colors I've heard about are white and the beautiful ice blue and ice green. I suspect this is a Fenton product, but have no verification of this. The rose and leaf spray is on one side of the rim only and is rather faint, much like the Kittens bowl.

ROSE TREE

Make no mistake about it, this is a very scarce and desirable Fenton bowl pattern. I believe this was the Fenton answer to the Imperial Lustre Rose, but apparently it was made in small quantities. The colors known are marigold and cobalt blue, and the size is a generous 10" diameter.

Rose Band

Rosalind Variant (Millersburg)

Rose Show Variant

Rose and Greek Key Plate

Rose Column

Rose Garden

Rose Show

Rose Spray Compote

Rose Tree

ROSES AND FRUIT

This beautiful little compote is unique in several ways and is a very hard-to-find Millersburg item. It measures 5¼" from handle to handle and is nearly 4" high. Notice the deep bowl effect (so often used by Millersburg on compotes and bonbons) and the pedestal base. In addition, observe the unusual stippling around the edge of the interior, and, of course, the combination of roses, berries, and pears are quite distinctive. It is found in green and amethyst mostly, but was made in marigold and blue too.

ROSES AND RUFFLES LAMP (RED)

I'm frankly not too taken with Gone With the Wind Lamps, but the beautifully iridized ones are in a class by themselves. The very few ones known are simply beautiful. The Roses and Ruffles lamp is 22" tall. It has excellent fittings of brass and is quality all the way. The mold work on the glass is quite beautiful and the luster superior.

ROSETTE

Combining several well-known Carnival glass patterns, including Stippled Rays, Beads and Prisms, this Northwood pattern isn't the easiest thing to find. In arrangement it reminds one of the Greek Key patterns, but Rosette stands on its own. Found only on generous sized bowls, the colors are marigold and amethyst. Green may be a possibility but I haven't seen one.

ROSE WINDOWS

I find this tumbler one of the prettiest geometric designs I've ever seen and wish other shapes were known. It has been seen in both a flashed light finish as well as the beautiful marigold shown. It stands 4½" tall, flares at both top and bottom and is quality all the way.

ROUND-UP

As I stated earlier, Round-Up, Fanciful, and Apple Blossoms Twigs all have the same exterior pattern and shards of the latter two were found in the Dugan diggings. Found only on bowls, ruffled plates, and true plates, Round-Up is available in marigold, purple, peach opalescent, blue, amber, white, and a pale shade of lavender. The true plate is quite scarce and always brings top dollar.

ROYALTY

Perhaps one might mistake this for the Fashion pattern at first glance, but with a little concentrated study it becomes obvious they aren't the same. Royalty is a pattern formed from a series of hobstars above a series of diamond panels. Found on punch sets and two-piece fruit bowls, this Imperial pattern is mostly found in marigold, but the fruit bowl set has been reported in smoke.

RUFFLED RIB SPITTOON

This little Northwood spittoon could be called Fine Rib or Lustre and Clear, I guess, but I feel the name given is more appropriate. At any rate, the coloring is a good rich marigold, and the ribbing is on the interior. The spittoon stands 4" tall and has a rim diameter of 4½" with a collar base diameter of nearly 2".

Rose Windows

Roses and Fruit

Roses and Ruffles Lamp

Rosette

Round-Up

Royalty

Ruffled Rib Spittoon

RUSTIC

I would venture to say Rustic is one of the best known and most common of vase shapes for it is plentiful, found in many sizes and colors including marigold, blue, green, amethyst, aqua, vaseline, amber, white, peach opalescent, and red. It was pulled from the Fenton Hobnail vase shapes and can be found in sizes from 6" to 20".

S-REPEAT

Made in crystal, decorated crystal, and gilt glass prior to being made in Carnival glass, S-Repeat is found in only a small range of shapes in iridized glass. Besides the punch set shown, there is a rare toothpick that has been widely reproduced, and a handful of marigold tumblers that some believe are questionable. At any rate, in Carnival glass, Dugan's S-Repeat is a very scarce item.

SACIC ASHTRAY

This little ashtray is a real mystery in many ways. It reads: "NARAJA SACIC POMELO." Apparently it was meant to go to Brazil, but why an English glass maker would mold such an item escapes me. The color is quite good with a touch of amber in marigold.

SAILBOAT

Found in small bowls, plates, compotes, goblets, and wines, Sailboats is a well-known Fenton pattern that competes nicely with Imperial's Windmill pattern. Colors I've heard about are marigold, blue, green, vaseline, amber, and red, but not all colors are found in all shapes.

SAWTOOTH BAND

From the Heisey company this pretty enameled tumbler is much like others except for the bands just above the base. This same pattern has been seen without the enameling also. All are marigold, and all are rare.

SAWTOOTH PRISMS

Despite not having a great deal of lustre, this cute jelly jar has a lot of character. It measures just over 3" in diameter and stands 4¼" tall. The sawtooth edges fit the lid and the bottom together nicely. Marigold is the only color reported.

SCALE BAND

While not too original, this Fenton pattern of smooth rays and bands of scale filler does quite nicely in the shapes chosen: bowls, plates, pitchers, and tumblers. The color most seen is, of course, marigold. However, Scale Band can also be found in green, amethyst, peach opalescent, aqua opalescent (quite rare), and red.

SCARAB HATPIN

I have always avoided showing hatpins or buttons, but the one here is so pretty, I couldn't resist. It is on a very deep amethyst base color and has super luster. It measures 1¾" x 1⅜".

Sawtooth Band

Scarab Hatpin

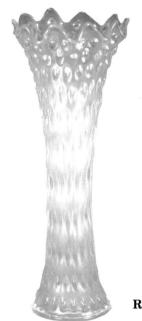

Rustic

S-Repeat

Sacic Ashtray

Sailboats

Scale Band

Sawtooth Prisms

SCOTCH THISTLE

What a pretty pattern this is for the interior of a compote! As you can see, the exterior is plain like so many compotes, but the edges have a very interesting ruffled effect. Colors I've seen are marigold, blue, green, and amethyst, but others may certainly exist. This pattern was manufactured by Fenton.

SCOTTIE

Surely there isn't a collector that hasn't seen these in the flea markets in Scotties, poodles, deer, duckies, or rabbits. They are all covered powder jars, all marigold and made near the end of the Carnival glass heyday. Still the coloring is usually respectable, and they are cute little critters.

SCROLL AND FLOWER PANELS

I've always been intrigued by this stylish Imperial pattern even though it was reproduced in the 1960's with a flared top. As you can see, the mold work, while very busy, is quite satisfying and the coloring is super. I've seen this vase in marigold and purple, but green is a possibility. The vase stands 10" tall on a collar base with a many-rayed star.

SCROLL AND GRAPE (MILLERSBURG)

Nothing pleases me more than showing an unlisted pattern, especially if it is Millersburg! The only example reported of this Multi-Fruits and Flowers punch bowl interior is such a find. From the center four strings of acanthus leaves extend to four clusters of grapes, all topped by a rich scroll. What a shame this wasn't a standard pattern! It's as pretty as anything Millersburg ever made.

SCROLL EMBOSSED (IMPERIAL)

As I said earlier, while this pattern originated at the Imperial factory, it was later produced in England on Carnival glass, notably on the Diving Dolphins bowl and on a four-handled sauce dish. The Imperial version is used with File pattern exterior on bowls with Easter Star as an exterior pattern on large compotes, as well as alone on bowls and smaller compotes. The usual colors are green, marigold, or purple, but smoke does exist. A scarce plate shape is shown.

SCROLL EMBOSSED VARIANT (ENGLISH)

Much like its Imperial counterpart, this English version is found on small bowls, small handled ashtrays, compotes, and the Diving Dolphins bowls. Without the exterior design it would be impossible to say who made which. However, the English version is known in marigold, blue, green, and amethyst.

SEAFOAM

Difficult to show in a photo, this Dugan pattern is an exterior one on the Constellation compotes. In design, it much resembles S-repeat, and it may have been a spin-off design. It does have a fine stippling around the rolling curves and is quality all the way.

SEA GULLS BOWL

If one rarity in this book stands as an example of "scarce but not prized," the Sea Gulls bowl is that rarity. Certainly there are far fewer of these to be found than many items that bring 10 times the money, but for some strange reason, these cuties are not sought by most collectors. The two bird figures are heavily detailed as is the bowl pattern. The color, while not outstanding, is good and is iridized both inside and out. The diameter of the bowl is 5¾" and the depth is 2⅞". I believe the manufacturer was Dugan.

Scroll and Grape (Millersburg)

Interior of Scroll and Grape

Scotch Thistle

Scottie

Scroll and Flower Panels

Scroll Embossed

Scroll Embossed Variant

Sea Gulls Bowl

Seafoam

SEA GULLS VASE

This rare vase has been traced to the Eda Glassworks of Sweden, adding to their growing importance as a non-American maker of iridized glass. The only color reported is a rich marigold with a good deal of amber hue.

SEACOAST PINTRAY

Pintrays are not common in Carnival glass, and this one from Millersburg is one of the nicest ones. The irregular shaping, the beautiful coloring and fine detail make this an outstanding item. It measures 5½" x 3¾" and rests on an oval collar base. The colors are marigold, green, amethyst, and a fine deep purple.

SEAWEED

Can you imagine a more graceful pattern than this one from Millersburg? The curving leaves and snail-like figures seem to be drifting back and forth in the watery depths, and the bubbles of beading add just the right touch. Usually found on fairly large bowls, Seaweed has three mold marks. The colors are marigold, green, and amethyst. Also a rare plate and a rare small bowl have been found.

SEAWEED LAMP

I've heard of four of these lamps in two different base shapes, but all with the Seaweed design circling the body. All were in marigold ranging from quite good to poor. The example shown measures 12" to the top of the font. The maker is unknown, but the lamp is a rare one.

SHELL

I've always felt this was a superior Imperial pattern – simple yet effective. This is especially true on the few plates I've seen. The pattern is a well-balanced one of eight scalloped shells around a star-like pattern. The background may or may not be stippled – I've seen it both ways. The shapes are smallish bowls, plates, and a reported compote I haven't seen. The colors are marigold, green, purple, smoke, and amber.

SHELL AND JEWEL

Easily found, this Westmoreland pattern was made only in the shapes shown in colors of marigold, amethyst, and green (white has been reported but not confirmed). The pattern is a copy of the Nugget Ware pattern of the Dominion Glass Company of Canada. Shell and Jewel has been reproduced, so buy with caution.

SHRINE CHAMPAGNE (ROCHESTER)

Shown is one of three known stemmed champagnes manufactured by the U.S. Glass Company, to be given away at Shrine conventions (a rare toothpick holder is also known). The 1911 Rochester, NY champagne has painted scenes of Rochester and Pittsburgh with a gilt decoration. The other champagnes are the 1910 New Orleans and Tobacco Leaf (Louisville, KY – 1909). Each is a premium example of the glass maker's skill.

SILVER QUEEN

While this Fenton pattern has never been one of my favorite enameled water sets, it is certainly not all that easy to find and has good color and finish. It is found only in marigold with the wide silver band and white scroll and only in water sets.

Sea Gulls Vase

Seacoast Pintray

Seaweed

Seaweed Lamp

Silver Queen

Shell

Shell and Jewel

Shrine Champagne (Rochester)

SINGING BIRDS

Found in custard glass, crystal, and Carnival glass, Singing Birds is one of the better known Northwood patterns. The shapes are berry sets, table sets, water sets, and mugs in vivid and pastel colors.

SINGLE FLOWER FRAMED

Much like the Single Flower pattern, this one has odd framing of double wavy lines that encircle the flowers. The pattern is exterior, the colors the usual Dugan ones. Shapes are large and small bowls, and the interior of the one shown shows a Fine Rib pattern.

SIX PETALS

Nearly always seen in shallow bowls in peach opalescent, Six Petals is occasionally found in a rare plate. The other colors available are purple, green, blue, and white. It is a Dugan product shown in black amethyst in exterior view.

SIX-SIDED CANDLESTICKS

What a beauty this candlestick is! Not only is the near-cut design quite imaginative, but the workmanship is just super. The Six-Sided Candlestick is 7½" tall and has a base diameter of 3¾". It has been seen in a rich marigold, an outstanding purple, smoke, and green. It has been reproduced by Imperial in crystal, so be cautious in your selection!

SKI STAR

While this Dugan pattern is found occasionally on small bowls in purple, blue and green, it is on the larger dome-footed bowls in peach opalescent where the pattern has its "day in the sun." These are found in many variations, some crimped with one side turned down, others with both sides pulled up to resemble a banana bowl. The exterior usually carries the Compass pattern, an interesting geometric design, or is plain.

SLIPPER (LADY'S)

Here's another novel miniature from U.S. Glass so ornamental yet appealing. Needless to say, very few of these were ever iridized, so all are rare. The Lady's Slipper is 4½" long and 2¾" high and is a good marigold. The entire piece is covered with stippling.

SMALL RIB

The compote shown has been pulled into the rose bowl shape, but versions of the lip opened out are also known. Coloring is much like the Daisy Squares pieces and may have the same common maker.

SMOOTH PANELS

Since I first showed this vase in marigold iridescence on milk glass, I've seen many sizes and colors. These vases remind one of the Imperial Flute pattern around their base. Found in sizes ranging from 8" tall to 18", the lip is often widened to 7". Colors are marigold, amethyst, green, purples, peach opalescent, amber, teal, red, and several colors over milk glass including marigold, amber, and a beautiful smoke.

Smooth Panels

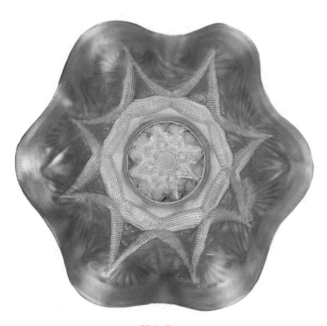

Ski Star   182

Singing Birds

Six Petals

Six Petals

Single Flower Framed

Six-Sided Candlesticks

Slipper (Lady's)

Small Rib Compote

SMOOTH RAYS (WESTMORELAND)

Like most of the other major manufacturers, Westmoreland had a try at a Smooth Rays pattern in compotes and various size bowls with both flat and dome bases. Here is one of theirs in a beautiful blue milk glass iridized, but these were made in marigold, amethyst, green, marigold milk glass, amber, and teal as well.

SNOW FANCY

Known in small bowls as well as a creamer and sugar breakfast set, this scarce near-cut pattern is one not with which many collectors are familiar. The bowl has been seen in green as well as a frosty white, and the breakfast set is shown in marigold; other colors may exist, but I haven't seen them. It is a McKee product.

SODA GOLD

Much confused with Tree of Life and Crackle shown elsewhere in this book, Imperial's Soda Gold differs from either in that the veins are much more pronounced and are highly raised from the stippled surface. It is found only on short candlesticks, a rare 9" bowl, and beautiful water sets in marigold or smoke.

SODA GOLD SPEARS

Similar to Tree of Life and Crackle patterns, this all-over design is easy on the eye and a good background to hold iridescence well. The bowl shown is the 8" size, but 5" bowls and plates are known in both marigold and clambroth.

SOLDIERS AND SAILORS (ILL.)

One of two known such commemorative plates, this is the Illinois version. It features the Soldiers and Sailors Home in Quincy, IL and measures 7½". On the exterior is found Fenton's Berry and Leaf Circle design. The colors known are marigold, amethyst, and blue.

SOUTACHE PLATE

I've long believed this to be a Northwood pattern, and while I've seen it on both bowls and lamp shades, this is the first footed plate I've run across. It measures 8¾" in diameter and has peach opalescent edging. The foot is a dome base and is of clear glass.

SOWERBY WIDE PANEL

While there isn't much special about this bowl — a wide panel exterior with a many rayed star base, it does have very good color and finish and the scalloping around the rim adds a touch of class. It is English and made by Sowerby.

SPIRAL CANDLE

Like the Premium Candlesticks also made by Imperial, these heavy, practical candlesticks were sold in pairs and were made in green, smoke, and marigold. They measure 8¼" from the base to the top and, as far as I know, did not have a console bowl to match. The smoke coloring is particularly beautiful with many fiery highlights.

SPIRALEX

This is the name used in England to describe these lovely vases, so I've continued using it. The colors are marigold, amethyst, green, and blue, and all I've seen are outstanding with very rich iridescence. Sizes range from 8" to 14".

**Smooth Rays
(Westmoreland)**

Soda Gold Spears

Sowerby Wide Panel

Snow Fancy

Soda Gold

Soldiers and Sailors (Ill.)

Spiralex

Soutache Plate

Spiral Candle

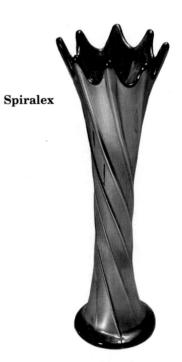

SPLIT DIAMOND

I'm very happy to show the complete table set in this Davison pattern, for while the creamer is easily found, the covered butter and sugar are quite scarce in this country. The only color is a good strong marigold with fine luster and superior mold.

SPOKES

Similar to the Corinth patterns, this Fostoria bowl is 10" across and is often seen in crystal. This is the first iridized one I've seen and it has outstanding pink and blue highlights.

SPRING OPENING

Made from the standard Millersburg small berry bowl mold, this interesting hand-grip advertising plate is a seldom-seen, always attractive item from the Ohio company. It measures 6½" in diameter, has the typical many-rayed base, and is known only in amethyst. The lettering says: "Campbell & Beesley Co. Spring Opening 1911."

SPRINGTIME

In many ways this pattern is similar to Northwood's Raspberry pattern, especially since both are bordered at the bottom with versions of a basketweave. Springtime, however, is really its own master and bears panels of wheat, flowers and butterflies above and throughout the basketweave. Found in berry sets, table sets, and very scarce water sets in marigold, green, amethyst, and also in pastels, Springtime is a very desirable pattern.

SQUARE DIAMOND (COLUMN FLOWER)

Sometime after I gave this vase the above name, another author called it Column Flower, so you have a choice. It was made at the Riihimaki Glassworks in Finland and has been seen only in blue.

STAG AND HOLLY

This is probably the best known animal pattern in all Carnival glass other than the Peacock, and certainly it remains one of Fenton's best efforts. Often brought out at Christmas time, the Stag and Holly is found mainly on footed bowls, rare footed plates, and rare rose bowls. Colors are marigold, blue, green, amethyst, aqua, peach opalescent, and red.

STAR

While there may not be a great deal of inventiveness to this English pattern, it certainly serves a useful purpose and does it with a good deal of attractiveness. The clear center shows off the star on the base quite well, and the two tiny rows of rope edging add a bit of interest. Marigold is the only color I've heard about.

STAR AND FAN CORDIAL SET

This pattern is not the same as the vase with the same name but has a close tie with the other cordial sets like Zipper Stitch which were made in Czechoslovakia. It is a rare grouping and the only complete set known.

STAR AND FAN VASE

I've been privileged to see the two Imperial marigold vases shown, but a beautiful cobalt blue example also exists, and it must be something, for the marigold ones are very beautiful examples of the glassmaker's art. The glass itself is thick and very clear. The luster is rich and even, and the design is flawless. Star and Fan is 9½" tall.

Spokes

Spring Opening

Square Diamond (Column Flower)

186

Star and Fan Cordial Set

Split Diamond

Springtime

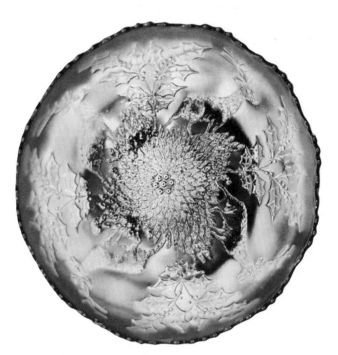

Stag and Holly

Star and Fan Vase

Star

STAR AND FILE

Very much like Star Medallion in concept, Imperial's Star and File doesn't have the cane effect, but uses panels of file, hobstars and sunbursts in a well-balanced design. Found in bowls, breakfast sets, a water set, a wine decanter set, handled vases, a rare rose bowl, and a large compote, Star and File is known in marigold, smoke, purple, and green.

STAR AND HOBS

This very attractive 9" rose bowl has much to offer in both quality and looks. The color is a deep purple glass with beautiful gold luster, and while the base pattern resembles Ohio Star, I believe this to be a European product.

STARBURST

This beautiful and rare spittoon whimsey shape comes from the Riihimaki glassworks of Finland. It is found mostly in bowls, table set pieces, and a vase shape and has been reported in cobalt blue; however, this is the first spittoon about which I've heard.

STAR FISH

As you can see, this little compote is a real cutie. The design is strong and interesting, and the quality is top notch. Star Fish is from the Dugan company and is seen in marigold, green, purple, and the beautiful peach opalescent.

STARLYTE SHADE

Imperial made several very attractive light shades, and this is certainly one of them. The Starlyte shade stands 4" tall and has a bell diameter of 8". The pattern is a series of panels containing graduated hobstars on a stippled background. Colors are a rich marigold and clambroth, but I suspect smoke and green are also possibilities.

STAR MEDALLION

Star Medallion is a much-overlooked but well designed near-cut Imperial pattern. Apparently, it was a very popular pattern in its day for it is found in many shapes, including bowls of all shapes, a table set, a handled celery, a 9" plate, milk pitcher, punch cup, tumbler, goblet, and a very beautiful compote. Colors are a rich marigold, smoke, and occasionally a beautiful helios green.

STAR OF DAVID

For some unknown reason, only small amounts of this beautiful Imperial pattern must have been produced, for it is seldom seen today. As you can see, it is simply a Star of David half-stippled on a plain background with smooth ribbing to the edge of the bowl. The example shown measures 8¾" in diameter and is the famous helios green of Imperial with a silver finish, but the pattern is also known in marigold, smoke, and purple. The exterior carries the Arcs pattern.

STAR OF DAVID AND BOWS

The Northwood version of this figure (Imperial also produced a Star of David bowl) is a very attractive dome-footed bowl and is a tribute to the Jewish religion. The Star is interlaced and is beaded while a graceful border of flowers, tendrils, and bows edge the stippled center. The exterior is the Vintage pattern, and the colors are marigold, green, and amethyst.

STAR SPRAY

This smallish (7½") Imperial bowl can be found in crystal as well as iridized glass in marigold and smoke. The pattern is all exterior and intaglio and very well done.

Starburst

Star and Hobs

188

Star and File

Star Fish

Starlyte Shade

Star Spray

Star of David

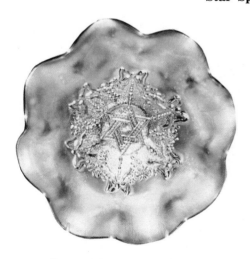

Star of David and Bows

Star Medallion

STARFLOWER

I certainly wish I could provide a manufacturer of this rare and beautiful pitcher (no tumblers known), but I can't. Known in both blue and marigold, the pitcher has turned up in two heights. The mold work is outstanding and the design flawless. Please notice how much the design resembles that of Millersburg's Little Star pattern.

STIPPLED ACORNS

The covered candy dish shown comes rather late in Carnival glass production but is still attractive enough to be of interest. It stands 6½" tall on a 3½" footing. I've seen these in marigold, blue, and amethyst. It was made by Jeanette.

STIPPLED DIAMOND SWAG

This beautifully designed English compote seems to be the only shape known in this pattern, and while Mrs. Presznick reports green and blue ones, I've seen only the rich marigold shown. The compote is 5" tall and measures 5¾" across the top with a 3½" base.

STIPPLED PETALS

While this Dugan pattern isn't uncommon in peach opalescent bowls, the pretty handled basket sets it well above the ordinary. Made from the 9" bowl, this basket is a large one and has been seen in amethyst as well as the beautiful peach shown.

STIPPLED RAMBLER ROSE

Most trails seem to lead to the Dugan company with this seldom-discussed pattern, but I have no proof they made it. The shape shown is the only one I've seen, and the colors are marigold and blue only.

STIPPLED RAYS (FENTON)

While Stippled Rays was used by both Northwood and Millersburg too, the Fenton version is perhaps the most commonly known and is available in bowls, bonbons, compotes, plates, creamers, and sugars. The colors found are marigold, amethyst, green, blue, and a rare red.

STIPPLED RAYS (IMPERIAL)

Only this footed breakfast set has been reported so far in this Imperial version of Stippled Rays. Most have plain interiors, but the one shown has a duplicate pattern inside as well. Colors reported are marigold, cobalt blue, purple, green, amber, and smoke.

STIPPLED RAYS (NORTHWOOD)

The Northwood company had several versions of this pattern, but most are marked and can be easily spotted. On some the rays are evenly finished some distance from the outer edge while on others, they extend almost to the lip. Mostly on dome-based bowls and compotes, colors are marigold, blue, green, amethyst, white, and rarely smoke.

Stippled Acorns

Stippled Petals

Starflower

Stippled Diamond Swag

Stippled Rambler Rose

Stippled Rays (Fenton)

Stippled Rays (Imperial)

Stippled Rays (Northwood)

STIPPLED STRAWBERRY

While this pattern has been reported previously in a tumbler only, it obviously wasn't limited to that shape, and it is a real pleasure to show this rare spittoon shape. It stands 3½" tall and measures 4½" across its widest part. The coloring is nothing spectacular but adequate. Along the spittoon's lip is a checkerboard pattern. The manufacturer is the Jenkins company.

STORK ABC PLATE

Long a favorite with collectors, the child's plate known as the Stork ABC plate was a product of the Belmont Glass company. Advertisements for this 7½" item show it was made in pink, green, frosted green, and the iridized version. It has a raised rim and flat base.

STORK AND RUSHES

Stork and Rushes is another pattern whose shards were found in the Dugan diggings, and since it has features that are typical of Northwood, I'm afraid it's difficult to state whether Dugan or Northwood made this pattern. At any rate, it is available in berry sets, punch sets, water sets, hats, and mugs. I've seen only marigold, purple, and blue with purple which is probably the hardest color to find.

STORK VASE

Much like the Swirl vase in concept, the Stork Vase was made by Jenkins and is usually found in a pale marigold glass. The Stork is on one side only with stippling covering the other side. The Stork Vase stands 7½" tall.

STRAWBERRY (FENTON)

This little bonbon shape has been seen in all sorts of glass including crystal, custard, milk glass, and Carnival glass where the colors range from marigold, cobalt, amethyst, and green to the rare red amberina shown and a good rich all red. The design qualities aren't all that good, but the iridescence is usually adequate and on the whole, the Fenton bonbon comes off nicely.

STRAWBERRY (MILLERSBURG)

Like its close relatives, Grape and Blackberry Wreaths, this beautiful pattern is the culmination of the design. Its detailing is much finer than either of the other patterns, and the glass is exceptional. The coloring is a true grape purple, and the iridescence is a light even gold. Like other Millersburg patterns, the shapes vary, but the deep tri-cornered bowl with candy-ribbon edge is my favorite. A rare compote exists in the usual colors.

Stork and Rushes

Stippled Strawberry

Stork ABC Plate

Strawberry (Fenton)

Strawberry (Millersburg)

STRAWBERRY (NORTHWOOD)

Available in only bowls of various sizes and plates in either flat or hand grip styles, the well-known Northwood pattern comes either plain or stippled. On the stippled version there are three narrow rings around the outer edge; these are absent on the plain pieces. Colors are both vivid and pastel with the purple showing off the pattern to its best.

STRAWBERRY EPERGNE

The Strawberry Epergne is very much like the Fish Net one also made by Dugan; however, the former is much rarer and has not been reported in peach opalescent yet. As you can see, the bowl exterior is plain, and the base is domed.

STRAWBERRY SCROLL

Much like the rare Lily of the Valley in design, this rare Fenton water set is a real beauty that can stand along side of the best designs in Carnival glass. The shape, like that of the Blueberry set, is very artistic also. Colors reported are marigold and blue, but I suspect amethyst and green are possibilities.

STRAWBERRY INTAGLIO

I showed this pattern in *Millersburg, The Queen of Carnival Glass* as a questionable Millersburg pattern. Since then we've been able to trace it to the Northwood company through both a "goofus" bowl and a gilt decorated one, both bearing the famous trademark. The glass is thick, the design deeply impressed, and the iridescence only so-so. I've seen large and small bowls only.

STREAM OF HEARTS

The same heart shape employed by Fenton on the Heart and Vine, and Heart and Trees designs is found here on the scale fillers swirls that form a peacock's tail. Usually found on the compote shape, often with Persian medallion as an exterior companion, Stream of Hearts is available on a 10" footed bowl also. Colors are marigold, blue, and white.

STRETCH

Made with virtually the same process as carnival glass but with an additional step to give it an "onion skin" appearance, Stretch Glass was made by most of the major companies in the mid-1920's. Shown is the iced tea pitcher and tall tumbler.

STRETCHED DIAMONDS AND DOTS

Very little information seems to be available on this tumbler. It is 4½" tall, comes from a two part mold, and has an unusual star design in the base. The pattern of diamonds filled with large buttons above stretched diamonds is very attractive, despite the color being rather light.

**Stretched Diamonds
and Dots**

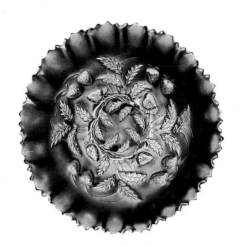

Strawberry (Northwood)

Strawberry Epergne

Strawberry Scroll

Strawberry Intaglio

Stream of Hearts

Stretch

STRUTTING PEACOCK

The only shapes in this Westmoreland pattern are the creamer and sugar, and the only colors I've heard about are green or amethyst. The design is much like Shell and Jewel, also a Westmoreland product, but beware; these have been reproduced.

STUDS

Studs is found in a large tray, milk pitcher, and footed juice tumbler. It is reported to be from Imperial, but I've always had a doubt about this. Marigold is the only color.

SUN-GOLD EPERGNE

Although I question the origin of this beautiful epergne, I don't for one minute doubt its desirability. The base is of highly polished pierced brass while the bowl and lily are of an unusual pinkish-marigold Carnival glass. The epergne is 12" tall, and the bowl has a 9¼" diameter. The glass is clear and mirror-like and has good even iridescence.

SUNFLOWER

Sunflower must have been a very popular pattern in its day, for numerous examples have survived to the present time. It's quite easy to see why it was in demand. It's a pretty, well-designed Northwood pattern that holds iridescence beautifully. The bowl is footed and carries the very pleasing Meander pattern on the exterior. It is also found, rarely, on a plate. The colors are marigold, green, amethyst, and a rare teal blue.

SUNFLOWER AND DIAMOND

Long felt to be a Jenkins pattern, this well done vase is now known to be of Swedish origin, and an example in blue has been reported. The usual color is a good marigold. The pattern is all intaglio and very deep.

SUNFLOWER PINTRAY

Like its companion piece, the Seacoast Pintray, this Millersburg item joins the list of a select few. It is 5¼" long and 4½" wide and also rests on a collar base. The most unique feature is, of course, the open handle, and the colors are marigold, purple, amethyst, and a rich green.

SUNKEN HOLLYHOCK

Probably found more readily than the other "Gone With the Wind" lamps, Sunken Hollyhock can be found in marigold (often with a caramel coloring) and a very rare red. The lamp stands an impressive 25" tall and certainly is a show stopper.

Studs

Strutting Peacock

Sun-Gold Epergne

Sunflower

Sunflower and Diamond

Sunken Hollyhock

Sunflower Pintray

SUNRAY COMPOTE

These small compotes, found on marigold over milk glass, are very pretty in their own plain way. Fenton made many such items, and I strongly feel this compote came from that company also.

SUPERB DRAPE

This beautiful and quite rare piece stands 6½" tall and has a 7" diameter. Its design of gently draped folds and the rolling top are truly superb. Known in both marigold and the aqua opalescent shown, the Superb Drape vase is a true find.

SWAN, PASTEL

Of all the shards of patterns I catalogued from the Dugan dump site, I'm sure this pattern surprised me more than any other. For years I considered these small novelties either Fenton or Westmoreland products with my vote leaning toward the latter. However, we now can say with some positiveness that they are Dugan. Found in pink, ice blue, ice green, marigold, peach, and purple. The darker colors and peach are the scarcest and demand greater prices. A variant by Fenton is known, however.

SWEETHEART

Besides the rare and beautiful covered cookie jar shown, this Cambridge pattern is known in a very rare tumbler shape in marigold. The cookie jar has been seen in marigold, green and amethyst, and as you can see, the mold work and finish are superior.

SWIRL (IMPERIAL)

This 7" vase is shown in old Imperial catalogs, and I've heard of it in marigold, smoke, green, and white. The design is nothing outstanding, but the useful shape and the iridescence are adequate.

SWIRL (NORTHWOOD)

I've seen this pattern on a beautiful tankard water set and the mug shape in marigold. The tumbler is shown in the Owens book in green and is known in amethyst. While the tumblers are often marked, the mug isn't. Now and then, the tankard pitcher is found with enameled flowers added. Naturally, the pitcher is scarce, and the mug is considered rare.

SWIRL CANDLESTICK

This very attractive candlestick is the same pattern as the rare mug I showed in previous books and was apparently a product of either Northwood or Dugan. While other colors may exist, I haven't heard of any. The luster is top notch, and the glass is quality all the way.

SWIRL HOBNAIL

This is a little Millersburg jewel in either the rose bowl or the lady's spittoon, and once you own either piece, wild horses couldn't drag it away. The glass is simply sparkling and the iridescence outstanding. The spittoon has an irregular scalloped edge opening, and both shapes have a many-rayed base. The usual colors prevail, but the green is extremely difficult to locate. Swirl Hobnail can also be found in a vase shape.

Swirl Hobnail

Sunray Compote

Superb Drape

Swirl Candlestick

Sweetheart

Swirl (Imperial)

Swirl (Northwood)

SWIRLED FLUTE VASE

This little Fenton vase is a real charmer for such simplistic design. The wide panel is quite pronounced at the base and the color and iridescence are quite good. These little vases average about 9" in height and are found in red, marigold, green, amethyst, blue, and white.

SWIRLED THREADS

What a very pretty piece of glass this stemmed goblet is. The coloring is dark and rich, and the stem ending in a ball shape gives it a nice touch. The threadings are all interior. I'd guess it came from Europe but can't be sure.

SYDNEY

While this Fostoria pattern is known in other shapes in crystal, the tumbler and smaller champagne glass are the only shapes reported in carnival glass. The color is an amber-like marigold that is well iridized. The tumbler is nearly 4" tall, and the champagne measures 3¼".

TAFFETA LUSTRE CANDLESTICKS

These very rare Fostoria candlesticks were manufactured in 1916 or 1917 (according to an old Fostoria catalog) in colors of amber, blue, green, crystal, or orchid. They were part of a "flower set" which included a centerpiece bowl 11" in diameter. The candlesticks themselves came in 2", 4", 6", 9", and 12" sizes, and as you can see, these shown still have the original paper labels on the bottom. When held to the light, the ultra-violet color is fantastic, and the iridescence is heavy and rich. Fostoria made very small amounts of iridized glass, and certainly these examples of their Taffeta Lustre line are quite rare.

TARGET VASE

This seldom seen vase pattern is from the Dugan-Diamond Glass Company. It can be found in marigold, amethyst, blue, peach opalescent, and a smoky blue. The example shown has a very unusual butterscotch hue to the peach coloring and is heavy with opalescence on both the hobnail-like projections and the panels, as well as flames on the top edges.

TEN MUMS

Found on beautiful water sets, large impressive bowls, and rare plates, Fenton's Ten Mums is a very realistic pattern. The mold work is unusually fine, especially on the bowl shape. Colors are marigold, cobalt blue, green, peach opalescent, and white, but not all shapes are found in all colors.

THIN RIB (NORTHWOOD)

Here is an exterior pattern every one must know for besides the famous basketweave, it is found on some of Northwood's best known bowl patterns, including Good Luck and Strawberry. It is simple enough, but held to the light, it adds greatly to the design.

THIN RIB AND DRAPE

Much like the other Thin Rib vases, this one has an interior drape pattern, adding to the interest. It can be found in several colors including marigold, green, and amethyst. I suspect Fenton is the maker but can't be sure.

Sydney

200

Thin Rib (Northwood)

Swirled Flute Vase

Swirled Threads

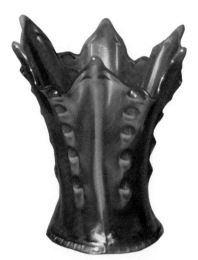

Target

Taffeta Lustre Candlesticks

Ten Mums

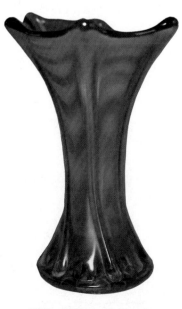

Thin Rib and Drape

THISTLE

Fairly typical of many Fenton bowl patterns, Thistle is artistically true with the thistles and leaves realistic and graceful. Found on bowls, plates, and a rare compote, the colors seen are marigold, green, blue, and occasionally amethyst. Now and then a bowl appears with advertising on the base.

THISTLE AND THORN

British in origin, this nicely designed pattern is found on a variety of shapes, all footed, including bowls, sugars, creamers, plates, and nut bowls. Colors are usually marigold, but I've had blue reported.

THISTLE BANANA BOAT

This beautiful Fenton banana boat is another of the underrated patterns in Carnival glass. Massive in concept, bold in design with the thistle on the interior and cattail and waterlily outside, the four-footed banana boat is usually found on marigold, amethyst, green, or cobalt blue. The iridescence is quite heavy, usually with much gold.

THISTLE VASE

What a pretty little vase this is. Standing 6" tall with a soft amber shading to the glass, the Thistle vase is a well-designed bit of color for vase lovers. The maker is unknown.

THREE FRUITS

So very close in design to the Northwood Fruits and Flowers pattern shown earlier in this book, the two substantial differences are the absence of the small flowers and the addition of an extra cluster of cherries to this pattern. Found in bowls of all sizes, including flat and footed ones, and average size plates. Northwood's Three Fruits is available in all vivid colors as well as pastels.

THREE FRUIT MEDALLION

The difference between this and the other examples of Northwood's Three Fruits patterns is center medallion of leaves rather than the usual fruit center. The exterior can be either the Meander pattern or Basketweave. The first is always footed while the latter is collar based. Colors are green, marigold, amethyst, black amethyst, blue, horehound, and aqua opalescent.

THREE FRUITS VARIANT

If you'll compare this beautiful 9" plate with the Northwood version, you'll see a good deal of similarities and some obvious differences. While this version has been credited to Fenton, I strongly suspect it was a Dugan product.

THREE-IN-ONE

Originally called "Number One" in the crystal line, this well-known Imperial bowl pattern (plates also exist) is always easy to spot because of the two rows of near-cut diamond designs, separated by a center area of flutes. I've seen bowls in 4½", 7½", 8¾" sizes and in colors of deep marigold, green, purple, and smoke. The iridescence is usually quite good and the glass heavy, clear, and sparkling.

THREE-IN-ONE VARIANT

This beautifully made toothpick holder has been iridized on only the center sections and is exactly like the Three-In-One pattern except for the file work within the top and bottom row of diamonds. Beyond any question, it is an old one.

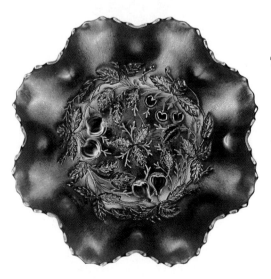

Three Fruits Medallion

Three-In-One Variant

202

Thistle

Thistle and Thorn

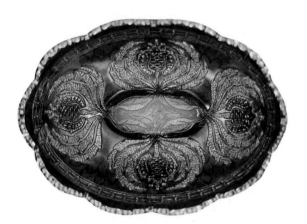

Thistle Banana Boat

Thistle Vase

Three Fruits Variant

Three Fruits

Three-In-One

THREE MONKEYS BOTTLE

I'm not sure how many of these are around, but not many I'd guess. The one shown is the reported example in all the previous pattern books, so it may have only a few brothers. The Three Monkeys bottle is of clear glass with good iridescence, stands 8" tall, and bears the words "Patent Pending – 8 oz." on the base. It is a rare find for bottle lovers.

THREE ROLL TUMBLE UP

Another of those European patterns that are rather non-descript, the Three Roll items shown, both parts of a tumble-up or bedroom set, have a good lustre but tend to appear a bit glossy. I suspect other shapes may well exist in this pattern but so far haven't seen any. Amethyst is also a possibility for color but hasn't been reported.

THREE ROW VASE

I was very impressed when I saw this beautiful Imperial rarity. The color was truly fabulous and the iridescence fine enough to rival the Farmyard bowl. I have heard of only this one piece in beautiful purple, but others may exist. It is 8" tall and 4½" wide, and the mold work is quite deep and sharp. There is also a variant called Two Row vase which is quite similar.

THUMBPRINT AND OVAL

Standing only 5½" tall, this well-molded Imperial pattern is known in marigold and purple. Either color is scarce, and Thumbprint and Oval is much sought.

THUNDERBIRD (SHRIKE)

Called Thunderbird in America, the bird shown in actually a shrike. The flora is, of course, wattle. This Australian pattern can be found in both large and small bowls in marigold or purple.

TIERED THUMBPRINT

Again here is a pattern with thin iridization but a very nice pattern that fills the glass much like Moonprint; Tiered Thumbprint may well be a British pattern too, but I can't be sure. It has been seen in two sizes of bowls also and certainly other shapes may exist.

TIGER LILY

It really is a shame this well-done Imperial pattern was used only on the water set. It would have been quite effective on any number of other shapes including table sets and punch sets. The mold work is some of Imperial's best, all intaglio, and very sharp and precise. Tiger Lily is found in marigold, green, and rarely purple. It has been reproduced in pastels, so beware!

TINY COVERED HEN (LITTLE)

The Imperial novelty item shown is a really well-conceived miniature that until recently had not been reproduced; however, I saw one of these in a gift shop in blue glass (not Carnival) not long ago. At any rate, the one shown is old and rare. The coloring is a very nice clambroth, richly iridized with a fiery finish. It measures 3½" long and 3¼" tall.

TINY HOBNAIL LAMP

In all my years in collecting I've seen just two of these miniature oil lamps even though they do come late in Carnival glass history. The base is 3" high and has a diameter of 2¼". The shade, which matches, is clear. I haven't a notion as to the maker, but they are scarce and cute as can be.

TOBACCO LEAF (U.S. GLASS)

Here is another souvenir champagne, but the one shown is a real rarity. Please note that the finish is gold, not the usual clear iridized! As the owner says, this must have been for someone very special at the convention.

TOMAHAWK

This lovely miniature (7¼" long and 2" wide) is a real "show stopper." Now known to have been a product of the Cambridge Glass Company, the rare Tomahawk is a very deep cobalt blue with heavy iridescence. It has been seen in pieces other than Carnival glass and has been reproduced in aqua and vaseline glass, but as far as I know, no iridized reproductions were made.

Tobacco Leaf (U.S. Glass)

Tiny Hobnail Lamp

Three Monkeys Bottle

Three Row Vase

Thumbprint and Oval

Thunderbird (Shrike)

Tiger Lily

Tomahawk

Tiny Covered Hen

Tiered Thumbprint

Three Roll Tumble Up

TORNADO
Perhaps because it is one of the most unusual vases in all of Carnival glass, Northwood's Tornado is always a favorite with collectors. Available in both plain and ribbed, the size may vary considerably, and I've seen a mini-version in marigold. The colors are marigold, green, purple, white, and ice blue. The Northwood trademark is found on the inside of the vase.

TORNADO VARIANT
This extremely rare variant is one inch taller that the regular Tornado vase. The base closely resembles that of Northwood's Corn vase, and the top is tightly crimped. The only color reported is a deep rich marigold, iridized both inside and out.

TOWN PUMP
Certainly there isn't one collector of Carnival glass who isn't familiar with this very famous pattern. The Town Pump is almost 7" tall and is mostly on purple, although marigold and green are found in limited quantities. The design is simple but very pleasing – ivy twining over a stippled background with a crude tree bark spout and handle. No Carnival glass collection would be complete without this pattern, and certainly it deserves a prominent place in any Northwood collection.

TRACERY
This pattern comes as quite a surprise to many Millersburg fans because of its delicate patterning, but Millersburg it certainly is. It is found on bonbons of rather deep, oval shape and is usually seen in green or amethyst. It measures 7½" long and 5½" wide. The base is 3" in diameter and has a many-rayed center. The exterior is plain and has two mold marks.

TREE BARK
As you can see, this is a simplistic pattern, turned out as a giveaway or inexpensive item. The only shapes I've heard of are water sets with either open or lidded pitchers, and the only color is marigold, usually of a deep, rich hue. While it certainly does not show the artistry the Imperial company was known for, Tree Bark does fulfill its purpose of being an available bit of color for the average housewife's table.

TREE BARK VARIANT
The main difference in this pattern and the regular Tree Bark are the even spacings of the bark lines rather than being randomly done. Shapes I know about are a water set, planter, an ornate candle holder on a brass cherub and marble base as well as a vase shape. This pattern was made by Jeanette.

TREE OF LIFE
There has always been a great deal of confusion surrounding this pattern and Crackle and Soda Gold patterns, because they are so similar, but there is really no need for the confusion. As you can see, Tree of Life has no stippling whatsoever, thus the filler area is plain. The pitcher shown is a scarce shape in this pattern, and as you can see, the iridescence is thin and light. The shapes known are water sets, plates, and perfume bottles.

TREE TRUNK
Simple but effective is the bark-like pattern for this popular North-wood vase. Apparently it was a well-liked pattern when it was being manufactured for many examples exist in sizes from 8" to tall 20" ones. The colors are marigold, blue, purple, green, white, and aqua opalescent.

TRIANDS (AND TOWERS VASE)
Triands is a product of Sowerby and is found in a covered butter dish, creamer, sugar, celery, and spooner (both shown). The only color reported is a good rich marigold. The other small hat shape shown is called Towers and is a vase pattern also from Sowerby.

Triands (and Towers Vase)

Tornado

Tornado Variant

Town Pump

Tracery

Tree Bark

Tree of Life

Treebark Variant

Tree Trunk

TROPICANA VASE

The maker of this intriguing vase is unknown, but I suspect it may be English. It stands 9" tall and has a very rich marigold coloring.

TROUT AND FLY

Of course, this is a companion piece to the Big Fish pattern and except for the added fly and a few changes in the water lilies and blossoms, is much the same. The bowls usually measure about 9¼" in diameter and have a wide panel exterior. The detail is good, and the coloring excellent. The shape may vary and even square bowls and a rare plate shape have been found in this Millersburg pattern.

TULIP (MILLERSBURG)

This beautiful and rare compote is exactly like the Flowering Vine one shown elsewhere except it has no interior design. It stands about 9" tall, and the bowl measures roughly 6" across. The only colors I've seen are marigold and amethyst, but green was more than likely made. In addition to this size, a 7" variant is known in amethyst.

TULIP AND CANE (IMPERIAL)

Seldom found, this old Imperial pattern is seen in iridized glass only on two sizes of wine goblets, a claret goblet and a rare 8 oz. goblet in marigold and smoke.

TULIP SCROLL (MILLERSBURG)

Only a few of these attractive Millersburg vases seem to show up from time to time, mostly in amethyst, but once in a while in green or the quite rare marigold. I've seen them as tall as 11", but most are about 7" and less stretched out. They are always quickly snatched up and are a popular vase pattern.

TWIGS

A kissing cousin to the Beauty Bud vase shown earlier, the Twigs vase has small branch-like stems growing from the base to the body of the vase. These little gems can be found in all sizes from 3" to 12" tall and are mostly seen in marigold or purple. These, like the Beauty, were made by Dugan-Diamond Glass.

TWINS

Like Imperial's Fashion pattern, Twins is another geometric design manufactured in large quantities in berry sets, a rare bride's basket, and the familiar fruit bowl and stand. Pieces have been found in a good rich marigold and a very beautiful smoke, and the berry set has been found in green, as shown. Needless to say, a purple fruit bowl and stand would be a treasure!

TWO FLOWERS

Once again the scale filler, water lilies, and blossoms are used by Fenton to form an artistic presentation. Known in footed and flat bowls of various sizes and a scarce bowl shape, Two Flowers is seen in blue, marigold, amethyst, red, green, and occasionally white.

TWO FRUITS

Once this Fenton pattern was felt to be an Imperial product, but we know from old advertisements that it came from Fenton. The background is Fenton's Stippled Rays and, as you can see, there are four sections to the divided bonbon. Each section contains one fruit – either a pear or an apple. Colors I've heard about are marigold, blue, and amethyst, but certainly green may exist.

UNIVERSAL HOME BOTTLE

While I normally shy away from utility bottles, this one is a bit special. It has very rich color and an interesting side panel of measurements by ounces and centimeters. It is a one quart bottle and is impressed "Universal Home Bottle". The maker is unknown as is what it originally held.

Twigs

Universal Home Bottle

Tropicana Vase

Trout and Fly

Tulip and Cane

Tulip Scroll

Tulip (Millersburg)

Twins

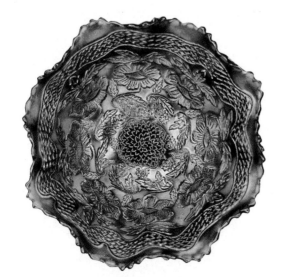

Two Flowers

Two Fruits

UNSHOD

The owner says this pitcher came with tumblers in the Unshod pattern, so we've listed the pitcher as that pattern. If anyone knows differently, I'm sure I'll hear about it. The styling look very much like the Millersburg Cherry, but that's only an observation.

URN VASE

This unusually shaped vase has been seen in white as well as marigold Carnival glass and is a product of the Imperial company. It stands 9" tall and has a finely grained stippling over the surface.

VENETIAN

While credited to the Cambridge company, there is evidence that this pattern was iridized at the Millersburg factory. It is shown in old Cambridge ads, however, and the vase was used as a lamp base. Colors are green and a scarce marigold. The base design is quite similar to the Hobstar and Feather rose bowl. A rare lidded sugarbowl is shown in marigold.

VICTORIAN

This impressively large bowl is another pattern from the Dugan factory in Indiana, PA and is both rich and desirable. Mostly found in a rich purple, one example in a rare peach opalescent has turned up and rates with the best of bowls.

VINEYARD

Here is another pattern whose shards I catalogued from the Dugan diggings, but actually it didn't come as too much of a surprise. The same design was made in 1905 in crystal, opaque glass, and opalescent ware under the name, Grape and Leaf. Known in iridescent glass, in a water set only, the colors are marigold, purple, and rarely peach opalescent. Often the tumblers are poorly formed, and the glass tends toward being bubbled.

VINEYARD HARVEST (AUSTRALIAN GRAPE)

It now appears this tumbler, like so many to be encountered in the last ten years, is a product of Czechoslovakia. It was first publicized by Muriel Triplett, and at that time she called it Australian Grape. It stands 5½" tall and measures 3⅝" across the top. Found only in marigold, it is considered rare.

VINING LEAF

There are two variants of the English pattern – one with small berries along portions of the stylized leaves. The examples shown, a rather small bud vase and an ample lady's spittoon, give us the pattern nicely. Please note the frosted effect around the leaves.

VINTAGE (FENTON)

Here is the Fenton premier grape pattern, and it is just as well done as Northwood's. It can be found in bowls, plates, rosebowls, compotes, punch sets, small ferneries, and a one-lily epergne. Colors are marigold, blue, green, amethyst, amber, pastel marigold, amberina, red, and reverse amberina.

VINTAGE (MILLERSBURG)

What makes Vintage unique is the hobnail exterior (the hobnail and the honeycomb seem to have been patterns used as standard fillers by Millersburg). It has a many-rayed star in the base and is usually seen on the medium size, shallow bowls. The Millersburg Vintage pattern is a scarce one and is certainly a credit to any collection. Colors are green, marigold, amethyst, and blue. And both 9" and 5" bowls are known.

VINTAGE BANDED

Often seen in the mug shape, this Dugan pattern is rather scarce in the footed pitcher shape, and the tumbler is rare and much sought. Please note the grapes are almost identical to those found in the Golden Grape pattern, and the banding is quite similar to that found in the Dugan pattern called Apple Blossoms.

Vintage (Millersburg)

Vintage (Fenton)

Vineyard Harvest

Urn Vase

Venetian

Victorian

Unshod

Vineyard

Vining Leaf

Vintage Banded

VINTAGE LEAF (FENTON)
Over the years, I've never been able to accept this design with the center leaf as the standard Fenton Vintage pattern, so I've given in to my conscience and given it a name all its own. It is found in berry sets in marigold, green, blue, and amethyst and is Fenton, not Millersburg, despite the radium finish.

VIOLET BASKETS
Here are two of the dainty little baskets designed to hold small bouquets like violets. One has its own glass handle, while the other fits into a handled sleeve. The File pattern in the glass is much like that on some Stork and Rushes pieces, and I suspect both of these baskets come from the Dugan company.

VIRGINIA BLACKBERRY
Known to be a variant of a U.S. Glass pattern called Virginia or Galloway, this small pitcher has turned up on a child's water set in crystal without the berries. The example shown in blue Carnival is the only reported one that is iridized, making it a very rare item indeed.

VOTIVE LIGHT
Also bearing the strange "M-inside-a-C" mark like Oklahoma, this very hard-to-find novelty has a beautiful marigold finish. It stands 4¼" tall and is a candle vase. The side shown is the Bleeding Heart of Jesus. On the opposite side is a raised cross measuring nearly 2" tall.

WAFFLE BLOCK
This Imperial pattern was originally made in many shapes. The pitcher is hard to come by and, of course, the tumblers are rather rare, but other shapes, including a handled basket, rose bowl, punch set, vases, bowls, parfait glass and shakers are known. Colors are marigold, clambroth, aqua, and amethyst.

WASHBOARD
Also called Diamonds and Petals, this pattern has been found in a small creamer shape, and I suspect there is a matching sugar, possibly a stemmed open compote type. The tumbler is tall, some 4⅞" with a flared top opening of 3". The pattern is known in crystal, but iridized pieces are rare.

WATER LILY
This very well done Fenton pattern is found on bonbons, flat and footed berry sets, and the very rare large footed plate shape. The pattern is made up of water lilies, leaves, lotus-like flowers, and other flora. Colors are marigold, blue, green, amethyst, amber, white, and red.

WATER LILY AND CATTAILS (FENTON)
While both Fenton and Northwood had versions of this pattern, the Fenton one is best known and is available in more shapes, including water sets, table sets, berry sets, and a rare spittoon whimsey. Colors are marigold and amethyst, but certainly blue or green may exist but have not been reported.

WATER LILY AND CATTAILS (NORTHWOOD)
Here is a pattern used in different degrees by both the Northwood and Fenton companies, and at times it's rather hard to tell who made what. The obvious Fenton rendition is the exterior pattern used on the Thistle banana boat, but it is believed they made other shapes in Water Lily and Cattails, including a whimsey toothpick. This is the Northwood water set.

WATER LILY AND DRAGONFLY
This large (10½") shallow bowl and matching frog is called a flower set and was used much like an epergne. A large flannel flower is under the frog. In Australia these are also called "float bowls."

Waterlily and Cattails (Northwood)

Water Lily and Dragonfly

212

Vintage Leaf (Fenton)

Washboard

Virginia Blackberry

Violet Baskets

Votive Light

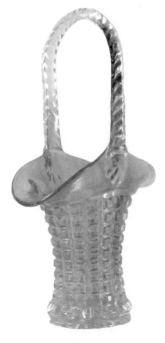

Waffle Block

Water Lily

Water Lily and Cattails (Fenton)

WEBBED CLEMATIS
I apologize for the weak photo of this huge vase (12½" tall), but it was the only one available. I suspect the vase is Scandinavian, and it reminds me of several others from that area. The color is light marigold.

WEEPING CHERRY
While we know this is a pattern from the Dugan factory, it seems few examples turn up for sale, and this is the first I've ever had an opportunity to show. It can be found in both flat and dome based bowls in marigold, amethyst, peach opalescent, and white. The center design reminds one of the Nippon design, and the four smooth ribs that divide the designs are very unusual.

WESTERN THISTLE
From Finland the Western Thistle is a very pretty pattern, deeply intaglio with rows of diamonds below a band of thistle flowers and leaves. It has been seen in both marigold and is just a tad over 4" tall.

WHEAT
Make no mistake about it, this is a very rare Northwood pattern, known in only a covered sweetmeat (two known) and a single covered bowl in colors of green and amethyst. Surfacing in Carnival glass circles only in the last 10 years, these rarities have caused much excitement and brought astonishing prices where they've been shown. The sweetmeat is the same shape as the Northwood Grape pattern. What a pity we don't have more of this truly important pattern.

WHIRLING LEAVES
What a simple but effective pattern for large bowls! Four flowing leaves and four star-like blossoms – what could be simpler? Please note that the flowers are very much like those found on the Little Stars bowls. This pleasing pattern is not especially difficult to find and does not sell for nearly as much as most Millersburg patterns, but it is worth owning.

WHIRLING STAR
While this Imperial pattern had never brought many raves, it is a nice, well-planned design found on punch sets, bowls and an attractive compote. Colors are mostly marigold, but an occasional piece in green is found.

WHITE OAK
After years of doubt about the maker of this rare tumbler (no pitcher known), I'm half convinced it was a Dugan product. The bark-like background and the general shape are much like the Vineyard tumbler. Of course, I could be wrong.

WICKERWORK (ENGLISH)
Sometimes only the bowl without the base of these is found, but here is the complete set. The bowl measures 8½" in diameter. The only color I've seen is the marigold. Apparently, this was a cookie or sandwich tray.

WIDE PANEL (IMPERIAL)
Like the other major Carnival glass companies, Imperial produced a Wide Panel pattern. These are found primarily in goblets of two sizes and a covered candy jar. Colors known are marigold, ice blue, ice green, vaseline white, pink, and red. Most have a stretch effect around the edge.

WIDE PANEL (FENTON)
Shown is the typical Fenton Wide Panel bowl exterior found on so many patterns. Like the rest, it has a beginning and an end and doesn't just drift away at the bowl's edge. The example shown is on the back of a green vintage bowl and is beautifully iridized.

Webbed
Clematis

Wickerwork
(English)

Weeping Cherry

Wide Panel (Fenton)

Whirling Leaves

Western Thistle

Whirling Star

Wheat

White Oak

Wide Panel Imperial

WIDE PANEL EPERGNE

This beauty is the most stately epergne in Carnival glass and is a product of the Northwood factory. Colors are white, marigold, green, amethyst, and ultra-rare aqua opalescent.

WIDE PANEL VARIANT

Rather plain for a Northwood product, this water set relies on symmetry and grace for its charm. It can be found in marigold and white as well as enameled in both colors and a beautiful Persian blue.

WIDE PANELED CHERRY

Unlisted until now, this very interesting pattern is similar to the Stippled Strawberry spittoon I showed in *Rarities In Carnival Glass* some years ago. The shape is a very small pitcher, possibly used for syrup or cream and to date I've heard of no matching pieces.

WIDE PANELS SHADE

Shown is one of the most beautiful light shades I've run across. The emerald green coloring is spectacular as is the iridescence. The owner says she was told it came from the Northwood Company which certainly is possible, since they made many fine shades, both marked and unmarked.

WIDE RIB VASE

While several glass companies produced these wide rib vases, the one shown came from the Dugan factory. Colors I've seen are marigold, green, blue, amethyst, smoke, white, amber, peach opalescent, and aqua opalescent.

WILD BLACKBERRY

Very much in design like the other Fenton Blackberry patterns, this is strictly a bowl pattern easily identified by the four center leaves and the wheat-like fronts around the outer edges. Colors are marigold, blue, green, and amethyst. The exterior has the wide panel pattern.

WILD FLOWER (MILLERSBURG)

This deeply cupped, clover-based compote is just over 6" tall and is 4½" wide. The very graceful pattern of four large leaves, four small leaves, and eight blossoms is quite effective. The iridescence is found only on the inside of the compote and has the usual radium finish. This is not an easy compote to find, and anyone having one should be proud. This Millersburg pattern is found in marigold, green, amethyst, and a rare vaseline.

WILD FLOWER (NORTHWOOD)

The only place I've ever seen this pattern is on the outside of Northwood's Blossomtime compotes, and that's a real shame. It is a beautiful pattern and certainly deserves better.

WILD GRAPE

I recently encountered this pattern for the first time and at first glance thought it to be a Palm Beach bowl, but as you can clearly see, it isn't. The color is weak, but the design is good, and the dome base looks like many Dugan bowls.

WILD LOGANBERRY (DEWBERRY)

Since I first showed this Westmoreland pattern in the pitcher and announced the existence of wine and goblets, other shapes have turned up including a covered compote, creamer, sugar, and an open compote. All except the marigold wine have been iridized milk glass, but other colors may exist.

WILD ROSE

This well-known Northwood pattern is used on the exterior of two types of bowls. The first is an average flat bowl, often with no interior pattern. The second, however, is an unusual footed bowl, rather small, with an edge of open work in fan-like figures. Certainly, the intricacy of this open work took much care and skill. The colors are marigold, amethyst, green, and occasionally pastels.

**Wide Panels
Shade**

Wild Grape

Wide Panel Epergne

Wide Rib Vase

Wild Blackberry

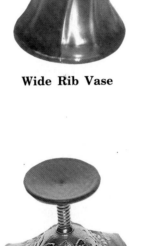

Wildflower (Northwood)

Wild Loganberry Pitcher

Wild Flower (Millersburg)

Wild Rose

Wide Panel Variant

Wide Paneled Cherry

WILD ROSE LAMP

Long felt to be a Millersburg product, this scarce to rare lamp can be found in three sizes and three colors besides the crystal version. The pattern is a primrose-like flower and leaves that wind around the base above a filler of sunken dots. Occasionally, the large size can be found with three medallions with busts of women on the underside. Colors are green, amethyst, and marigold.

WILD ROSE SHADE

Rose Presznick called this shade Wild Rose, and I will honor that name despite so many other patterns with the same name. The shade is a strong marigold and has a series of stippled panels, separated by beading with each panel holding a spray of leaves, stems, and a flower that forms the outer edge of the shade.

WILD ROSE SYRUP

Seen only in marigold of rich color and adequate lustering, the Wild Rose Syrup is very attractive. The maker is thus far unknown, but the mold work is quite similar to that of many of Harry Northwood's products. Measuring 6½" tall, the syrup holds 12 fluid ounces and has a metal top.

WILD ROSE WREATH (MINIATURE INTAGLIO)

The Butler Brothers ad showing this rare and desirable miniature calls it a "stemmed almond," so we know it was intended as a nut cup and was made by U.S. Glass. It stands 2½" tall and is usually about 3" across the top. The design is intaglio, and the only color reported is marigold.

WILD STRAWBERRY

One might think of this as the "grown-up" version of the regular Northwood Strawberry, since it is much the same. The primary difference is the addition of the blossoms to the patterning and, of course, the size of the bowl itself, which is about 1½" larger in diameter.

WINDFLOWER

Not one, but two shards of this pattern were excavated at the Dugan site including a marigold bit and a sizeable chunk of an ice blue nappy with a portion of the handle attached. To the best of my knowledge, this pattern has not been reported previously in pastels. Windflower is an uncomplicated, well-balanced design with the background stippled and a geometric bordering device. The exterior is plain. Windflower is found on bowls, plates, and handled nappies. The colors are marigold, cobalt, ice blue, and ice green.

WINDMILL

Again, here is one of the best-selling Imperial patterns, reproduced in the 1960's. It is still rather popular with collectors of old Carnival glass, especially in the darker colors. Originally, Windmill was made in a wide range of shapes, including berry sets, water sets, fruit bowls, pickle dishes, dresser trays, and milk pitchers. The colors were marigold, green, purple, clambroth, and smoke.

WINE AND ROSES

Please note the similarities between this scarce Fenton cider set, the well-known Lotus and Grape pattern shown elsewhere in this book, and the very rare water set called Frolicking Bears. Wine and Roses can be found in marigold in both pitcher and wine, and the wine is known in blue and the rare aqua.

WISHBONE

I personally feel that this Northwood pattern is one of the most graceful in Carnival glass. The lines just flow, covering much of the allowed space. Found on very scarce water sets, flat and footed bowls, plates and a very stately one-lily epergne, Wishbone is usually accompanied by the basketweave pattern on the exterior. My favorite color is the ice blue, but Wishbone is available in marigold, green, purple, blue, white, and ice green. There is also a variant to this pattern.

Wild Rose Shade

Wild Rose Lamp

Wild Rose Syrup

**Wild Rose Wreath
(Miniature Intaglio)**

Wild Strawberry

Windflower

Windmill

Wine and Roses

Wishbone

WISHBONE AND SPADES

I've always had misgivings about attributing this pattern, and I'm listing it here as a questionable Dugan one. As you can see, the design is a good one, well balanced and artistically sound. The shapes are berry sets, and large and small plates and colors include peach opalescent, purple, and green.

WISHBONE FLOWER ARRANGER

Similar in many ways to the Windsor Flower Arranger, for years I confused the two until one collector was kind enough to point out the differences. The Wishbone has an open top and none of the points touch while this isn't true with the Windsor.

WISTERIA

What a beautiful pattern this is! Certainly a first cousin to the Grape Arbor pattern in iridescent glass as well as the Lattice and Cherry pattern in crystal, Wisteria is unfortunately found only on water sets. While only tumblers in ice green have surfaced, both pitchers and tumblers are known in white and a really outstanding ice blue. What a shame no vivid colors are available in this Northwood masterpiece.

WOODEN SHOE

It seems as if good things come in bunches, and that's how it's been with miniatures in this book. However, one could never tire of seeing them, and they are so rare, so here is another. The Wooden Shoe is 4½" long and 3" high. Its coloring is a light, watery amber, and the glass is heavy.

WOODLANDS VASE

Once again I show a rare vase that is very impressive even though it measures only 5½" tall. The coloring is a rich marigold with heavy luster, and the pattern is all smooth and raised. The design has a simple, well-balanced attractiveness that raises it above the everyday. And, of course, not many are known.

WOODPECKER VASE

The Woodpecker vase is 8¼" long and measures 1⅝" across the top. The only color I've run into is marigold, usually of good color. Perhaps this is strictly a Dugan pattern, and if so, it would explain the lack of other colors or shapes. These vases were usually hung in doorways or used as auto vases and were quite popular in their day.

WREATHED CHERRY

For many years collectors have been puzzled by certain pieces of this pattern turning up with the Diamond Glass Company trademark, notably the covered butter. Now, since the Dugan shards have been catalogued, it becomes apparent this was a Dugan pattern. Known in berry sets consisting of oval bowls, table sets, water sets, and a scarce toothpick holder, the colors are marigold, fiery amethyst, purple, and white (often with gilt). The toothpick has been widely reproduced in cobalt, white, and marigold, so beware! The only color in the old ones is amethyst.

WREATH OF ROSES (FENTON)

Known in bonbons with or without stems, compotes, bowls, and the punch sets shown. Fenton's Wreath of Roses is a beautifully executed pattern. Two interior patterns are known. Colors are marigold, green, blue, amethyst, peach opalescent, and white. The luster is very fine and the mold work excellent.

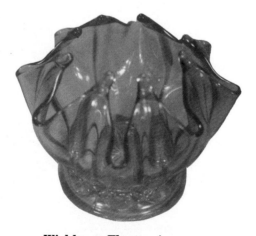

Wishbone Flower Arranger

Wishbone and Spades

Wisteria

Wooden Shoe

Woodlands Vase

Woodpecker Vase

Wreathed Cherry

Wreath of Roses

WREATH OF ROSES ROSE BOWL (DUGAN)

Apparently one of the inexpensive, mass-produced patterns made for wide sales, this Dugan pattern is found only on the small rosebowl shapes and ruffled bowl shapes from the same mold. The only colors I've seen are amethyst, marigold, lavender, and a rare amber in the spittoon whimsey shape.

WREATH OF ROSES VARIANT (DUGAN)

While Northwood, Fenton and Dugan all made similar patterns with this name, the Dugan is least known and valued. It hasn't all that much going for it, since the design is weak and doesn't fill the space to advantage. Colors are amethyst, blue and marigold – at least the ones I've seen, but white, green and peach opal may exist.

ZIG-ZAG (FENTON)

I suspect the same mold shape was used for this nicely done Fenton water set and the Fluffy Peacock pattern. The Zig-Zag was brought along in the enameled Carnival period and can be found in marigold, blue, green, amethyst, ice green, and white. The floral work may vary slightly from piece to piece.

ZIG-ZAG (MILLERSBURG)

This lovely Millersburg bowl pattern is an improved version of a stippled ray theme but with a twist, resulting in a beautiful sunburst effect. This, coupled with a curious star and fan design on the exterior base, creates a unique and intriguing pattern. Colors are green, marigold, and amethyst.

ZIPPERED HEART

Recent evidence that this is an Imperial pattern is a catalog from the company illustrating the Zippered Heart pattern in crystal in many shapes, including table sets, vases, compotes, rose bowls, a milk pitcher, punch sets, and water sets. However, in iridized glass the shapes I've seen are a berry set and the famous Queen's vase. While a beautiful purple is most encountered, marigold is known. Shown is a rare 5" vase.

ZIPPER LOOP

While the Zipper Loop lamp is the most frequently encountered of all the kerosene lamps, it is a scarce item in itself. Known in four sizes, including a small hand lamp, the Zipper Loop is found in a good rich marigold color as well as a sparkling smoke finish. It has been reproduced in the former in the large size, so be cautious when buying.

ZIPPER STITCH

This attractive piece shown is the tray for a lovely cordial set consisting of a decanter, six stemmed cordials and the tray. These were made in Czechoslovakia and are known only in marigold.

ZIPPER VARIANT

I suspect this nicely done covered sugar is of British origin but can't be sure. The color is quite good as is the mold work. Note the interesting finial on the lid.

Wreath of Roses Variant (Dugan)

Wreath of Roses Rose Bowl

Zig-Zag (Fenton)

Zig-Zag (Millersburg)

Zippered Heart

Zipper Loop

Zipper Stitch

Zipper Variant

The Standard
Carnival Glass
Price Guide

The current values in this book should be used only as a guide. They are not intended to set prices, which vary from one section of the country to another. Auction prices as well as dealer prices vary greatly and are affected by condition as well as demand. Neither the Author nor the Publisher assumes responsibility for any losses that might be incurred as a result of consulting this guide.

Color Code

M—Marigold
A—Amethyst or Purple
B—Blue
G—Green
PO—Peach Opalescent
AO—Aqua Opalescent
BO—Blue Opalescent
IG—Ice Green
IB—Ice Blue
SM—Smoke
CL—Clear
CM—Clambroth
V—Vaseline
R—Red
Pas—Pastel
AQ—Aqua
AM—Amber
IM—Iridized Moonstone
HO—Horehound
RenB—Renniger Blue
PH—Pastel Horehound
HA—Honey Amber
CT—Citrene
EB—Electric Blue
EmG—Emerald Green

PL—Pearl Opalescent
AB—Amberina
RA—Reverse Amberina
LV—Lavender
IC—Iridized Custard
VO—Vaseline Opalescent
PM—Pastel Marigold
W—White
TL—Teal
PeB—Persian Blue
CeB—Celeste Blue
AP—Apricot
BA—Black Amethyst
LG—Lime Green
RG—Russet Green (olive)
PK—Pink
MO—Milkglass Opalescent
LO—Lime Opalescent
RS—Red Slag
WS—Wisteria
CHP—Champagne
NG—Nile Green
MC—Marigold Custard
SMG—Smoke Milkglass

* Denotes a speculative price for an item that is rare and hasn't been on the market recently.

Note: While many prices have had an explosion of growth, especially on Northwood plates, red carnival and pastels, certain items after many years of growth have declined slightly or have remained constant. This price guide reflects these changes as well as is possible with today's ever-changing market. Please remember it takes months to print a price guide such as this, and in that time carnival glass sales do not remain static. While I have tried to allow for this passage of time from compilation to print, I cannot guess the future. Still, with over 33,000 price listings, this remains the most complete price source for carnival glass in the world, and I'm proud of the results.

Acorn Burrs

Apple Blossom Twigs

Apple Tree

Art Deco

	M	A	G	B	PO	AO	Pas	R
ACANTHUS (IMPERIAL)								
Bowl, 8"-9½"	65	90	110	90			75SM	
Plate, 10"	200						275SM	
ACORN (FENTON)								
Bowl, 7"-8½"	65	140	85	55	290	750	500AM	850
Plate, 9", Scarce		600		575				
ACORN (MILLERSBURG)								
Compote, Rare	3,000	1,800	1,900				2,850V	
ACORN BURRS (NORTHWOOD)								
Bowl, Flat, 10"	90	135	175				500	
Bowl, Flat, 5"	30	40	50				100	
Punch Bowl and Base	550	700	850	2,000		25,000	4,500W	
Punch Cup	45	90	100	75		575	100W	
Covered Butter	300	400	950				700	
Covered Sugar	225	300					450	
Creamer or Spooner	200	260					390	
Water Pitcher	500	600	1,000					
Tumbler	65	80	100					
Whimsey Vase, Rare	3,000	3,500+						
ACORN AND FILE								
Ftd Compote, Rare							1,500V	
A DOZEN ROSES (IMPERIAL)								
Bowl, Footed, 8½"-10", Rare	650	750	850					
ADVERTISING ASHTRAY								
Various Designs	60+							
AFRICAN SHIELD (ENGLISH)								
Toothpick Holder (or Bud Holder)	115							
AGE HERALD (FENTON)								
Bowl, 9¼", Scarce		1,200						
Plate, 10", Scarce		2,000						
AMARYLLIS (NORTHWOOD)								
Small Compote	225	200		275			450W	
Whimsey (Flattened)		600						
AMERICAN (FOSTORIA)								
Tumbler, Rare	95		125					
APOTHECARY JAR								
Small Size	60							
APPLE BLOSSOMS (DUGAN)								
Bowl, 7½"	40	58	70		175		150W	
Plate, 8¼"	250	275			260		300W	
APPLE BLOSSOM (ENAMELED) (NORTHWOOD)								
Tumbler				90				
APPLE BLOSSOM TWIGS (DUGAN)								
Bowl	40	160	170			185	150W	
Plate	200	250	300	190		400	225W	
APPLE PANELS (ENGLISH)								
Creamer	35							
Sugar (open)	35							
APPLE AND PEAR INTAGLIO (NORTHWOOD)								
Bowl, 10"	90							
Bowl, 5"	40							
APPLE TREE (FENTON)								
Water Pitcher	225			500			750W	
Tumbler	40			65			150W	
Pitcher, Vase Whimsey, Rare	1,800			2,000				
APRIL SHOWERS (FENTON)								
Vase	55	110	150	130			200	
ARCADIA BASKETS								
Plate, 8"	50							
ARCHED FLEUR-DE-LIS (HIGBEE)								
Mug, Rare	250							
ARCHED PANELS								
Tumbler	85							
ARCS (IMPERIAL)								
Bowls, 8½"	40	60	50				175W	
Compote	65	90						
ART DECO (ENGLISH)								
Bowl, 4"	38							
ASTERS								
Bowl	60							
Compote	90							
ASTRAL								
Shade	55							
AUGUST FLOWERS								
Shade	42							
AURORA								
Bowl, 2 Sizes Decorated	400	700					950IM	
AUTUMN ACORNS (FENTON)								
Bowl, 8¼"	55	75	80	70				4,800
Plate, Rare		1,000	1,000	1,200				

Aztec

Banded Rib

Basket

Beaded Acanthus

	M	A	G	B	PO	AO	Pas	R
AZTEC (McKEE)								
Pitcher, Rare	1,300							
Tumbler, Rare	650							
Creamer	250						250CM	
Sugar	250						250CM	
Rosebowl							400CM	
BABY BATHTUB (U.S. GLASS)								
Miniature Piece							500	
BABY'S BOUQUET								
Child's Plate, Scarce	115							
BAKER'S ROSETTE								
Ornament	75	90						
BALL AND SWIRL								
Mug	120							
BALLARD-MERCED, CA. (NORTHWOOD)								
Plate								
Bowl		950						
BALLOONS (IMPERIAL)								
Cake Plate	85						110SM	
Compote	65						90SM	
Perfume Atomizer	60						90SM	
Vase, 3 Sizes	75						100SM	
BAMBI								
Powder Jar w/lid	30							
BAMBOO BIRD								
Jar, Complete	800							
BAND (DUGAN)								
Violet Hat	30	40			75			
BANDED DIAMONDS & BARS								
Decanter, Complete	175							
Tumbler, Rare	425							
BANDED DIAMONDS & BARS (FINLAND)								
Tumbler, 4" tall	550							
Tumbler, 2¼" tall	550							
BANDED DIAMOND AND FAN (ENGLISH)								
Toothpick Holder	80							
BANDED DIAMONDS (CRYSTAL)								
Water Pitcher, Rare	900	1,250						
Tumbler, Rare	500	400						
Bowl, 10"	100	125						
Bowl, 5"	50	75						
BANDED GRAPE (FENTON)								
Water Pitcher	200		500	400			750W	
Tumbler	40		75	50			95W	
BANDED GRAPE AND LEAF (ENGLISH)								
Water Pitcher, Rare	650							
Tumbler, Rare	100							
BANDED KNIFE AND FORK								
One Shape	75							
BANDED PANELS (CRYSTAL)								
Open Sugar	45	60						
BANDED PORTLAND (U.S. GLASS)								
Puff Jar	80							
BANDED RIB								
Tumbler	25							
Pitcher	125							
BANDED ROSE								
Vase, Small	175							
BARBELLA (NORTHWOOD)								
Tumbler							225VAS	
BARBER BOTTLE (CAMBRIDGE)								
Complete	575	750	750					
BASKET (NORTHWOOD)								
Either Shape, Ftd	225	125	365	1,350		550	900CeB	
BASKETWEAVE (FENTON)								
Hat Shape-Advertising	50		65					
Vase Whimsey, Rare	750		900					450
Basket-Open Edge Jip	50	180	275	110			370IG	
Open Edge Plate, 10"	1,000			1,600			2,000IB	
Open Edge Bowl, 8"	140	175		190			290IG	
Open Edge Bowl, 5"	45	50	55	50			100W	
BASKETWEAVE AND CABLE (WESTMORELAND)								
Creamer, Complete	50	75	100				250W	
Sugar, Complete	50	75	100				250W	
Syrup Whimsey	180							
BEADED								
Hatpin		45						
BEADED ACANTHUS (IMPERIAL)								
Milk Pitcher	75		260				170SM	

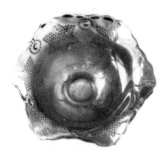

Beaded Star

Beauty

Bernheimer

Big Basketweave

	M	A	G	B	PO	AO	Pas	R
BEADED BAND AND OCTAGON								
Kerosene Lamp	250							
BEADED BASKET (DUGAN)								
One shape	45	55	80	60			120V	
BEADED BERRY (FENTON)								
Exterior Pattern Only								
BEADED BULLSEYE (IMPERIAL)								
Vase, 8"-14"	47	125	140				130SM	
BEADED CABLE (NORTHWOOD)								
Rose Bowl	60	95	150	160	900	1,000	425W	
Candy Dish	50	70	80	85		500	200W	
BEADED HEARTS (NORTHWOOD)								
Bowl	50	85	90					
BEADED PANELS (IMPERIAL)								
Bowl, 8"	45							
Bowl, 5"	25							
Powder Jar w/lid	50							
BEADED PANELS (WESTMORELAND)								
Compote	45	55				115		
BEADED PANELS & GRAPES (CHECHOSLOVACIA)								
Tumbler	275							
BEADED SHELL (DUGAN)								
Bowl, Ftd, 9"	75	95						
Bowl, Ftd, 5"	35	40						
Mug	200	95						
Covered Butter	130	150						
Covered Sugar	90	110						
Creamer or Spooner	75	90						
Water Pitcher	500	650						
Tumbler	60	70		180				
Mug Whimsey		450						
BEADED SPEARS (CRYSTAL)								
Pitcher, Rare	490	560						
Tumbler, Rare	190	200						
BEADED STARS (FENTON)								
Plate, 9"	110							
Bowl	40				90			
Rose Bowl	60							
Banana Boat	110							
BEADED SWIRL (ENGLISH)								
Compote	50			60				
Covered Butter	70			85				
Milk Pitcher	75			90				
Sugar	50			55				
BEADS (NORTHWOOD)								
Bowl, 8½"	45	60	70					
BEADS AND BARS (U.S. GLASS)								
Spooner	55							
BEAUTY BUD VASE (DUGAN)								
Regular Size	40	85					80SM	
Twig Size, Rare	150	175						
BEAUTY BUD VASE VT.								
No Twigs	30						35SM	
BEETLE ASHTRAY (ARGENTINA)								
One Size, Rare				350				
BEETLE HATPIN								
Complete		85						
BELL FLOWER (DUGAN)								
Compote, handled				450				
BELLAIRE SOUVENIR (IMPERIAL)								
Bowl, Scarce	185							
BELLS AND BEADS (DUGAN)								
Bowl, 7½"	45	90	115	120				
Nappy	60	95			100			
Plate, 8"		170						
Hat Shape	40	60						
Compote	70	75						
Gravy Boat, Handled	55	70			140			
BERNHEIMER (MILLERSBURG)								
Bowl, 8¾", Scarce				1,900				
BERRY BASKET								
One Size	55							
Matching Shakers, Pair	75							
BIG BASKETWEAVE (DUGAN)								
Vase, 6"-14"	90	120			140	275	150W	
Basket, Small	45	60						
BIG CHIEF								
One Shape		95						
BIG FISH (MILLERSBURG)								
Bowl, Various Shapes	500	600	650				6,500V	
Banana Bowl, Rare		2,000	2,000					
Bowl, Tri-Cornered	1,050	2,000	2,000				2,000V	
Rose Bowl, Very Rare							7,500V	
Square Bowl, Very Rare	900	1,500	1,500				6,000V	

	M	A	G	B	PO	AO	Pas	R
BIG THISTLE (MILLERSBURG)								
Punch Bowl and Base								
Only, Rare		10,000						
BIRD OF PARADISE (NORTHWOOD)								
Bowl, Advertising.................		395						
Plate, Advertising.................		450						
BIRD WITH GRAPES (COCKATOO)								
Wall Vase............................	75							
BIRDS AND CHERRIES (FENTON)								
Bon-bon	45	65	65	65			90	
Bowl, 9½", Rare	200	325		375				
Bowl, 5", Rare.....................	65	90						
Compote	45	60	65	60			95	
Plate, 10", Rare....................	1,200		1,600	1,500				
BLACK BOTTOM (FENTON)								
Candy Jar	60						60	
BLACKBERRY (FENTON)								
Open Edge Hat	40	45	50	40		175	80	475
Spittoon Whimsey, Rare	3,200			3,600				
Vase Whimsey, Rare	750			900			700W	
Plate, Rare	800			400				
BLACKBERRY (NORTHWOOD)								
Compote..............................	55	65		75			100	
Bowl, Ftd, 9".......................	50	60						
BLACKBERRY BANDED (FENTON)								
Hat Shape	35		55	45	90			
BLACKBERRY BARK								
Vase, Rare		1,900*						
BLACKBERRY BLOCK (FENTON)								
Pitcher................................	265	1,250	1,500	600			6,500V	
Tumbler	50	150	85	75			300V	
BLACKBERRY BRAMBLE (FENTON)								
Bowl....................................				60				
Compote..............................	40	50	70	55				
BLACKBERRY, MINIATURE (FENTON)								
Compote, Small	125	250	350	265			590W	
Stemmed Plate, Rare				450				
BLACKBERRY SPRAY (FENTON)								
Bon-bon	35	45	50	45				
Compote..............................	40	50	55	50				
Hat Shape	45	55	200	40		225	115V	485
BLACKBERRY WREATH (MILLERSBURG)								
Plate, 10", Rare....................	4,700	5,000						
Plate, 6", Rare.....................	2,250	2,700	2,900				90CM	
Bowl, 5"...............................	50	70	75					
Bowl, 7"-9"	65	90	90					
Bowl, 10", Ice Cream	175	200	250	1,100				
Spittoon Whimsey, Rare			3,800					
Plate, 8" Rare......................			4,200					
BLOCKS AND ARCHES								
Creamer	42							
BLOCKS AND ARCHES (CRYSTAL)								
Pitcher, Rare.......................	100	140						
Tumbler, Rare	75	90						
BLOSSOMS AND BAND (IMPERIAL)								
Bowl, 10".............................	38	45						
Bowl, 5"..............................	20	30						
Wall Vase, Complete	45							
BLOSSOM AND SPEARS								
Plate, 8"...............................	52							
BLOSSOMTIME (NORTHWOOD)								
Compote..............................	135	200	350					
BLOWN CANDLESTICKS								
One Size, Pair	90							
BLUEBERRY (FENTON)								
Pitcher, Scarce....................	500			700				
Tumbler, Scarce	60			100				
BO PEEP (WESTMORELAND)								
ABC Plate, Scarce...............	550							
Mug, Scarce	125							
BOOT								
One Shape...........................	150							
BORDER PLANTS (DUGAN)								
Bowl, Flat, 8½"		125			180			
Bowl, Ftd, 8½"		600			250			
BOUQUET (FENTON)								
Pitcher................................	285			550			750W	
Tumbler	37	80		55			90W	

Black Bottom

Blackberry

Blackberry Wreath

Blocks and Arches

Boutonniere

Brocaded Acorns

Broacaded Palms

Butterfly

	M	A	G	B	PO	AO	Pas	R
BOUQUET AND LATTICE								
Various Shapes From $5.00-15.00 each, Late Carnival								
BOUQUET TOOTHPICK HOLDER								
One Size	75							
BOUTONNIERE (MILLERSBURG)								
Compote..............................	175	195	225					
BOW AND ENGLISH HOB (ENGLISH)								
Nut Bowl	50			60				
BOXED STAR								
One Shape, Rare							110	
BRIAR PATCH								
Hat Shape	40	50						
BRIDLE ROSETTE								
One Shape............................	85							
BROCADED ACORNS (FOSTORIA)								
BROCADED DAFFODILS								
BROCADED PALMS								
BROCADED ROSES								
BROCADED SUMMER GARDENS								
All Related Patterns in Similar Shapes and Colors								
Wine....................................							70	
Bon-bon							65	
Cake Tray............................							110	
Ice Bucket							100	
Covered Box							95	
Tray							100	
Cake Plate, Center Handle ...							110	
Vase							120	
Rose Bowl............................							70	
Bowls, Various Sizes............							85	
Flower Set, 3 Pieces							190	
Center Bowl, Ftd..................							120	
BROKEN ARCHES (IMPERIAL)								
Bowl, 8½"-10"	45	50	75					
Punch Bowl and Base..........	365	595						
Punch Cup	30	30						
BROCKER'S (NORTHWOOD)								
Advertising Plate.................		1,700						
BROOKLYN								
Bottle w/stopper..................	75	95						
BROOKLYN BRIDGE (DUGAN)								
Bowl, Scarce........................	350							
Unlettered Bowl, Rare..........	1,200							
BUBBLE BERRY								
Shade..................................							75	
BUBBLES								
Hatpin.................................		65						
Lamp Chimney							50	
BUDDHA (ENGLISH)								
One Shape, Rare	900						1,100IB	
BULL DOG								
Paperweight........................	350							
BULL'S EYE (U.S. GLASS)								
Oil Lamp	210							
BULL'S EYE AND LEAVES (NORTHWOOD)								
Bowl, 8½"	40	55	50					
BULL'S EYE AND LOOP (MILLERSBURG)								
Vase, 7"-11", Rare...............	300	400	500					
BULL'S EYE AND SPEARHEAD								
Wine....................................	90							
BUMBLEBEES								
Hatpin.................................		70						
BUNNY								
Bank	35							
BUTTERFLIES (FENTON)								
Bon-bon	60	70	75	65			90	
Card Tray	55			60				
BUTTERFLIES AND BELLS (CRYSTAL)								
Compote..............................	120	145						
BUTTERFLIES AND WARATAH (CRYSTAL)								
Compote, Large	120	200						
BUTTERFLY								
Pintray	40						50	

232

Butterfly and Berry

Butterfly and Tulip

Button and Daisy Hat

Cannon Ball Variant

	M	A	G	B	PO	AO	Pas	R
BUTTERFLY (FENTON)								
Ornament, Rare..................	190	220	225	200			300W	
BUTTERFLY (NORTHWOOD)								
Bon-bon, Regular	65	75	90	325				
Bon-bon, Ribbed Exterior		250					575IB	
BUTTERFLY (U.S. GLASS)								
Tumbler, Rare	5,800		6,000					
BUTTERFLY LAMP								
Oil Lamp	1,500							
BUTTERFLY AND BERRY (FENTON)								
Bowl, Ftd, 10"	100	200	250	225			750W	1,200
Bowl, Ftd, 5"	35	40	45	40			95W	
Covered Butter	150	240	300	225				
Covered Sugar	100	160	200	175				
Covered Creamer	100	150	200	170				
Nut Bowl Whimsey		700						
Spooner............................	90	125	190	160				
Pitcher.............................	350	500		490			1,200W	
Tumbler	40	70	80	70			100W	
Hatpin Holder, Rare............	790			650				
Vase, Rare	40	55	200	50			500W	700
Spittoon Whimsey, 2 Types..		2,600		2,600				
Bowl Whimsey (Fernery)	850	1,200		1,400				
Plate, Ftd (Whimsey)............				1,500				
BUTTERFLY BOWER (CRYSTAL)								
Compote............................	95	130						
Cake Plate, Stemmed...........		200						
BUTTERFLY BUSH (CRYSTAL)								
Compote, Large	120	175						
BUTTERFLY AND CORN (NORTHWOOD)								
Vase, Rare							4,000V	
BUTTERFLY AND FERN (FENTON)								
Pitcher.............................	450	575	650	960				
Tumbler	55	60	85	65				
BUTTERFLY AND TULIP (DUGAN)								
Bowl, Ftd, 10½", Scarce	490	2,500						
Bowl, Whimsey Shape, Rare ..	900	1,500						
BUTTERMILK, PLAIN (FENTON)								
Goblet	60	70	80					
BUTTON AND FAN								
Hatpin...............................		60						
BUTTONS AND DAISY (IMPERIAL)								
Hat (Old Only)							70CM	
Slipper (Old Only)							80CM	
BUTTRESS (U.S. GLASS)								
Pitcher, Rare......................	400							
Tumbler, Rare	300							
BUZZ SAW								
Shade................................	45							
BUZZ SAW (CAMBRIDGE)								
Cruet, Small 4", Rare..........			400					
Cruet, Large 6", Rare	400		400					
CACTUS (MILLERSBURG)								
Exterior Pattern								
CANADA DRY								
Bottle................................	55							
CANDLE LAMP (FOSTORIA)								
One Size	110						150AM	
CANE (IMPERIAL)								
Bowl, 7½"-10"	40						50	
Pickle Dish	32						46	
Wine	65						75	
Compote.............................	80						115	
CANE AND DAISY CUT (JENKINS)								
Vase	150							
Basket, Handled, Rare.........	220						250	
CANE AND SCROLL (SEA THISTLE) (ENGLISH)								
Rose Bowl..........................	55			75				
Creamer or Sugar	45							
CANNONBALL VT.								
Pitcher.............................	240			285			400W	
Tumbler	50			65			90W	
CANOE (U.S. GLASS)								
One Size	150							
CAPITOL (WESTMORELAND)								
Mug, Small	140							
Bowl, Ftd, Small		70		70				

Captive Rose

Cartwheel

Checkerboard

Cherry (Dugan)

	M	A	G	B	PO	AO	Pas	R
CAPTIVE ROSE (FENTON)								
Bowl, 8½"-10"	75	90	90	80			250BA	
Compote	65	80	90	160				
Plate, 7"	140	190	210	200			550	
Plate, 9"	225	410	425	400				
Bon-bon	50		70	60			160	
CARNATION (NEW MARTINSVILLE)								
Punch Cup	57							
CARNIVAL BELL								
One Size	425							
CARNIVAL HONEYCOMB (IMPERIAL)								
Bon-bon	40	55	60				75AM	
Creamer or Sugar	35							
Plate, 7"		95						
Bowl, Handles, 6"	30							
CAROLINA DOGWOOD (WESTMORELAND)								
Bowl, 8½"	80	110			260MO	500		
Plate, Rare					320MO			
CAROLINE (DUGAN)								
Bowl, 7"-10"	70				190			
Banana Bowl					210			
Basket, Scarce					400			
CARRIE (ANCHOR-HOCKING)								
One Size	60							
CARTWHEEL #411 (HEISEY)								
Compote	50							
Goblet	75							
CATHEDRAL (SWEDEN) (Also know as Curved Star)								
Chalice, 7"	145		190					
Pitcher, Rare			3,700					
Bowl, 10"	50							
Flower Holder	75							
Epergne, Scarce	245							
Compote, 2 Sizes	60		80					
Creamer, Ftd	60							
Butterdish, 2 Sizes	240							
CATHEDRAL ARCHES (ENGLISH)								
Punch Bowl, 1 Piece	350							
CATTAILS								
Hatpin		50						
CENTRAL SHOE STORE (NORTHWOOD)								
Bowl, 6"-7"		1,200						
CHAIN AND STAR (FOSTORIA)								
Tumbler, Rare	900							
Covered Butter, Rare	1,500							
CHATELAINE (IMPERIAL)								
Pitcher, Rare		3,700						
Tumbler, Rare		510						
CHATHAM (U.S. GLASS)								
Compote	75							
Candlesticks, Pair	90							
CHECKERBOARD BOUQUET								
Plate, 8"		85						
CHECKERBOARD (WESTMORELAND)								
Cruet, Rare							750CL	
Pitcher, Rare		3,800						
Tumbler, Rare	750	550						
Goblet, Rare	350	425						
Punch Cup	90							
Wine, Rare	295							
Vase		2,700						
CHECKERBOARD PANELS (ENGLISH)								
Bowl	70							
CHECKERS								
Ashtray	47							
Bowl, 4"	28							
Bowl, 9"	40							
Butter, 2 Sizes	200							
Plate, 7"	90							
CHERRY (DUGAN)								
Bowl, Flat, 5"	40	50			90			
Bowl, Flat, 8"	65	70			210			
Bowl, Ftd, 8½"	210	310			400			
Plate, 6"		200			410			
Cruet, Rare							650W	
CHERRY (FENTON) (See Mikado Compote)								

Cherry Chain

Cherry Circle

Circle Scroll

Classic Arts

	M	A	G	B	PO	AO	Pas	R
CHERRY								
(MILLERSBURG)								
Bowl, 4"..................	60	85	90	600				
Bowl, 5", Hobnail								
Exterior Rare				900				
Bowl, 7", Rare....................	135	95	130					
Bowl, 9", Scarce..................	90	125	150					
Bowl, Ice Cream, 10"	250	375	350	1,800				
Bowl, 9", Hobnail								
Exterior Rare	900	1,250		2,700				
Compote, Large, Rare	1,250	1,495	1,600	4,000			5,000V	
Banana Compote, Rare........		4,000						
Milk Pitcher, Rare................	1,100							
Plate, 6", Rare.....................	1,050							
Plate, 7½", Rare		1,100	1,150					
Plate, 10", Rare	4,600							
Powder Jar, Rare			1,950					
Covered Butter	250	375	450					
Covered Sugar....................	170	300	325					
Creamer or Spooner	150	275	275					
Pitcher, Scarce....................	1,150	1,000	1,450					
Tumbler, 2 Variations	145	190	210					
CHERRY BLOSSOMS								
Pitcher..............................				150				
Tumbler				40				
CHERRY AND CABLE								
(NORTHWOOD)								
Pitcher, Rare......................	1,450							
Tumbler, Rare	425							
Bowl, 5", Scarce.................	75							
Butter, Rare........................	450							
Sugar, Creamer,								
Spooner, Each, Rare	210							
Bowl, 9", Scarce..................	125							
CHERRY AND CABLE INTAGLIO								
(NORTHWOOD)								
Bowl, 10"..........................	75							
Bowl, 5".............................	50							
CHERRY CHAIN (FENTON)								
Bon-bon	50	60	65	55				
Bowl, 6½"-10"	50	90	90	95				
Plate, 7"-9"	85			140				
CHERRY CIRCLES								
(FENTON)								
Bon-bon	50	65		75				7,400
Bowl, 8"..............................	50	65		70				
Compote.............................	70	80		80			130W	
Plate, 9", Rare.....................	550			210			210W	
CHERRY AND DAISIES								
(FENTON)								
Banana Boat	950			1,050				
CHERRY SMASH								
(U.S. GLASS)								
Bowl, 8".............................	65							
Butter	150							
Tumbler	190							
CHERRY STIPPLED								
Tumbler	110							
CHERUB								
Lamp, Rare.........................							150	
CHIPPENDALE SOUVENIR								
Creamer or Sugar	65	80						
CHRISTMAS COMPOTE								
Large Compote, Rare	4,200	4,700						
CHRYSANTHEMUM								
(FENTON)								
Bowl, Flat, 9"......................	130	60	95	80				5,700
Bowl, Ftd, 10".....................	80	75	110	120			600BA	
CHRYSANTHEMUM DRAPE								
Oil Lamp, Rare							900	
CIRCLE SCROLL (DUGAN)								
Compote, Scarce..................		150						
Bowl, 10"............................	65	80						
Bowl, 5"..............................	40	45						
Pitcher, Rare.......................	2,000	2,800						
Tumbler, Rare	400	600						
Hat Shape, Rare	60	100						
Creamer or Spooner	150	225						
Vase Whimsey, Rare	135	160						
Butter or Sugar	375	425						
CLASSIC ARTS (CZECH)								
Vase, 7" (Egyptian)...............	700							
Powder Jar..........................	575							
Rose Bowl..........................	525							
Vase, 10", Rare	750							
CLEOPATRA								
Bottle	110							

Cleveland Memorial

Cobblestone

Colonial

Concord

	M	A	G	B	PO	AO	Pas	R
CLEVELAND MEMORIAL (MILLERSBURG)								
Ashtray, Rare	5,800	5,700						
COAL BUCKET (U.S. GLASS)								
One Size	400		500					
COBBLESTONES (DUGAN)								
Bowl, 9"	65	150						
Bowl, 5"	40	80						
COBBLESTONES (DUGAN-IMPERIAL)								
Plate, Rare		1,300						
COBBLESTONES (IMPERIAL)								
Bowl, 5"	35	40	50					
Bowl, 8½"	75	275	115					
Bon-bon	45	75	70				95AM	
COIN DOT (FENTON)								
Bowl, 6"-10"	35	40	40	65		260	100LV	1,200
Plate, 9", Rare	200	250	275	260				
Pitcher, Rare	350	500	550	525				
Tumbler, Rare	190	250	265	225				
Basket Whimsey, Rare	75		100					
Rose Bowl	90							1,600
COIN DOT VT. (WESTMORELAND)								
Compote	60				175MO	270	350IBO	
Rose Bowl	40	75					320TL	
Bowl	40	60	70				90	
COIN SPOT (DUGAN)								
Compote	45	60	70	65	200	375		
Goblet, Rare							390IG	
COLOGNE BOTTLE (CAMBRIDGE)								
One Size, Rare	600		850					
COLONIAL (IMPERIAL)								
Lemonade Goblet	75							
Vase	40	60						
Toothpick Holder	60	110	95					
Open Sugar or Creamer	47							
Candlesticks, Pair	200							
COLONIAL LADY (IMPERIAL)								
Vase, Rare	1,000	1,150						
COLUMBIA (IMPERIAL)								
Vase	45	55	50					
Compote	60	75	65					
COLUMBUS								
Plate, 8"	45							
COMPASS (DUGAN)								
(Exterior Pattern Only)								
COMPOTE VASE								
Stemmed Shape	50	65	72	76				
CONCAVE DIAMONDS (DUGAN)								
Pitcher w/lid			450RG				550V	
Tumbler			425RG				190V	
Pickle Castor, Ornate Holder	475						395CeB	
Tumble-Up, Complete, Rare							230V	
Coaster, Not Iridized							20	
Vase							100CeB	
CONCAVE FLUTE (WESTMORELAND)								
Rose Bowl	50		65					
Vase	40	65	65					
CONCORD (FENTON)								
Bowl, 9", Scarce	175	300	400	250			350AM	
Plate, 10", Rare	800	1,200	1,300				1,000AM	
CONE AND TIE (IMPERIAL)								
Tumbler, Rare		950						
CONNIE (NORTHWOOD)								
Pitcher							750W	
Tumbler							125W	
CONSTELLATION (DUGAN)								
Compote	150	60			200		175V	
CONTINENTAL BOTTLE								
2 Sizes	45							
COOLEEMEE, NC (FENTON)								
Advertising Plate, Rare (Heart and Vine)	1,500							
CORAL (FENTON)								
Bowl, 9"	200		395	400			500W	
Compote, Rare	450		500				650W	
Plate, 9½", Rare	1,000		1,200	1,200				
CORINTH (DUGAN)								
Bowl, 9"	40	50			200			
Banana Dish	55	75			300			
CORINTH (WESTMORELAND)								
Vase	30	50	75	450BO	150		60TL	
Bowl	40	60					75TL	
CORN BOTTLE (IMPERIAL)								
One Size	285		250				275SM	

Corn Cruet

Corn Vase

Coronation

Covered Swan

	M	A	G	B	PO	AO	Pas	R
CORN CRUET								
One Size, Rare							1,100W	
CORN VASE								
(NORTHWOOD)								
Regular Mold	1,150	800	900	2,200		4,800	2,500TL	
Pulled Husk, Rare		7,500	7,500					
Fancy Husk,								
Rare (Dugan)	950							
CORNING (CORNING)								
Insulator	35+							
CORNUCOPIA								
(FENTON)								
Candlestick, pair, 5"	80						190W	
Vase, 5"	70						110W	
Candle Holder, 6½"							110W	
CORONATION								
(ENGLISH)								
Vase, 5"								
(Victoria Crown Design)	250							
COSMOS								
(MILLERSBURG)								
Bowl, 5"			70					
COSMOS AND CANE								
Bowl, 10"	75						90W	
Bowl, 5"	40						45W	
Compote, Tall, Rare	350						300W	
Butter, Covered	200						300W	
Covered Sugar or Creamer...	135						200W	
Flat Tray, Rare							275W	
Spooner.............................	100						195W	
Stemmed Dessert							150W	
Pitcher, Rare......................	750						1,450W	
Tumbler, Rare	115						250W	
Advertising Tumbler, Rare ...							110AM	
Rose Bowl, Large	1,275	1,500					2,000AM	
Rose Bowl Whimsey.............	1,700							
Spittoon Whimsey, Rare							4,200W	
Chop Plate, Rare..................	1,450						1,600W	
Breakfast Set, 2 Pieces							500W	
COSMOS & HOBSTAR								
Bowl (on metal stand)	450							
COSMOS VT. (FENTON)								
Bowl, 9"-10"	40	65	75				75V	485
Plate, 10", Rare...................	175	210		400				
COUNTRY KITCHEN								
(MILLERSBURG)								
Bowl, 9", Rare.....................	265							
Bowl, 5", Rare.....................	90							
Spittoon Whimsey, Rare		4,600						
Covered Butter, Rare	650	750						
Sugar, Creamer or Spooner..	400	500	800				900V	
Vase Whimsey, Rare	600	700						
COURTHOUSE								
(MILLERSBURG								
Lettered (Round or Ruffled),								
Scarce		950						
Unlettered, Rare		2,500						
COVERED FROG								
(HEISEY)								
One Size..............................	375	450	500	275			650	
COVERED HEN								
(ENGLISH)								
One Size	110			145				
COVERED LITTLE HEN								
(TINY)								
Miniature, 3½", Rare............							90CM	
COVERED MALLARD								
(U.S. GLASS)								
One Shape...........................							450CM	
COVERED SWAN								
(ENGLISH)								
One Size	150	250						
COVERED TURKEY								
(HEISEY)								
One Size		400						
COVERED TURTLE								
(HEISEY)								
One Size			475				600PK	
CR (ARGENTINA)								
Ash Tray..............................	90			135				
CRAB CLAW (IMPERIAL)								
Bowl, 5"	25	37	40					
Bowl, 10"	50	65	65				70SM	
Fruit Bowl w/base..............	110							
Pitcher, Scarce....................	650							
Tumbler, Scarce	140							
Cruet, Rare.........................	950							

	M	A	G	B	PO	AO	Pas	R
CRACKLE (IMPERIAL)								
Auto Vase	30	35	35					
Bowl, 9"	25	30	30					
Bowl, 5"	15	18	18					
Candy Jar w/lid	30							
Candlestick, 3½"	25							
Candlestick, 7"	30							
Plate	45	55	60					
Punch Bowl and Base	55							
Punch Cup	10							
Pitcher, Dome Base	90	150	160					
Spittoon, Large	45							
Tumbler, Dome Base	20	30	30					
Wall Vase	40							
Window Planter, Rare	110							
CROCUS VT.								
Tumbler	45	65						
CRUCIFIX (IMPERIAL)								
Candlestick, Rare, Each	650							
CRYSTAL CUT (CRYSTAL)								
Compote	75							
CUBA (McKee)								
Goblet, Rare	45							
CURTAIN OPTIC (FENTON)								
Pitcher							450VAS	
Tumbler							150VAS	
Guest Set (tumble-up)							350VAS	
CUT ARCHES (ENGLISH)								
Banana Bowl	80							
CUT ARCS (FENTON)								
Bowl, 7½"-10"	40							
Compote	55	60		55				
Vase Whimsey (From Bowl)	40	50		50			80W	
CUT COSMOS (MILLERSBURG)								
Tumbler, Rare	450							
CUT CRYSTAL (U.S. GLASS)								
Compote, 5½"	110							
Water Bottle	185							
CUT FLOWERS (JENKINS)								
Vase, 10"	200							
CUT OVALS (FENTON)								
Candlesticks, pair	175						210	700
Bowl, 7"-10"	60						75	425
CUT SPRAYS								
Vase, 9"	45			75				
DAHLIA (DUGAN)								
Bowl, Ftd, 10"	95	125					290W	
Bowl, Ftd, 5"	40	50					190W	
Butter	120	155					350W	
Sugar	90	100					250W	
Creamer or Spooner	75	90					220W	
Pitcher, Rare	500	950					800W	
Tumbler, Rare	90	145					170W	
DAHLIA (FENTON)								
Twist Epergne, One Lily	250						300W	
DAHLIA AND DRAPE (FENTON)								
Tumble-Up, Complete	150						190IB	
DAINTY BUD VASE								
One Size	55							
DAISY (FENTON)								
Bon-bon, Scarce	250			300				
DAISY BASKET (IMPERIAL)								
One Size	65						85SM	
DAISY BLOCK (ENGLISH)								
Rowboat, Scarce	250	300					300AQ	
DAISY AND CANE (ENGLISH)								
Vase	75							
Decanter, Rare	90							
Spittoon, Rare				250				
DAISY CHAIN								
Shade	50							
DAISY CUT BELL (FENTON)								
One Size, Rare	500							

Crucifix

Cut Flowers

Daisy

Daisy and Cane

Daisy and Plume

Diamond and Daisy Cut

Diamond Flutes

	M	A	G	B	PO	AO	Pas	R
DAISY AND DRAPE (NORTHWOOD)								
Vase	300	375	2,200	550		700	400W	
DAISY DEAR (DUGAN)								
Bowl......................	40	48			55		70W	
DAISY IN OVAL PANELS (U.S. GLASS)								
Creamer or Sugar, Each	55							
DAISY AND PLUME (NORTHWOOD)								
Rose Bowl, 2 Shapes............	75	100	105	110	175	2,000	550	
Compote.............................	60	110	90	100	160			
Candy Dish	70	90	90	100	165			
DAISY SQUARES								
Rose Bowl	600		675				650IG	
Goblet, Rare	700	900					800AM	
Compote, Rare....................	500						700AM	
DAISY WEB (DUGAN)								
Hat, Rare.............................	180	500			650			
DAISY WREATH (WESTMORELAND)								
Bowl, 8"-10"		250				600	500MO	
DANCE OF THE VEILS (FENTON)								
Vase, Rare	3,000							
DANDELION (NORTHWOOD)								
Mug......................................	500	575	675	500		650	750BO	
Pitcher.................................	395	620	700	900			7,500IB	
Tumbler	175	190	200	250			475IG	
Vase Whimsey, Rare		850						
DAVISON'S SOCIETY CHOCOLATES (NORTHWOOD)								
Plate, Handgrip...................		700						
DECO LILY								
Bulbous Vase	140							
DEEP GRAPE (MILLERSBURG)								
Compote, Rare....................	1,200	1,500	1,700	3,000				
Compote, Ruffled Top, Rare......................................		2,400						
Rose Bowl, Stemmed			8,000					
DeVILBISS								
Atomizer, Complete..............	65+							
Perfumer	60+							
DIAMONDS (MILLERSBURG)								
Pitcher.................................	285	395	350				490AO	
Tumbler	70	100	85				190AO	
Punch Bowl and Base, Rare ..	2,800	2,300	2,500					
Pitcher Oddity (No Spout)		550	550					
Spittoon Whimsey, Very Rare............................	8000*							
DIAMOND BAND (CRYSTAL)								
Open Sugar	45	60						
Float Set..............................	400	550						
DIAMOND BAND AND FAN (ENGLISH)								
Cordial Set, Complete, Rare...	900							
DIAMOND CHECKERBOARD								
Cracker Jar	85							
Butter	90							
Bowl, 9"................................	40							
Bowl, 5"................................	25							
Tumbler	100							
DIAMOND DAISY								
Plate, 8"...............................	95							
DIAMOND AND DAISY CUT (U.S. GLASS)								
Vase, Square, 10"	125							
Compote...............................	55	70		75				
Pitcher, Rare........................	400			450				
Tumbler, Rare	50			60				
DIAMOND AND DAISY CUT VT (JENKINS)								
Punch Bowl/Base, Rare.......	600							
DIAMOND AND FILE								
Banana Bowl	65							
Bowl, 7"-9"	50						70	
DIAMOND FLUTES (U.S. GLASS)								
Creamer	45							
Parfait	55							

239

	M	A	G	B	PO	AO	Pas	R
DIAMOND FOUNTAIN (HIGBEE)								
Cruet, Rare	750*							
DIAMOND LACE (IMPERIAL)								
Bowl, 10"-11"	65	110						
Bowl, 5"	30	40						
Pitcher		295						
Tumbler	190	70					250W*	
DIAMOND OVALS (ENGLISH)								
Compote (Open Sugar)	40							
Creamer	40							
DIAMOND PINWHEEL (ENGLISH)								
Compote	45							
Butter	75							
DIAMOND POINT								
Rose Bowl	700							
Basket, Rare	1,350	1,400		1,500				
DIAMOND POINT COLUMNS (IMPERIAL)								
Bowl, 4½"	20							
Compote	30						40	
Plate, 7"	35							
Vase	40	55					55	
Butter	70							
Creamer, Sugar or Spooner, Each	40							
Powder Jar w/lid	40							
Milk Pitcher	35							
DIAMOND POINTS (NORTHWOOD)								
Vase, 7"-14"	45	90	80	175	300	395	275TL	
DIAMOND PRISMS (ENGLISH)								
Compote	58							
DIAMOND AND RIB (FENTON)								
Vase, 7"-12"	45	100	90	80			70SM	
Funeral Vase, 17"-22"	700	900	1,000	1,000			800W	
Vase Whimsey			900					
DIAMOND RING (IMPERIAL)								
Rose Bowl, Rare	400*	650*					450*SM	
Bowl, 9"	40	50					55SM	
Bowl, 5"	25	30					32SM	
Fruit Bowl, 9½"	65	90					60SM	
DIAMOND STAR								
Mug, 2 sizes	120+							
Vase, 8"	80							
DIAMOND AND SUNBURST (IMPERIAL)								
Bowl, 8"	50	55	55				50AM	
Decanter	110	150	150					
Wine	55	60	60					
Oil Cruet, Rare		900*						
DIAMOND TOP (ENGLISH)								
Creamer	40							
Spooner	40							
DIAMOND VANE (ENGLISH)								
Creamer, 4"	35							
DIVING DOLPHINS (ENGLISH)								
Bowl, Ftd, 7"	200	260	280	270				
DOG								
Ashtray	85							
DOGWOOD SPRAYS (DUGAN)								
Compote	270				360			
Bowl, 9"	250	270			370			
DOLPHINS (MILLERSBURG)								
Compote, Rare		1,850	2,000	6,000				
DORSEY AND FUNKENSTEIN (NORTHWOOD)								
Plate		600						
DOTS AND CURVES								
Hatpin		55						
DOTTED DAISIES								
Plate, 8"	90							
DOTTED DIAMONDS & DAISIES								
Tumbler	90							

Diamond Ovals

Diamond Pinwheel

Diamond Point

Double Dutch

Double Scroll

Double Stem Rose

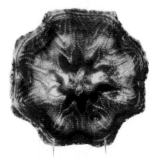

Dragon's Tongue

	M	A	G	B	PO	AO	Pas	R
DOUBLE DOLPHINS (FENTON)								
Bowl, Ftd, 9"-11"							115	
Cake Plate, Center Handle							85	
Candlesticks, pair							90	
Compote							70	
Fan Vapse							70	
Covered Candy Dish, Stemmed							80	
Bowl, 8"-10", Flat							65	
DOUBLE DUTCH (IMPERIAL)								
Bowl, 9", Ftd	50	75	75				85SM	
DOUBLE LOOP (NORTHWOOD)								
Creamer	155	160	170	190		275		
Sugar	155	160	170	190		290		
DOUBLE SCROLL (IMPERIAL)								
Bowl	45	55	55				65	210
Candlesticks, pair	75	80	80				80	260
Punch Cup	25							
DOUBLE STAR (CAMBRIDGE)								
Pitcher, Scarce	750	650	500					
Tumbler, Scarce	280	140	60					
Spittoon Whimsey, Rare			3,000					
Bowl, 9", Rare			400					
DOUBLE STEM ROSE (DUGAN)								
Bowl, Dome Base, 8½"	100	90	115	100	190		600CeB	
DOUGHNUT BRIDLE ROSETTE								
One Size		95						
DRAGON AND LOTUS (FENTON)								
Bowl, Flat, 9"	185	150	195	115	240	2,400	875AM	4,800
Bowl, Ftd, 9"	180	195	175	190	200		85LV	4,500
Plate, 9½", Rare	2,800	1,350		1,600	1,100		1200	9,000
DRAGON AND STRAWBERRY (FENTON)								
Bowl, Flat, 9", Scarce	450		900	950		2,300		
Bowl, Ftd, 9", Scarce	400		900	795				
Plate (Absentee Dragon), Rare	3,700							
DRAGON VASE								
Square Vase		250						
DRAGONFLY								
Shade							65	
DRAGONFLY LAMP								
Oil Lamp, Rare							1,800	
DRAGON'S TONGUE (FENTON)								
Bowl, 11", Scarce	950							
Shade	40				115			
DRAPE AND TASSEL								
Shade	45							
DRAPERY (NORTHWOOD)								
Vase	45	235	110	225EB		250	250IG	
Rose Bowl	240	135	170	120		700	600W	
Candy Dish	65	140	200	110		550	200AO	
DRAPERY VT. (FENTON)								
Pitcher, Rare	510							
Tumbler, Scarce	90							
DREIBUS PARFAIT SWEETS (NORTHWOOD)								
Plate, Handgrip, 6"		550						
DUCKIE								
Powder Jar w/lid	40							
DUGAN FAN (DUGAN)								
Sauce, 5"	40	55			145			
Gravy Boat, Ftd	65	75			210		100	
DUGAN'S MANY RIBS								
Vase	60	80		75	110			
Hat Shape	50	70		60	100			
DUNCAN (NATIONAL GLASS)								
Cruet	600							
DURAND (FENTON)								
Bowl - Grape and Cable					1,200			
DUTCH MILL								
Plate, 8"	50							
Ashtray	65							

Elks (Millersburg)

Embroidered Mums

Engraved Grape

Estate

	M	A	G	B	PO	AO	Pas	R
DUTCH PLATE								
One Size, 8"	55							
DUTCH TWINS								
Ashtray	50							
E.A. HUDSON FURNITURE (NORTHWOOD)								
Plate		1,000						
EAGLE FURNITURE (NORTHWOOD)								
Plate		800						
EAT PARADISE SODA (NORTHWOOD)								
		595						
EBON								
Vase		110BA						
ELEGANCE								
Bowl, 8¼", Rare	2,800						3,200IB	
Plate, Rare							4,800IB	
ELKS (DUGAN)								
Nappy, Very Rare		4,200						
ELKS (FENTON)								
Detroit Bowl, Scarce	1,300	900	750	700				
Parkersburg Plate, Rare			1,450	1,300				
Atlantic City Plate, Rare			1,800	1,200				
Atlantic City Bowl				1,325				
1911 Atlantic City Bell, Rare				2,200				
1917 Portland Bell, Rare				15,000*				
1914 Parkersburg Bell, Rare				2,300				
ELKS (MILLERSBURG)								
Bowl, Rare		1,500						
Paperweight, Rare		1,500	1,700					
EMBROIDERED MUMS (NORTHWOOD)								
Bowl, 9"	475	400	585	450		3,900	1,950IG	
Stemmed Bon-bon							1,250W	
Plate	600	550	695	650			2,500IG	
EMU (CRYSTAL)								
Bowl, 5", Rare	75							
Bowl, 10", Rare	245						550AM	
ENAMELLED GRAPE (NORTHWOOD)								
Pitcher				400				
Tumbler				45				
ENAMELED PANEL								
Goblet	190							
ENGLISH BUTTON BAND (ENGLISH)								
Creamer	45							
Sugar	45							
ENGLISH HOB AND BUTTON (ENGLISH)								
Bowl, 7"-10"	60	80	95	70				
Epergne (metal base), Rare	125			145				
ENGRAVED DAISY & SPEARS								
Goblet, 4½"	75							
ENGRAVED FLORAL (FENTON)								
Tumbler			95					
ENGRAVED GRAPES (FENTON)								
Vase, 8"	65						75	
Candy Jar w/lid	85							
Juice Glass	30							
Pitcher, Squat	120							
Tumbler	30							
Pitcher, Tall	145							
Tumble-Up	150							
ESTATE (WESTMORELAND)								
Mug, Rare	75							
Perfume							1,100SM	
Creamer or Sugar	55				90	190BO	110AQ	
Bud Vase, 6"	50						65	
ESTATE, STIPPLED (WESTMORELAND)								
Vase, 3"					190		200	

242

	M	A	G	B	PO	AO	Pas	R
ETCHED DECO								
Plate, ftd. 8"	60							
EVELYN (FOSTORIA)								
Bowl (1940's)			1,000*					
EXCHANGE BANK (NORTHWOOD)								
Plate, 6"		500						
EYE CUP								
One Size	90							
FAMOUS								
Puff box	75							
FANCIFUL (DUGAN)								
Bowl, 8½"	90	350		500EB		250	175W	
Plate, 9"	175	550		350		500	250W	
FANCY (NORTHWOOD) (Interior on some "Fine Cut and Roses" Rose Bowls)								
FANCY CUT (ENGLISH)								
Miniature Pitcher, Rare	225							
Miniature Tumbler	60							
FANCY FLOWERS (IMPERIAL)								
Compote	120		175					
FANS (ENGLISH)								
Pitcher	185							
Cracker Jar (metal lid)	150							
Tumbler	150							
FANTAIL (FENTON)								
Bowl, Ftd, 5"	80			220			145	
Bowl, Ftd, 9"	110			275			180	
Compote	90			195				
Plate, Ftd, Rare				1,600				
FARMYARD (DUGAN)								
Bowl, 10", Rare		3,200	8,500		10,000			
Plate, 10½", Very Rare		12,000						
FASHION (IMPERIAL)								
Creamer or Sugar	42	125					50	
Fruit Bowl and Base	70						75	
Punch Bowl and Base	85	195					90	
Punch Cup	24	40					30	
Pitcher	250	1,000					600SM	
Tumbler	20	225					100SM	
Bowl, 9"	40		90				55SM	
Bride's Basket	125						140	
Butter	75	200						
Rose Bowl, Rare	450	1,300	950					
FEATHER AND HEART (MILLERSBURG)								
Pitcher, Scarce	600	750	850					
Tumbler, Scarce	75	150	200					
FEATHER STITCH (FENTON)								
Bowl, 8½"-10"	60	80	90	80				
FEATHER SWIRL (U.S. GLASS)								
Vase	65							
Butter	165							
FEATHERED ARROW (ENGLISH)								
Bowl, 8½"	50							
FEATHERED SERPENT (FENTON)								
Bowl, 5"	30	40	45	42				
Bowl, 10"	60	75	70	65				
Spittoon Whimsey, Rare		4,000						
FEATHERS (NORTHWOOD)								
Vase, 7"-12"	60	85	95	105				
FELDMAN BROTHERS (NORTHWOOD)								
Bowl		550						
FENTONIA								
Bowl, Ftd, 9½"	60	85	75	70				
Bowl, Ftd, 5"	30	50	40	40				
Fruitbowl, 10"	85			90				
Butter	115			185				
Creamer, Sugar or Spooner	75			85				
Pitcher	390			600				
Tumbler	50			75				
FENTONIA FRUIT (FENTON)								
Bowl, Ftd, 6"	45			55				
Bowl, Ftd, 10"	120			160				
Pitcher, Rare	575			700				
Vase Whimsey, Rare	140			160				
Tumbler, Rare	150			200				
FENTON'S ARCHED FLUTE (FENTON)								
Toothpick Holder	85			100			140	

Evelyn

Fan-Tail

Fan

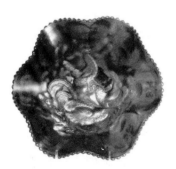

Farmyard

Field Flower

File

Fine Cut and Roses

Fine Prisms and Diamonds

	M	A	G	B	PO	AO	Pas	R
FENTON'S BASKET (FENTON)								
Two Row or Three Row								
(Open Edge)	45		225	150			325CeB	460
Advertising	65							
FERN (FENTON)								
Bowl, 7"-9", Rare				900*				
FERN (NORTHWOOD)								
Bowl, 6½"-9"	50	65	70					
Compote	55	70	85	100			110	
Hat, Rare	90	120	135				160	
FERN BRAND CHOCOLATES (NORTHWOOD)								
Plate		800						
FERN PANELS (FENTON)								
Hat	45		60	50			495	
FIELD FLOWER (IMPERIAL)								
Pitcher, Scarce	165	350	365	400			360AM	
Tumbler, Scarce	35	60	70	150			90AM	1,500
Milk Pitcher, Rare	180	200	220				225AM	
FIELD THISTLE (U.S. GLASS)								
Plate, 6", Rare	180							
Plate, 9" Rare	350							
Butter, Rare	125							
Sugar, Creamer or								
Spooner, Rare	80							
Compote, Large	90							
Pitcher, Scarce	160							
Tumbler, Scarce	45							
Breakfast Set, 2 Pc, Rare							350IB	
Bowl, 6"-10"	45						290LG	
Vase	65							
FILE (IMPERIAL AND ENGLISH)								
Pitcher, Rare	265	445						
Tumbler, Scarce	150							
Bowl, 5"	30	40						
Bowl, 7"-10"	45+	50					60	
Compote	40	50					60	
Vase	75							
Butter	190							
Creamer or Spooner	100							
Sugar	120							
FILE AND FAN								
Bowl, Ftd, 6"	40				160			
Compote						290	125MO	
FINE BLOCK (IMPERIAL)								
Shade			45					
FINE CUT FLOWERS AND VT. (FENTON)								
Compote	50		75					
Goblet	50		75					
FINE CUT HEART (MILLERSBURG)								
(Primrose Bowl Exterior Pattern)								
FINE CUT OVALS (MILLERSBURG)								
(Whirling Leaves Exterior Pattern)								
FINE CUT RINGS (ENGLISH)								
Oval Bowl	40							
Vase	50							
Celery	60							
Butter	70							
Creamer	45							
Stemmed Sugar	45							
Stemmed Cake Stand	75							
Round Bowl	35							
Jam Jar w/lid	65							
FINE CUT AND ROSES (NORTHWOOD)								
Rose Bowl, Ftd	100	115	200	220		1,000	1,000IG	
Candy Dish, Ftd	85	90	170	185		900	260W	
(Add 25% for Fancy Interior)								
FINE PRISMS AND DIAMONDS (ENGLISH)								
Vase, 7"-14"							90AM	
FINE RIB (NORTHWOOD, FENTON AND DUGAN)								
Bowl, 9"-10"	50	60	75					
Bowl, 5"	30	35	40					
Plate, 9"	80	90	135					
Vase, 7"-15", 2 Types	40	55	90	50			160W	500
Compote					165			
FISH NET (DUGAN)								
Epergne		450			475			
FISH VASE (CZECH)								
One shape, Marked "Jain"	450	400	500	450				

Fleur De Lis (Czech)

Floral and Grape

Floral and Wheat

Flower Pot

	M	A	G	B	PO	AO	Pas	R
FISHERMAN'S MUG (DUGAN)								
One Size	400	210		550	1,450		255LV	
FISHSCALE AND BEADS (DUGAN)								
Bowl, 6"-8"	35	45			150		70	
Bride's Basket, Complete					140			
Plate, 7"	50	200			185			
FIVE HEARTS (DUGAN)								
Bowl, Dome Base, 8¼"	95	110			165			
FIVE LILY EPERGNE								
Complete, Metal Fittings	175	250						
FIVE PANEL								
Candy Jar, Stemmed	70							
FLANNEL FLOWER (CRYSTAL)								
Compote, Large	120	155						
Cake Stand	140	195						
FLARED PANEL								
Shade					75MO			
FLARED WIDE PANEL								
Atomizer, 3½"	90							
FLEUR-DE-LIS (CZECH)								
Vase	1,100							
FLEUR-DE-LIS (MILLERSBURG)								
Bowl, Flat, 8½"	240	350	300				240CM	
Bowl, Ftd, 8½"	260	370	400					
Compote, Very Rare			5,000*					
Rose Bowl, Either Base, Rare		4,500						
FLICKERING FLAMES								
Shade							50	
FLORA (ENGLISH)								
Float Bowl			90					
FLORABELLE								
Pitcher							600IG	
Tumbler							200IG	
FLORAL								
Hatpin							75AM	
FLORAL FAN								
Etched Vase	57							
FLORAL AND GRAPE (DUGAN)								
Pitcher	145	200		185			450W	
Tumbler	20	30		50			50W	
Hat, Whimsey	40							
FLORAL AND GRAPE VT. (FENTON)								
Pitcher, 2 Variations	195	285	290	270				
Tumbler	30	35	40	30				
FLORAL AND OPTIC (IMPERIAL)								
Bowl, Ftd, 8"-10"	35				150		40SM	400
Bowl, Flat, 8"-10"	30						20SM	
Cake Plate, Ftd					180		50SM	650
Rose Bowl, Ftd					190		185AQ	
FLORAL OVAL (HIG-BEE)								
Bowl, 8"	50							
Plate, 7", Rare	90							
Creamer	60							
FLORAL AND SCROLL								
Shade, Various Shapes	45							
FLORAL SUNBURST								
Vase	175							
FLORAL AND WHEAT (DUGAN)								
Compote	40	45		45	150			
Bon-bon, Stemmed	40	45		45	155			
FLORENTINE (FENTON AND NORTHWOOD								
Candlesticks, pair	120		160RG	150CeB			140IG	1,050
FLORENTINE (IMPERIAL)								
Hat Vase							95	
FLOWER BASKET								
One Size	50							
FLOWER AND BEADS								
Plate, 6 Sided, 7½"	95	115						
Plate, Round, 8½"	95							
FLOWER MEDALLION								
Tumbler, very rare	800							
FLOWER POT (FENTON)								
One Size, Complete	60							
FLOWERING DILL (FENTON)								
Hat	40		45	40			75	550
FLOWERING VINE (MILLERSBURG)								
Compote, Tall, Very Rare		4,200	4,200					

Flute (Millersburg)

Flute #3

Footed Prism Panels

Formal

	M	A	G	B	PO	AO	Pas	R
FLOWERS AND FRAMES (DUGAN)								
Bowl, 8"-10"	70	200	85		300		95	
FLOWERS AND SPADES (DUGAN)								
Bowl, 10"	50	90	85		210			
Bowl, 5"	25	40	37		80			
FLUTE (BRITISH)								
Sherbet, Marked "British"	50							
FLUTE (MILLERSBURG)								
Vase, Rare	300	400	425					
Bowl, 4" (Variant)		45						
Compote, 6" (Marked "Krystol," Very Rare)	450	500						
Punch Bowl and Base, Rare.	265	320						
Punch Cup	27	30						
Bowl, 10"	65	90						
Bowl, 5"	25	40						
FLUTE (NORTHWOOD)								
Creamer or Sugar	75	85	95					
Salt Dip, Ftd	32						75V	
Sherbet	35	50	45				55CeB	
Pitcher, Rare	395		600					
Tumbler, 3 Varieties	50							
Ringtree, Rare	175							
Bowl, 10"	45	55						
Bowl, 5"	25	30						
Butter	135	170	185					
FLUTE #3 (IMPERIAL)								
Covered Butter	180	240	210					
Sugar, Creamer or Spooner	90	105	95					
Celery, Rare		390						
Punch Bowl and Base	295	500	470					
Punch Cup	25	40	38					
Pitcher	300	595	510	450				
Tumbler	40	195	185	100			300AQ	300
Handled Toothpick Holder	85							
Toothpick Holder, Regular	70	65	75	95			300AQ	
Bowl, 10"		225						
Bowl, 5"	30	70						
Custard Bowl, 11"		300	300					
Cruet	90							
FLUTE AND CANE (IMPERIAL)								
Pitcher, Stemmed, Rare	400							
Wine	50							
Champagne, Rare	135							
Milk Pitcher	115							
Punch Cup	25							
Tumbler, Rare	450							
FLUTED SCROLL (DUGAN)								
Rose Bowl, Ftd, Very Rare		975						
FLYING BAT								
Hatpin, Scarce	195	200	200				350	
FOLDING FAN (DUGAN)								
Compote		75		85	120	295		
FOOTED DRAPE (WESTMORELAND)								
Vase	50						55W	
FOOTED PRISM PANELS (ENGLISH)								
Vase	85		120	100				
FOOTED RIB (NORTHWOOD)								
Vase	50	80	90	75		190	110	
Vase, Advertising						250	150	
FOOTED SHELL (WESTMORELAND)								
Large, 5"	40	50	55	55			75AM	
Small, 3"	45	55	60	60	100MO		70AM	
FORGET-ME-NOT (FENTON)								
Pitcher	165	285	300	320			350W	
Tumbler	30	40	50	45			55W	
FORKS (CAMBRIDGE)								
Cracker Jar, Rare			500					
FORMAL (DUGAN)								
Hatpin Holder, Rare	175	170						
Vase, Jack-In-Pulpit, Rare	125	100					150	
49'ER (IMPERIAL)								
Tumbler	75							
Wine	80							
Decanter	125							
Pitcher, Squat	210							
FOSTORIA #600 (FOSTORIA)								
Napkin Ring	75							
FOSTORIA #1231 (FOSTORIA)								
Rose Bowl							145	

Four Flowers Variant

French Knots

Frolicking Bears

Fruits and Flowers

	M	A	G	B	PO	AO	Pas	R
FOSTORIAL #1299 (FOSTORIA)								
Tumbler	150*							
FOUNTAIN LAMP								
Complete, Scarce	290							
FOUR FLOWERS								
Plate, 6½"		210	200		290			
Plate, 9"-10½"		700			560			
Rose Bowl, Rare		850*						
Bowl, 6¼"		45	50	70	190			
Bowl, 10"		180	185	190	220			
FOUR FLOWERS VT.								
Bowl, 9"-11"	70	75	70		210		170LV	
Bowl, Ftd, 8½"		80	90					
Plate, 10½", Rare		450	470				400TL	
Bowl on Metal Base, Rare		350LV			300		350TL	
FOUR PILLARS (NORTHWOOD AND DUGAN)								
Vase	50	60	75	60	110	175	75CT	
474 (IMPERIAL)								
Bowl, 8"-9"	60		85					
Punch Bowl and Base	220	700	600					
Cup	30	40	35					
Covered Butter	100	150	125					
Creamer, Sugar or Spooner	65	90	85					
Milk Pitcher, Scarce	225		475				600LV	
Pitcher, 2 Sizes, Scarce	210	510	480				610PK	
Tumbler, Scarce	35	80	65				120PK	
Goblet	50	90	65					
Wine, Rare	75							
Cordial, Rare	90	210						
Vase, 7", Rare								3,200
Vase, 14", Rare	950		1,100					
FRENCH KNOTS (FENTON)								
Hat	40	50	50	45				
FRENCH GRAPE								
Bowl, 4"	175							
FROLICKING BEADS (U.S. GLASS)								
Pitcher, Rare			10,000					
Tumbler, Rare			8,000					
FROSTED BLOCK (IMPERIAL)								
Bowl, 6½"-7½"	30						35CM	
Bowl, 9"	35						40CM	
Celery Tray	40							
Covered Butter	70							
Creamer or Sugar	50							
Rose Bowl	50						75CM	
Compote	85						120CM	
Milk Pitcher, Rare	90							
Pickle Dish, Handled, Rare	60						65CM	
Bowl, Square, Rare	50						60CM	
Plate, 7½"	70						65CM	
Plate, 9"							170CM	
Vase, 6"							100SM	
25% More if Marked "Made in USA"								
FROSTED BUTTONS (FENTON)								
Bowl, Ftd, 10"							175	
FROSTED RIBBON								
Pitcher	85							
Tumbler	30							
FROSTY								
Bottle	30							
FRUIT BASKET (MILLERSBURG)								
Compote, Handled, Rare		1,950						
FRUIT AND BERRIES (ENGLISH)								
Bean Pot, Covered, Rare	385			425				
FRUIT AND FLOWERS (NORTHWOOD)								
Bowl, 9"	100	150	140				250	
Bowl, 5"	40	50	55				75	
Fruit Bowl, 10"	110	170					80	
Banana Plate, 7", Rare		350	325					
Bon-bon, Stemmed	60	100	85	275		380	350W	
Plate, 7"	185	250	195	240				
Plate, 9½"	235	270	260				385	
FRUIT JAR (BALL)								
One Size	65							
FRUIT LUSTRE								
Tumbler	40							
FRUIT SALAD (WESTMORELAND)								
Punch Bowl and Base, Rare	600	700			3,900			
Cup, Rare	30	40			60			

	M	A	G	B	PO	AO	Pas	R

Garden Mums

Garland

Golden Grape

Golden Honeycomb

	M	A	G	B	PO	AO	Pas	R
GAMBIER, MT. (CRYSTAL)								
Mug..........................	95							
GARDEN MUMS (NORTHWOOD)								
Bowl, 8½"-10"	60	75	80	85			110	
Plate, Regular or Handgrip, 7"....................	180	210	225	240			250	
Shallow Bowl, 5"................		200						
GARDEN PATH (DUGAN)								
Bowl, 8½"-10"	60	85			140			
Compote, Rare....................	200	365					500	
Fruit Bowl, 10"	90	115						
Plate, 6", Rare.....................	430	585		985				
Bowl, 5".............................				60				
GARDEN PATH VT. (DUGAN)								
Bowl, 9"..............................					175			
Fruit Bowl, 10"		375			410			
Plate, 11", Rare...................		10,465			3,300			
Rose Bowl, Rare	400							
GARLAND (FENTON)								
Rose Bowl, Ftd	55	70		60				
GAY 90'S (MILLERSBURG)								
Pitcher, Rare......................		8,500	9,500					
Tumbler, Rare	1,250	1,150						
GEO. GETZ PIANOS (NORTHWOOD)								
Plate..................................		2,000						
GEORGIA BELLE (DUGAN)								
Compote, Ftd......................	65	75	85		140			
Card Tray, Ftd, Rare............	75	80	95		175			
GERVUTZ BROTHERS (NORTHWOOD)								
Bowl...................................		750						
GOD AND HOME (DUGAN)								
Pitcher, Rare.......................				2,000				
Tumbler, Rare				275				
GODDESS ATHENA								
Epergne, Rare.....................			2,000				2,000AM	
GODDESS OF HARVEST (FENTON)								
Bowl, 9½", Rare	6,000	6,900		6,500				
Plate, Very Rare		7,800						
GOLD FISH								
Bowl...................................	145							
GOLDEN CUPIDS (CRYSTAL)								
Bowl, 9", Rare.....................							500	
Bowl, 5", Rare.....................							225	
GOLDEN FLOWERS								
Vase, 7½"...........................	95							
GOLDEN GRAPES (DUGAN)								
Bowl, 7".............................	35	45	60				50	
Rose Bowl, Collar Base	85							
GOLDEN HARVEST (U.S. GLASS)								
Decanter w/stopper.............	125	250						
Wine..................................	25	35						
GOLDEN HONEYCOMB (IMPERIAL)								
Bowl, 5".............................	25							
Plate, 7".............................	55							
Compote............................	50							
Creamer or Sugar	35							
Bon-bon	45	55	60				60AM	
GOLDEN OXEN								
Mug...................................	90							
GOLDEN WEDDING								
Bottle, Various Sizes............	40+							
GOOD LUCK (NORTHWOOD)								
Bowl, 8¼"...........................	235	400	475	450		1,300	4,200IB	
Plate, 9".............................	425+	700+	850+	1,100+			5000IB	
GOOD LUCK VT. (NORTHWOOD)								
Bowl, 8¼", Rare	300	400	450				600	
GOODYEAR								
Ashtray in Tire	60							
GOOSEBERRY SPRAY								
Bowl, 10"...........................	55	85	90	90			120	
Bowl, 5".............................		110	125	125			155	
Compote, Rare....................		225	260	250			260	
GOTHIC ARCHES								
Vase, 8"-12", Rare................	45	70	85	95			95SM	
GRACEFUL (NORTHWOOD)								
Vase	60	100	120	135			200W	
GRACEFUL TUMBLER								
Tumbler				800			500AMB	

Grape and Cable (Fenton)

Grape (Imperial)

Grape and Cable (Northwood)

	M	A	G	B	PO	AO	Pas	R
GRAND THISTLE (FINLAND)								
Pitcher, Rare				1,900				
Tumbler, Rare				400				
GRAPE (FENTON'S GRAPE AND CABLE)								
Orange Bowl, Ftd	110	220	240	200			265	
Orange Bowl, Advertising, Very Rare	1,900			2,200				
Bowl, Ftd, 8¾"	65	80	95	775				
Bowl, Flat, 8"	50	60	80	70		850	600	900
Plate, Ftd, 9"	145	350	200					1,600
Orange Basket, Very Rare		3,800						
Spittoon Whimsey, Rare	1,150							
GRAPE (IMPERIAL)								
Bowl, 10"	40	80	65				135AM	
Bowl, 5"	25	40	30				40SM	
Fruit Bowl, 8¾"	40	60	55					365
Compote	50	60	60				275SM	
Cup and Saucer	70	155	50					
Nappy	30		40				35SM	
Tray, Center Handle	45						65HA	
Goblet, Rare	40	75	65				70AM	
Plate, 7"-12"	90	290	175	1,750			150AM	
Plate, Ruffled, 8½"	45	65	50	55			70SM	
Pitcher	100	350	175				270SM	
Tumbler	25	45	30				40SM	
Punch Bowl and Base	135	390	275				300SM	
Cup	20	45	35				30AM	
Water Bottle, Rare	125	250	165				270CM	
Milk Pitcher	260	350	300				190CM	
Basket, Handled, Rare	75		90				130SM	
Rose Bowl, Rare	175	225	190					
Decanter w/stopper	135	270	170				150	
Wine	30	40	35				90SM	
Spittoon Whimsey	1,100		2,250					
GRAPE (NORTHWOOD'S GRAPE AND CABLE)								
Bowl, Flat, 9"-10"	200	75	85	75		3,200		
Bowl, Flat, 5½"							75W	
Scalloped Bowl, 5½"-11½"	80+	75+	100+	120			750IG	
Bon-bon	65	58	105	100			350W	
Banana Boat, Ftd	250	300	400	425			700IB	
Bowl, Ftd	60	80	105	90				
Ice Cream Bowl, 11"	150	325	350	500		1700	400IB	
Orange Bowl, Ftd		250		450				
Breakfast Set, 2 pcs	140	250	200					
Candlelamp, Complete	800	475	500					
Compote, Covered	2,500	350						
Compote, Open	500	375	1,100				750	
Sweetmeat w/lid	1,850	165		2,000				
Sweetmeat Whimsey	400	325						
Cookie Jar w/lid	350	500				9,000	2,350IG	
Centerpiece Bowl, Ftd	300	595	1,100	1,250			1,100IG	
Cup and Saucer, Rare	400	425						
Cologne w/stopper	180	195	220				600IB	
Perfume w/stopper	375	650						
Dresser Tray	175	250	295				550IB	
Pin Tray	395	195	250				250IC	
Hatpin Holder	275	300	275	900		12,000	2,000W	
Powder Jar w/lid	100	150	180	200				
Nappy	85	100	135	165				
Fernery, Rare	1,250	950	1,000				1,200W	
Hat	40	50	50				90	
Ice Cream Sherbet	40	50	60				90	
Plate, Flat, 6"-9½"	150	200	250	750			2,000TL	
Plate, Handgrip	140	200	220				240	
Plate, Ftd	65	95	110	135			1,200IG	
Plate, 2 Sides Up	200	170	375					
Shade	200	180						
Punch Bowl and Base (Standard)	380	500	500	900			900	
Punch Bowl and Base (Small)	300	600	700	850			10,000IB	
Plate, Advertising				375				
Punch Bowl and Base (Banquet)	2,000	2,300	3,000	4,200			16,000IB	
Cup	25	27	50	60			80W	
Butter	175	220	225				300	
Sugar w/lid	70	85	85				150	
Creamer or Spooner	45	85	75					
Tobacco Jar w/lid	350	525		1,350				
Pitcher, Standard	270	250	300				2,000IG	
Pitcher, Tankard	700	800	3,300				2,600IG	
Tumbler, Jumbo	60	75	90					
Tumbler, Regular	50	60	75				500IG	
Decanter w/stopper	650	700						
Shot Glass	125	285						
Spittoon, Rare	6,000	7,800	7,500					

249

Grape Arbor (Northwood)

Grapevine Lattice

Hammered Bell

Harvest Flower

	M	A	G	B	PO	AO	Pas	R
Grape (Northwood's Grape and Cable) Cont'd								
Orange Bowl, Blackberry Interior, Rare		1,800						
Hatpin Holder Whimsey, Rare .		3,500	4,000					
GRAPE ARBOR (DUGAN)								
Bowl, Ftd, 9½"-11"	150	400					150W	
GRAPE ARBOR (NORTHWOOD)								
Pitcher............................	320	650		3,000			550W	
Tumbler	45	70		375			400IG	
Hat.......................................	75			175			350IG	
GRAPE AND CHERRY (ENGLISH)								
Bowl, 8½", Rare	75			180				
GRAPE DELIGHT (DUGAN)								
Rose Bowl, Ftd, 6"	65	80		70			70W	
Nut Bowl, Ftd, 6"	65	120		180			80W	
GRAPE FIEZE (NORTHWOOD)								
Bowl, 10½", Rare							600IC	
GRAPE AND GOTHIC ARCHES (NORTHWOOD)								
Bowl, 10"........................	80	120	90	80	150PL			
Bowl, 5"........................	25	40	40	35	45PL			
Butter	100	140	140	125	420PL			
Sugar w/lid	75	120	110	90	125PL			
Creamer or Spooner	55	85	75	70	125PL			
Pitcher............................	200	385	400	360	750PL			
Tumbler	35	80	70	50	170PL		160CM	
GRAPE, HEAVY (DUGAN)								
Bowl, 5", Rare.....................	160	185			395			
Bowl, 10",........................	240	295			600			
GRAPE, HEAVY (IMPERIAL)								
Bowl, 9".............................	45	65						
Bowl, 5"..............................	25	30						
Nappy..................................	45	55						
Plate, 8"..............................	65	85	90				200AM	
Plate, 6"..............................	52	60	70				90	
Plate, 11".............................	265	375					350IG	
Fruit Bowl w/base...............	295							
Custard Cup	20	35	35					
Punch Bowl w/base.............	210	510	450					
GRAPE LEAVES (MILLERSBURG)								
Bowl, 10", Rare....................	600	800	900				850V	
GRAPE LEAVES (NORTHWOOD)								
Bowl, 8¼"	65	80	85	90			450IB	
Brides Basket, Complete......		300						
GRAPE WREATH (MILLERSBURG)								
Bowl, 5".............................	40	55	320					
Bowl, 7½"-9"	60	75	80	420				
Bowl, Ice Cream, 10"	120	175	175					
Spittoon Whimsey, Rare	3,200		3,800					
GRAPEVINE LATTICE (DUGAN)								
Bowl, 8½"	42	60	52	65			80W	
Plate, 7"-9"	75	95		90			150W	
Bowl, 5"..............................	30						60W	
Hat Shape, Jip.....................	75							
GRAPEVINE LATTICE (FENTON)								
Pitcher, Rare......................	325	600		650			850W	
Tumbler, Rare	55	75		95			100W	
GREEK KEY (NORTHWOOD)								
Bowl, 7"-8½"	90	120	150	375				
Plate, 9"-11", Rare	1,050	850	1,200	2,900		1,750*		
Pitcher, Rare......................	450	900	1,650					
Tumbler, Rare	85	195	210					
GREEK KEY VT.								
Hatpin................................		90						
GREENGARD FURNITURE (MILLERSBURG)								
Bowl, Rare...........................		1,295						
HAIR RECEIVER								
Complete...........................	75							
HAMMERED BELL CHANDELIER								
Complete, 5 Shades.............							600W	
Shade, Each							95W	
HAND VASE								
One Shape, 5½"-8"...............	180	280						450*
HANDLED TUMBLER								
One Size	55							
HANDLED VASE (IMPERIAL)								
One Shape...........................	47							
HARVEST FLOWER (DUGAN)								
Pitcher, Rare......................	1,250							
Tumbler	105	300	365					
HARVEST POPPY								
Compote.............................	320			450				

Heron

Heart and Flowers

Heavy Prisms

	M	A	G	B	PO	AO	Pas	R
HATCHET (U.S. GLASS)								
One Shape	150							
HATTIE (IMPERIAL)								
Bowl	47	115						
Rose Bowl	95						250AM	
Plate, Rare	875	700	500				900	
HAWAIIAN LEI (HIGBEE)								
Sugar	75							
Creamer	75							
HAWAIIAN MOON								
Pitcher	200						250CRAN	
Tumbler	75						90CRAN	
HEADDRESS								
Bowl, 9", 2 Varieties	47		60	52				
Compote	58		75	60				
HEART BAND								
One Shape (Salt)	45							
HEART BAND SOUVENIR (McKEE)								
Mug, Small	85		100				115AQ	
Mug, Large	90		115				127AQ	
HEART AND HORSESHOE (FENTON)								
Bowl, 8½"	900							
Plate, 9", Rare	1,150							
HEART AND TREES (FENTON)								
Bowl, 8¾"	165		215	200				
HEART AND VINE (FENTON)								
Bowl, 8½"	80	50	115	120			70LV	
Plate, 9", Rare	300	475	365	350				
Spector Plate, Advertising, Rare	900							
HEARTS AND FLOWERS (NORTHWOOD)								
Bowl, 8½"	525	450	750	650			1,200IG	
Compote	300	550	2,400	500		800	900IG	
Plate, 9", Rare	1,000	1,150	1,850	550		2,300	1,350IB	
HEAVY DIAMOND								
Nappy	40							
HEAVY DIAMOND (IMPERIAL)								
Bowl, 10"	45							
Creamer	30							
Sugar	35							
Vase	50		65				85SM	
Compote	45		55					
HEAVY HEART (HIGBEE)								
Tumbler	150							
HEAVY HOBNAIL (FENTON)								
Vase, Rare		550					465W	
HEAVY HOBS								
Lamp (Amber Base Glass)					300			
HEAVY PRISMS (ENGLISH)								
Celery Vase, 6"	85	115		95				
HEAVY SHELL (FENTON)								
Bowl, 8¼"							150	
Candleholder, Each							100	
HEAVY VINE								
Lamp	250							
Atomizer	85							
HEAVY WEB (DUGAN)								
Bowl, 10", Rare					1,300			
Plate, 11", Rare					1,800			
HEINZ								
Bottle							58	
HEISEY								
Breakfast Set							290	
HEISEY CARTWHEEL								
Compote							85	
HEISEY FLORAL SPRAY								
Stemmed Candy w/lid, 11"							85IB	
HEISEY FLUTE								
Punch Cup	35							
HEISEY SET								
Creamer and Tray	150						195	
HEISEY #357								
Water Bottle	190							
Tumbler	65							
HERON (DUGAN)								
Mug, Rare	1,000	375						
HERRINGBONE AND BEADED OVAL								
Compote, Rare	600*							

	M	A	G	B	PO	AO	Pas	R

Hobstar

Hobstar Band

Hobstar and Feather

Hobstar and Cut Triangles

	M	A	G	B	PO	AO	Pas	R
HERRINGBONE AND MUMS (JEANETTE)								
Tumbler, very rare	600							
HEXAGON AND CANE (IMPERIAL)								
Covered Sugar	90							
HEX BASE								
Candlesticks, pair	75	125	110				175SM	
HEX-OPTIC (JEANETTE)								
Pitcher							135CL	
Tumbler							50CL	
HICKMAN								
Castor Set, 4 pc	250						450	
HOBNAIL (FENTON)								
Vase, 5"-11"							95+W	
HOBNAIL (MILLERSBURG)								
Pitcher, Rare	1,800	1,900	2,200	1,600				
Tumbler, Rare	775	500	1,000	950				
Rose Bowl, Scarce	200	395	595					
Spittoon, Rare	900	1,000	1,800					
Butter, Rare	500	600	650	800				
Sugar w/lid, Rare	350	500	575	800				
Creamer or Spooner, Rare	275	375	450	500				
HOBNAIL VT. (MILLERSBURG)								
Vase Whimsey, Rare	600	750	750					
Rose Bowl, Rare	900							
Jardinere, Rare		950		1,100				
HOBNAIL, MINIATURE								
Tumbler, 2½"	50							
Pitcher 6", Rare	250							
HOBNAIL PANELS (McKEE)								
Vase, 8¾"							70CM	
HOBNAIL SODA GOLD (IMPERIAL)								
Spittoon, Large	50		75				60W	
HOBSTAR (IMPERIAL)								
Bowl, Berry, 10"	40						50	
Bowl, Berry, 5"	25						35	
Bowls, Various Shapes, 6"-12"	30						40	
Fruit Bowl w/base	50	85	75					
Cookie Jar w/lid	65		100					
Butter	80	195	185				90CM	
Sugar w/lid	65	100	90				60CM	
Creamer or Spooner	45	85	75				50CM	
Pickle Castor, Complete	450							
Bride's Basket, Complete	75							
Vase, Flared	350	200						
HOBSTAR AND ARCHES (IMPERIAL)								
Bowl, 9"	50	75	60				60SM	
Fruit Bowl w/base	60	90	75					
HOBSTAR BAND (IMPERIAL)								
Celery	85							
Compote, Rare	100							
Bowl, Rare	90							
Pitcher, 2 Shapes, Rare	275							
Tumbler, 2 Shapes, Rare	70							
HOBSTAR AND WAFFLE BLOCK (IMPERIAL)								
Basket	150						175SM	
HOBSTAR AND CUT TRIANGLES (ENGLISH)								
Rose Bowl	45	55	70					
Bowl	30	40	60					
Plate	70	100	110					
HOBSTAR DIAMONDS								
Tumbler, very rare	500							
HOBSTAR AND FEATHER (MILLERSBURG)								
Punch Bowl and Base (Open), Rare	1,800		3,800					
Punch Bowl and Base (Tulip), Rare		3,500						
Punch Cup, Scarce	30	40		275*				
Rose Bowl, Giant, Rare	3,000*	2,000	2,000					
Vase Whimsey, Rare		5,000	5,000					
Punch Bowl Whimsey, Rare			7,500					
Compote Whimsey (From Rose Bowl), Rare		5,500						
Bowl, Round, 5", Rare		450						
Bowl, Diamond, 5", Rare	400							
Bowl, Heart, 5", Rare	350							
Butter, Rare	1,500	1,800	1,800					
Sugar w/lid, Rare	900	1,000	1,000					
Creamer, Rare	700	800	800					
Spooner, Rare	700	800	800					
Dessert, Stemmed, Rare	650							
Compote, 6" Rare	1,500							

Hobstar Whirl

Holly

Honeycomb and Clover

Honeycomb and Hobstar

	M	A	G	B	PO	AO	Pas	R
Hobstar and Feather (Millersburg) Cont.								
Stemmed Whimsey								
Tray-Ftd, 4½", Very Rare....	750							
HOBSTAR AND FILE								
Pitcher, Rare.......................	1,700							
Tumbler, Rare	200							
HOBSTAR FLOWER (NORTHWOOD)								
Compote, Scarce.................	55	65	70	80				
HOBSTAR AND FRUIT (WESTMORELAND)								
Bowl, 6", Rare......................					100	300		
Bowl, 10", Rare...................					195			
Plate, 10½", Rare							400IB	
HOBSTAR PANELS (ENGLISH)								
Creamer	45							
Sugar, Stemmed	45							
HOBSTAR REVERSED (ENGLISH)								
Spooner..............................	45							
Butter	55	75		70				
Frog and Holder	50							
HOBSTAR WHIRL (WHIRLAGIG)								
Compote, 4½"	50	60		60				
HOLIDAY								
Bottle							75	
HOLIDAY (NORTHWOOD)								
Tray, 11", Rare	375							
HOLLY (FENTON)								
Bowl, 8"-10"	75	80	90	90			150W	1,400
Compote, 5"........................	45	50	85	50			85AM	1,100
Goblet	40	60		60			90W	600
Hat....................................	35	40	50	40			75LG	450
Plate, 9"............................	280	300	450	345			850BA	2,800
Rose Bowl..........................	400		900*	500				
HOLLY AND BERRY (DUGAN)								
Bowl, 7"-9"	40	47	50	50	70			
Nappy................................	45	55	60	55	70			
Gravy Boat, Handled		65		65	140			
HOLLY, PANELLED (NORTHWOOD)								
Bowl.................................		75	70					
Bon-bon, Ftd	60	90	75					
Creamer or Sugar	90							
Pitcher, Rare.......................		12,000*						
Spooner.............................	50							
HOLLY SPRIG VT. (MILLERSBURG)								
Bowl, Scarce.......................	290	320	350					
HOLLY SPRIG OR WHIRL (MILLERSBURG)								
Deep Sauce, Rare	175	275	350					
Nappy, Tri-Cornered, Rare...	85	115	120					
Bon-bon (Plain)...................	55	60	60					
Bon-bon (Isaac Benesch), Rare	125							
Bowl, Round or Ruffled, 7"-10"	50	65	60				60CM	
Compote, Very Rare	450	625					1,000V	
Rose Bowl Whimsey, Rare....							1,250V	
Bowl, Tri-Cornered, 7"-10"...	325	200	190					
HOLLOWEEN								
Pitcher, 2 sizes	485							
Tumbler, 2 sizes	175							
Spittoon	600							
HOLM SPRAY								
Atomizer, 3"	65							
HOMESTEAD								
Shade................................	50							
HONEYBEE (JEANETTE)								
Pot							85	
HONEYCOMB (DUGAN)								
Rose Bowl..........................	190				250			
HONEYCOMB AND CLOVER (FENTON)								
Bon-bon	40	60	60	50			70AM	
Compote............................	35	50	60	50				
Spooner, Rare.....................	95							
HONEYCOMB AND HOBSTAR (MILLERSBURG)								
Vase, 8¼", Rare...................		7,000		7,500				
HONEYCOMB ORNAMENT								
Hatpin...............................		80		90				

Horseshoe Shot Glass

Illinois Daisy

Imperial Paperweight

Intaglio Daisy

	M	A	G	B	PO	AO	Pas	R
HONEYCOMB PANELS								
Tumbler		175*						
HORN OF PLENTY								
Bottle	60							
HORN, POWDER (CAMBRIDGE)								
Candy Holder	200							
HORSES HEADS (FENTON)								
Bowl, Flat, 7½"	75		325	250			290W	1,200
Bowl, Ftd, 7"-8"	95		335	270			295W	1,200
Plate, 6½"-8½"...................	310			800				
Rose Bowl, Ftd	260			400			800V	
Nut Bowl, Rare		250						
HORSESHOE								
Shot Glass.........................	50							
HOT SPRINGS SOUVENIR								
Vase, 9⅞", Rare..................	115*							
HOURGLASS								
Bud Vase...........................	50							
HUMPTY-DUMPTY								
Mustard Jar	75							
HYACINTH								
Lamp.................................	1,900							
ICE CRYSTALS								
Bowl, Ftd..........................							85	
Candlesticks, pair...............							160	
Salt, Ftd							65	
IDYLL (FENTON)								
Vase, Rare	550	750		850				
ILLINOIS DAISY (ENGLISH)								
Bowl, 8".............................	40							
Cookie Jar w/lid.................	60							
ILLUSION (FENTON)								
Bon-bon	55		85					
Bowl..................................	60		90					
IMPERIAL BASKET (IMPERIAL)								
One Shape, Rare	65						80	
IMPERIAL DAISY (IMPERIAL)								
Shade................................	45							
IMPERIAL GRAPE (IMPERIAL)								
Shade................................	85							
IMPERIAL #5 (IMPERIAL)								
Bowl, 8".............................	40						50AM	
Vase, 6", Rare	95							
IMPERIAL #9 (IMPERIAL)								
Compote............................	40							
IMPERIAL PAPERWEIGHT (IMPERIAL)								
Advertising Weight, Rare......		1,050						
INCA								
Vase, 7", Rare	900	950						
Bottle	175*							
INDIAN CANOE								
Novelty Boat Shape.............	100							
INDIANA GOBLET (INDIANA GLASS)								
One Shape, Rare							800AM	
INDIANA STATEHOUSE (FENTON)								
Plate, Rare.........................	2,900			3,500				
INSULATOR (VARIOUS MAKERS)								
Various Sizes......................	35+							
INTAGLIO DAISY (ENGLISH)								
Bowl, 7½"	50							
Bowl, 4½"	30							
INTAGLIO FEATHERS								
Cup...................................	25							
INTAGLIO OVALS (U.S. GLASS)								
Bowl, 7"..............................						70		
Plate, 7½"						90		
INTAGLIO STARS								
Tumbler, Rare	600							
INTERIOR PANELS								
Mug...................................	75							
INTERIOR POINSETTIA (NORTHWOOD)								
Tumbler, Rare	485							
INTERIOR RAYS								
Sherbet	35							
INTERIOR RAYS (WESTMORELAND)								
Covered Butter	65							
Sugar, Creamer or Jam Jar, Each............................	40							
INTERIOR SWIRL								
Vase, Ftd, 9".......................	40							
Spittoon					95			

Inverted Coin Dot

Isaac Benesch Bowl

Jack-in-the-Pulpit (Dugan)

Jackman Whiskey

	M	A	G	B	PO	AO	Pas	R
INVERTED COIN DOT (NORTHWOOD-FENTON)								
Pitcher	325	450		400				
Tumbler	75	95		85				
Bowl	40	50	70	50			70	
Rose Bowl	50		60				85	
INVERTED FEATHER (CAMBRIDGE)								
Cracker Jar w/lid		1,000	395					
Covered Butter, Rare	450	500						
Sugar, Creamer or Spooner, Rare	400	325						
Pitcher, Tall, Rare	4,500							
Tumbler, Rare	500		600					
Compote	85							
Punch Bowl w/base, Rare	3,000		4,000					
Cup, Rare	60							
Wine, Rare	200							
Squat Pitcher, Rare	1,200							
INVERTED STRAWBERRY								
Bowl, 9"-10½"	190	300	295	350				
Bowl, 5"	40	55	50					
Sugar, Creamer or Spooner, Rare, Each	100			150				
Covered Butter		750						
Candlesticks, Rare, Pair	300	425	400					
Compote, Large, Rare	350	500	450					
Compote, Small, Rare	400			350				
Cruet Whimsey, Very Rare	1,500*							
Powder Jar, Rare	195							
Ladies Spittoon, Rare	900	1,000	1,000					
Milk Pitcher, Rare		1,850						
Pitcher, Rare	2,200	3,200	3,000					
Tumbler, Rare	300	250	350					
Table Set, 2 pcs, Rare (Stemmed)		1,275						
Celery, Rare		1,300	1,300	1,300				
Compote Whimsey, Rare	500							
INVERTED, THISTLE (CAMBRIDGE)								
Bowl, 9", Rare		350	350					
Spittoon, Rare		4,000						
Covered Box, Rare				400				
Pitcher, Rare	3,800	3,500						
Tumbler, Rare	425	300						
Butter, Rare	500	600	700					
Sugar, Creamer or Spooner, Rare	350	400	500					
Chop Plate, Rare		2,600						
Milk Pitcher, Rare		2,850						
Bowl, 5", Rare		200	200					
IOWA								
Small Mug, Rare	95							
IRIS (FENTON)								
Compote	50	60	60	75			275W	
Buttermilk Goblet, Scarce	55	65	65				80AM	
IRIS, HEAVY (DUGAN)								
Pitcher	400	750			1,000		1,200W	
Tumbler	90	80					150W	
IRIS HERRINGBONE (JEANETTE) Various Shapes, Prices range from $10.00 to $35.00 each in this late pattern.								
ISAAC BENESCH								
Advertising Bowl, 6½"		350						
Misspelled Version, Rare		1050*						
I.W. HARPER								
Decanter w/stopper	85							
JACK-IN-THE-PULPIT (DUGAN)								
Vase	45	75		80	110			
JACKMAN								
Whiskey Bottle	50							
JACOB'S LADDER								
Perfume	60							
JACOB'S LADDER VT. (U.S. GLASS)								
Rose Bowl	90							
JACOBEAN RANGER (CZECHOSLOVAKIAN AND ENGLISH)								
Pitcher	350							
Tumbler	195							
Juice Tumbler	180							
Miniature Tumbler	350							
Decanter w/stopper	250							
Wine	50							
Bowls, Various Sizes	60+							

	M	A	G	B	PO	AO	Pas	R
JARDINERE (FENTON)								
Various Shapes....................	350	500	500	600				
JELLY JAR								
Complete, Rare....................	65							
JEWEL BOX								
Ink Well	150							
JEWELED HEART (DUGAN)								
Bowl, 10"............................		95			135			
Bowl, 5".............................		40			65			
Pitcher, Rare......................	900							
Tumbler, Rare	100						575W	
Plate, 6"..........................	195				250			
JEWELS (IMPERIAL — DUGAN)								
Candlesticks, Pair..............	90	150	180	190			120CeB	395
Bowls, Various Sizes............		50	150	185			80	350
Hat Shape		65					90	300
Vase	100	150	150	175			195AM	250
Creamer or Sugar							70	235
JOCKEY CLUB (NORTHWOOD)								
Bowl, 7".............................		600						
KANGAROO (AUSTRALIAN)								
Bowl, 9½"	175	200						
Bowl, 5".............................	50	60						
KEYHOLE (DUGAN)								
Exterior Pattern of Raindrops Bowls								
KINGFISHER AND VARIANT (AUSTRALIAN)								
Bowl, 5"..............................	50	60						
Bowl, 9½"	175	200						
KITTEN								
Miniature Paperweight, Rare	250							
KITTENS								
Bottle							65	
KITTENS (FENTON)								
Bowl, 4", Scarce..................				775			500AQ	
Bowl, 2 Sides Up, Scarce	175	500		625			500LV	
Cup and Saucer, Scarce	250			650				
Spooner, 2½", Rare	175			275			250V	
Plate, 4½", Scarce	175			250			275SM	
Cereal Bowl, Scarce	275			500				
Vase or Toothpick holder, 3" ..	175			400			300V	
Spittoon Whimsey, Rare	1,200			1,500*				
KIWI (AUSTRALIAN)								
Bowl, 10", Rare...................	350	300						
KNIGHT TEMPLAR (NORTHWOOD)								
Advertising Mug, Rare	600						1,200IG	
KNOTTED BEADS (FENTON)								
Vase, 4"-12"........................	30+		40+	40+			85V	
KOKOMO (ENGLISH)								
Rose Bowl, Ftd	45		60	50				
KOOKABURRA AND VTS. (AUSTRALIAN)								
Bowl, 5"..............................	75	90						
Bowl, 10"............................	180	200						
LACY DEWDROP (WESTMORELAND)								
Pitcher...............................							650	
Compote, Covered							350	
Bowl, Covered.....................							280	
Banana Boat							375	
Tumbler							275	
Goblet							180	
Creamer							160	
Sugar							180	
(Note: All Items Listed Are in Pearl Carnival)								
LADY'S SLIPPER								
One Shape, Rare	250							
LARGE KANGAROO (AUSTRALIAN)								
Bowl, 5"..............................	60	65						
Bowl, 10"............................	195	210						
LATE ENAMELED BLEEDING HEARTS								
Tumbler	175							
LATE ENAMELED GRAPE								
Goblet	90							
LATE ENAMELED STRAWBERRY								
Tumbler, tall.......................	175							
LATTICE (DUGAN)								
Bowl, Various Sizes	60	70					85	

Jelly Jar

Keyhole (Dugan)

Kingfisher Vt.

Lacy Dewdrop

	M	A	G	B	PO	AO	Pas	R
LATTICE AND DAISY (DUGAN)								
Bowl, 9"..................	60							
Bowl, 5"..................	30							
Pitcher...........................	225			285			325	
Tumbler	30	60		50			60	
LATTICE AND GRAPE (FENTON)								
Pitcher........................	260	425	485	410	2,200		850W	
Tumbler	38	45	55	40	500		300W	
Spittoon Whimsey, Rare	2,600							
LATTICE HEART (ENGLISH)								
Bowl, 10"...................	50	75		70				
Bowl, 5"....................	30			40				
Compote...........................	60	90		85				
LATTICE AND LEAVES								
Vase, 9½"................	275			295				
LATTICE AND POINTS (DUGAN)								
Vase	40	45					65W	
LATTICE AND PRISMS								
Cologne w/stopper	65							
LATTICE AND SPRAYS								
Vase, 10½"...............	50							
LAUREL								
Shade...................	40						50	
LAUREL BAND								
Tumbler	40							
LAUREL AND GRAPE								
Vase, 6"	120							
LAUREL LEAVES (IMPERIAL)								
Plate............................	40	55					60SM	
LBJ HAT								
Ashtray	35							
LEA AND VT. (ENGLISH)								
Bowl, Ftd..................	40							
Pickle Dish, Handled	45							
Creamer, Ftd	45	50						
LEAF AND BEADS (NORTHWOOD-DUGAN)								
Bowl, 9".............................	150	275	700			275		
Plate Whimsey.....................	495*							
Candy Dish, Ftd	80	110	115			575	425	
Rose Bowl, Ftd	90	120	125	190		1,000	500W	
Nut Bowl, Rare						1,200		
(Note: Add 25% for Patterned Interior)								
LEAF CHAIN (FENTON)								
Bon-bon	40	55	60	50				
Bowl, 7"-9"	60	80	90	140		1,400	165W	750
Plate, 7½"	195			150				
Plate, 9¼"	460	150	175	135		2,350	225W	
LEAF COLUMN (NORTHWOOD)								
Vase	30	45	45		150		190IB	
Shade..............................							90	
LEAF AND LITTLE FLOWERS (MILLERSBURG)								
Compote, Miniature, Rare....	450	495	475					
LEAF RAYS (DUGAN)								
Nappy, Either Exterior.........	30	40			50		60W	
LEAF SWIRL (WESTMORELAND)								
Compote............................	55	75		65TL			70AM	
LEAF SWIRL AND FLOWER (FENTON)								
Vase	55						65W	
LEAF TIERS (FENTON)								
Bowl, Ftd, 10"......................	60							
Bowl, Ftd, 5"........................	30							
Butter, Ftd...........................	175							
Sugar, Ftd	90							
Creamer, Spooner, Ftd.........	85							
Pitcher, Ftd, Rare	475	650	650	695				
Tumbler, Ftd, Rare	75	90	90	95				
Banana Bowl Whimsey	200							
LIGHTNING FLOWER								
Nappy, Rare	450*							
LILY OF THE VALLEY (FENTON)								
Pitcher, Rare........................				3,900				
Tumbler, Rare	700			450				
LINED LATTICE (DUGAN)								
Vase, 7"-14"........................	40	110	90	80	160		60W	
Hat Shape	40							
LION (FENTON)								
Bowl, 7", Scarce...................	115			160				
Plate, 7½", Rare	900							

Lattice and Daisy

Leaf Chain

Leaf Column

Leaf Rays

	M	A	G	B	PO	AO	Pas	R
LITTLE BARREL (IMPERIAL)								
One Shape............................	175		195				210AM	
LITTLE BEADS								
Bowl, 8"................................	22				45			
Compote, Small	30				50	95	40AQ	
LITTLE DAISIES (FENTON)								
Bowl, 8"-9½", Rare	395			475				
LITTLE DAISY								
Lamp, Complete, 8"							500	
LITTLE DARLING								
Bottle	60							
LITTLE FISHES (FENTON)								
Bowl, Flat or Ftd, 10"..........	250		340	365			1,100W	
Bowl Flat or Ftd, 5½", ...	75	290	280	185			350W	
Plate, 10½", Rare				850			1,350W	
LITTLE FLOWERS (FENTON)								
Bowl, 9¼"	65	100	115	135			140AM	11,000
Bowl, 5½", Rare	40	80	70	75			80V	
Plate, 7", Rare.....................	245							
Plate, 10", Rare...................	795							
LITTLE JEWEL								
Finger Lamp, Rare	650							
LITTLE MERMAID								
One Shape...........................							90	
LITTLE OWL								
Hatpin, Rare........................	450*		1,100	1,200			800LV	
LITTLE STARS (MILLERSBURG)								
Bowl, 4", Rare......................			450					
Bowl, 7", Scarce..................	100	125	135	1,400			120CM	
Bowl, 9", Rare......................	450	550	575				400CM	
Bowl, 10½", Rare	600	700	750					
Plate, 7⅜", Rare			1,200					
LITTLE SWAN								
Miniature, 2"							75	
LOG								
Paperweight, 3" x 1¼", Rare....	150							
LOGANBERRY (IMPERIAL)								
Vase, Scarce	225	525	395				495AM	
Whimsey Vase		2,400						
LONG HOBSTAR								
Bowl, 8½"	45							
Bowl, 10½"	60							
Compote.............................	65							
Punch Bowl and Base.........	125						135CM	
LONG HORN								
Wine....................................	60							
LONG LEAF (DUGAN)								
Bowl, Ftd.............................					165			
LONG PRISMS								
Hatpin.................................		75						
LONG THUMBPRINT (DUGAN)								
Vase, 7"-11"	30	35	40	40	150			
Bowl, 8¾"	30	40						
Compote.............................	35	40	40					
Creamer, Sugar, ea	40						50SM	
Butter	70							
LOTUS AND GRAPE (FENTON)								
Bon-bon	45	65	70	60			195AQ	950
Bowl, Flat, 7".......................	50	50	55	60				
Bowl, Ftd, 7"........................	55		60	70				
Plate, 9½", Rare	190	495	650	500				
LOTUS LAND (NORTHWOOD)								
Bon-bon	1,500							
LOUISA (WESTMORELAND)								
Rose Bowl............................	55	65	70	67			150HO	
Candy Dish, Ftd	50	60	65				80AQ	
Bowl, Ftd.............................			50	50RG			70AQ	
Plate, Ftd, 8", Rare		155					190AG	
Mini-Banana Boat (old only) .	40	65						
LOVEBIRDS								
Bottle w/stopper.................	575							
LUCILE								
Pitcher, Rare........................	1,200			1,300				
Tumbler, Rare	750			800				
LUCKY BANK								
One Shape	40							
LUCKY BELL								
Bowl, 8¾", Rare	80							
LUSTER								
Tumbler	45							

Little Daisies

Little Stars

Long Hobstar

Long Thumbprint

Lustre Flute

Magpie

Many Stars

Maple Leaf

	M	A	G	B	PO	AO	Pas	R
LUSTRE AND CLEAR (FENTON)								
Fan Vase	40		60	55			90IG	
LUSTRE AND CLEAR (IMPERIAL)								
Pitcher	195							
Creamer or Sugar	40	65					60	
Bowl, 5"	20						30	
Bowl, 10"	40						50	
Shakers, pair	70							
Tumbler	40							
Butter Dish	75							
Console Set, 3 pcs.	60							165
LUSTRE AND CLEAR (LIGHTOLIER)								
Shade	45							
LUSTRE FLUTE (NORTHWOOD)								
Bowl, 5½"	35							
Bowl, 8"	40	55	54					
Bon-bon		60	60					
Creamer or Sugar	40	55	55					
Hat	30	40	40					
Compote		50	45					
Sherbet	30							
Nappy	40	45	40					
Punch Bowl and Base	150	165	150					
Cup	15	25	20					
LUSTRE ROSE (IMPERIAL)								
Bowl, Flat, 7"-11"	35	45	50				60CM	
Bowl, Ftd, 9"-12"	40	55	60	45			75	2,500
Fernery	50	60	65				275AM	
Plate, 6"-9"	58	70	75				140AM	
Butter	60	75	70				100AM	
Sugar	40	55	55				80AM	
Creamer or Spooner	40	55	55				70AM	
Berry Bowl, 8"-9"	40	40	48				40	
Berry Bowl, 5"	20	25	30				20	
Pitcher	85	100	110				100AM	
Rose Bowl	60	70	80				70CL	
Tumbler	25	30	40				50AM	
Milk Pitcher	60						120AM	
Plate Whimsey, Ftd	50						65CM	
LUTZ (McKEE)								
Mug, Ftd	60							
MAGNOLIA DRAPE								
Pitcher	275							
Tumbler	55							
MAGPIE (AUSTRALIAN)								
Bowl, 6"-10"	45	60						
MAIZE (LIBBEY)								
Vase, Celery, Rare							185CL	
Syrup, Rare							235CL	
MAJESTIC (McKEE)								
Tumbler, Rare	500							
MALAGA (DUGAN)								
Bowl, 9" Scarce	60	80						
Plate, 10", Rare		350					375	
MANHATTAN (U.S. GLASS)								
Decanter	250*							
Wine	40*							
MANY FRUITS (DUGAN)								
Punch Bowl w/base	450	900					1,400W	
Cup	25	30	40	45			60W	
MANY PRISMS								
Perfume w/stopper	75							
MANY STARS (MILLERSBURG)								
Bowl, Ruffled, 9", Scarce	350	575	475	2,000			1,850V	
Bowl, Round, 9½", Rare	500	1,000	700	2,100				
Tri-cornered Bowl, Rare		1,650						
MAPLE LEAF (DUGAN)								
Bowl, Stemmed, 9"	70	115		95				
Bowl, Stemmed, 4½"	30	35	50	30				
Butter	110	130		120				
Sugar	75	85		75				
Creamer or Spooner	50	65		60				
Pitcher	185	350		300				
Tumbler	30	50		40				

May Basket

Mikado

Mayan

Mayflower (Millersburg)

	M	A	G	B	PO	AO	Pas	R
MARIE								
(FENTON)								
Rustic Vase Interior								
Base Pattern								
MARILYN								
(MILLERSBURG)								
Pitcher, Rare....................	750	1,000	1,350					
Tumbler, Rare	150	275	400					
MARTEC (McKEE)								
Tumbler, Rare	500							
MARY ANN								
(DUGAN)								
Vase, 2 Varieties, 7"............	75	135						
Loving Cup, 3 Handles,								
Rare	310*							
MASSACHUSETTS								
(U.S. GLASS)								
Vase	175*							
MAYAN (MILLERSBURG)								
Bowl, 8½"-10"	2,500*		200					
MAY BASKET								
(ENGLISH)								
Basket, 7½"			95					
Bowl, 9", Rare.....................			160					
MAYFLOWER								
Bowl, 7½"	30	40			160		50	
Compote..............................	40	50					60	
Shade.................................	35							
Hat.....................................	40	50			150		60	
MAYFLOWER								
(MILLERSBURG)								
Exterior Pattern on Grape								
Leaves Bowls								
MAYPOLE								
Vase, 6¼"............................	45	55	60					
MELON RIB								
(IMPERIAL)								
Candy Jar w/lid	30							
Pitcher................................	60							
Tumbler	20							
Powder Jar w/lid	35							
Shakers, Pair......................	35							
Decanter	90							
MEMPHIS								
(NORTHWOOD)								
Bowl, 10"............................	100	195	200					
Bowl, 5".............................	35	45	50					
Fruit Bowl w/base...............	450	550	600	2,300			12,000IG	
Punch Bowl w/base.............	400	500	575				5,600IB	
Cup	30	40	45				75IB	
Sugar or Creamer		70						
MIKADO								
(FENTON)								
Compote, Large	250		2,400	700			650W	7,000*
MILADY								
(FENTON)								
Pitcher................................	500	700	800	975				
Tumbler	95	140	150	160				
MINIATURE BELL								
Paperweight, 2½"	60							
MINIATURE FLOWER BASKET								
(WESTMORELAND)								
One Shape...........................	75							
MINIATURE HOBNAIL								
Cordial Set, Rare	1,250							
MINIATURE INTAGLIO								
(WESTMORELAND)								
Nut Cup, Stemmed, Rare.....	585						700W	
(Note: Also Known as "Wild								
Rose Wreath")								
MINIATURE SHELL								
Candleholder, Each							75CL	
MIRRORED PEACOCKS								
Tumbler, Rare	400							
MIRRORED LOTUS								
(FENTON)								
Bon-bon	85		100	95				
Bowl, 7"-8½"	60		90	80			900CeB	
Plate, 7½", Rare	400			550			3,000CeB	
Rose Bowl, Rare	375			480			1,100W	
MITERED DIAMOND AND								
PLEATS (ENGLISH)								
Bowl, 4½"	25			30				
Bowl, 8½", Shallow	40			45				
MITERED OVALS								
(MILLERSBURG)								
Vase, Rare	7,000	7,500	6,700					

	M	A	G	B	PO	AO	Pas	R
MOON AND STAR (WESTMORELAND)								
Compote (Pearl Carnival)							385	
MOONPRINT (ENGLISH)								
Bowl, 8¼"	45							
Candlesticks, Rare, Each.....	50							
Compote............................	50							
Jar w/lid	60			85				
Vase	50							
Cheese Keeper, Rare	145							
Sugar, Stemmed	50							
Banana Boat, Rare	135							
Creamer	45							
Butter	100							
Bowl, 14"...........................	80							
Milk Pitcher, Scarce............	150							
MORNING GLORY (IMPERIAL)								
Vase, 8"-16".......................	50+	90+	80+				80+SM	
Funeral Vase	185	200	220				180SM	
MORNING GLORY (MILLERSBURG)								
Pitcher, Rare......................	9,100	9,400	10,000					
Tumbler, Rare	1,100	1,400	1,000					
MOXIE								
Bottle, Rare							90	
MULTI-FRUITS AND FLOWERS (MILLERSBURG)								
Dessert, Stemmed, Rare		1,050	1,050					
Punch Bowl w/base, Rare	2,000	2,300	2,600	3,700				
Cup, Rare...........................	50	75	90	175				
Pitcher, Rare (Either Base).....	3,400	3,600	4,000*					
Tumbler, Rare	900	1,250	1,400					
MUSCADINE								
Tumbler, Rare	450							
MY LADY								
Powder Jar w/lid	90							
MYSTIC (CAMBRIDGE)								
Vase, Ftd, Rare	165							
NAPOLEON								
Bottle							85	
NARCISSUS AND RIBBON (FENTON)								
Wine Bottle w/stopper, Rare	1,150							
NAUTILUS (DUGAN-NORTHWOOD)								
Lettered, Rare.....................		285			250			
Unlettered		200			170			
Giant Compote, Rare	3,000*							
Vase Whimsey, Rare	1,750*	1,750*						
NEAR CUT (CAMBRIDGE)								
Decanter w/stopper, Rare			3,500					
NEAR CUT SOUVENIR (CAMBRIDGE)								
Mug, Rare	190							
Tumbler, Rare	260							
NEAR CUT WREATH (MILLERSBURG)								
Exterior Pattern Only								
NELL (HIGBEE)								
Mug..................................	75							
NESTING SWAN (MILLERSBURG)								
Rose Bowl, Rare	3,000							
Bowl, Scarce, Round or Ruffled, 10"	250	395	500	2,800*			2,650V*	
Spittoon Whimsey, Rare		5,000*	5,000*					
Bowl, Tri-Cornered, Rare	500	1,200	1,200	3,500			750CM	
NEW ORLEANS SHRINE (U.S. GLASS)								
Champagne							150CL	
NIGHT STARS (MILLERSBURG)								
Bon-bon, Rare	500	450	400					
Card Tray, Rare..................		700						
Nappy, Tri-Cornered, Very Rare...........................		1,000						
NIPPON (NORTHWOOD)								
Bowl, 8½"	250	220	325	350			450IG	
Plate, 9"............................	400	550	650	700			600W	

Moonprint

Morning Glory

My Lady's Powder Box

Near Cut Decanter

Nu-Art Chrysanthemum

Number 270

Octagon

Ohio Star

	M	A	G	B	PO	AO	Pas	R
NORRIS N. SMITH								
(NORTHWOOD)								
Advertising Plate, 5¼"		1,800						
NORTHERN STAR								
(FENTON)								
Card Tray, 6"	40							
Bowl, 6"-7"	30							
Plate, 6½", Rare	90							
NORTHWOOD								
JACK-IN THE PULPIT								
Vase, Various Sizes	40	50	45	50	90	225	85	
NORTHWOOD'S LOVELY								
Bowl, 9"								
(Leaf and Beads Exterior),								
Rare	600	600						
NORTHWOOD'S NEARCUT								
Compote	85	130						
Goblet, Rare	195	140						
Pitcher, Rare......................	1,500*							
NORTHWOOD'S POPPY								
Bowl, 7"-8¾"	100	135		140	350*	595		
Pickle Dish, Oval	180	175	225	175		750	450IB	
Tray, Oval, Rare		300		375				
NU-ART								
(IMPERIAL)								
Plate, Scarce......................	850	950	3,000	5,500			1,200W	
Shade..............................	90							
NU-ART CHRYSANTHEMUM								
(IMPERIAL)								
Plate, Rare........................	950	1,100	3,800	5,400			1,500AM*	
NUGGATE								
Pitcher 6"			90					
NUGGET BEADS								
Beads		125						
NUMBER 4								
(IMPERIAL)								
Bowl, Ftd	30						40SM	
Compote.............................	40							
NUMBER 270								
(WESTMORELAND)								
Compote............................		90	140RG		115		140AQ	
NUMBER 2176 (SOWERBY)								
Lemon Squeezer	55							
NUMBER 2351								
(CAMBRIDGE)								
Bowl, 9", Rare....................			350*					
Punch Cup		65	65					
Punch Bowl/Base, Very Rare ..	1,500*							
NUMBER 600								
(FOSTORIA)								
Toothpick Holder	45							
OCTAGON								
(IMPERIAL)								
Bowl, 8½"	40		50				80	
Bowl, 4½"		35						
Goblet	65							
Butter	90		130					
Sugar	60		75					
Creamer or Spooner	55		65					
Toothpick Holder, Rare	70	85						
Pitcher...............................	120	400	240				200	
Tumbler	30	40	35				45	
Decanter, Complete	90	200	750					
Wine..................................	25	40	70					
Vase, Rare	90	140	125					
Milk Pitcher, Scarce............	150	200	170				150	
Cordial							70	
Shakers, Pair, Old Only		160						
OCTET								
(NORTHWOOD)								
Bowl, 8½"	60	100					90W	
OHIO STAR								
(MILLERSBURG)								
Vase, Rare	1,300	1,500	1,400			13,000*	4,000W*	
Compote, Rare.....................	1,100							
Vase Whimsey, Rare		1,800*	1,800*			12,000*		
OKLAHOMA								
(MEXICAN)								
Tumble-Up, Complete..........	200							
Pitcher, Rare......................	500*							
Tumbler, Rare	500							
Shade, Various Sizes,								
Rare							95CL	
OLYMPIC								
(MILLERSBURG)								
Compote, Small,								
Rare		3,500*	3,500*					

	M	A	G	B	PO	AO	Pas	R
OLYMPUS								
Shade	60							
OMNIBUS								
Tumbler, Rare	275		795	795				
OPEN FLOWER								
(DUGAN)								
Bowl, Flat or Ftd, 7"	35	45	50		85			
OPEN ROSE								
(IMPERIAL)								
Fruit Bowl, 7"-10"	40	65					70	
Bowl, Ftd, 9"-12"	65	45					95	
Bowl, Flat, 9"	45	40		50			65	
Bowl, Flat, 5½"	20	40					45	
Plate, 9"	65	180	185				185AM	
OPTIC								
(IMPERIAL)								
Bowl, 9"		75						
Bowl, 6"		50						
OPTIC AND BUTTONS								
(IMPERIAL)								
Bowls, 5"-8"	30							
Bowl, Handled, 12"	45							
Pitcher, Small, Rare	185							
Plate, 10½"	70							
Salt Cup	50							
Tumbler, 2 Shapes, Rare	110							
Goblet	60							
Cup and saucer, Rare	185							
OPTIC FLUTE								
(IMPERIAL)								
Bowl, 10"	45	80					55SM	
Bowl, 5"	30	45					30SM	
Compote	55							
OPTIC 66								
(FOSTORIA)								
Goblet	47							
ORANGE PEEL								
(WESTMORELAND)								
Punch Bowl w/base	200	225					225TL	
Cup	20	30					35TL	
Custard Cup, Scarce	25							
Dessert, Stemmed, Scarce	45	65	70RG				75TL	
ORANGE TREE								
(FENTON)								
Butter	250			350			340W	
Bowl, Flat, 8"-10"	55		235	95			500IM	1,400
Bowl, Ftd, 9"-11"	55		140	130			120W	
Ice Cream, w/stem, Small	30			35				
Bowl, Ftd, 5½"	40		45	48			900CeB	
Breakfast Set, 2 Pieces	180		230	220			250W	
Plate, 8"-9½"	235			450			400CM	
Powder Jar w/lid	75		500	95			130W	
Mug, 2 Sizes	70	80						
Loving Cup	160		350	275	4,500*	5,500*	500W	
Punch Bowl w/base	200		300	275	1,000MO*		400W	
Cup	30		36	32			38W	
Compote, Small	50	60	90	50				
Goblet, Large	90						85AQ	
Wine	25					75	70SM	
Sugar	65			75			150W	
Pitcher, 2 Designs	220			325			9,000LO*	
Tumbler	35			42			75W	
Creamer or Spooner	45			65			120W	
Rose Bowl	55	65	70	65			275W	1,900
Hatpin Holder	160		350	290			300W	
Hatpin Holder Whimsey, Rare				2,600				
Centerpiece Bowl, Rare	900		1,200	1,600				
Cruet Whimsey, Rare				1,250				
Orange Bowl Whimsey, 12"			650					
ORANGE TREE AND SCROLL								
(FENTON)								
Pitcher	495		600	550				
Tumbler	50		85	80				
ORANGE TREE ORCHARD								
(FENTON)								
Pitcher	400	500	550	500			650W	
Tumbler	40	50	55	50			120W	
ORIENTAL POPPY								
(NORTHWOOD)								
Pitcher	500	700	950	3,200			1,100W	
Tumbler	40	75	55	275			200W	
OSTRICH								
(AUSTRALIAN)								
Compote, Large, Rare	150	200						
Cake Stand, Rare	275	350						

Open Rose

Optic and Buttons

Oriental Poppy

Ostrich Cake Plate

Oval and Round

Palm Beach

Panelled Dandelion

Panelled Smocking

	M	A	G	B	PO	AO	Pas	R
OVAL AND ROUND								
(IMPERIAL)								
Plate, 10"..............................	65	75	80				90AM	
Bowl, 4".................................	20	30	30					
Bowl, 7".................................	30	36	40				45AM	
Bowl, 9".................................	35	45	50				60AM	
OVAL PRISMS								
Hatpin..................................		75						
OVAL STAR AND FAN								
(JENKINS)								
Rose Bowl............................	50	60						
OWL BANK								
One Size	40							
OWL BOTTLE								
One Shape.........................							65CL	
OXFORD								
Mustard Pot w/lid	70							
PACIFICA								
(U.S. GLASS)								
Tumbler	400							
PAINTED CASTLE								
Shade..................................	65							
PAINTED PANSY								
Fan Vase	50							
PALM BEACH								
(U.S. GLASS)								
Vase Whimsey	85	125					140W	
Bowl, 9"..............................	55						75	
Bowl, 5"..............................	30						50	
Butter	120						225	
Creamer, Spooner,								
Sugar, Each........................	75						125	
Pitcher................................	300						600W	
Tumbler	80						140W	
Plate, 9", Rare.....................	175	250					225	
Banana Bowl........................	100	200						
Rose Bowl Whimsey,								
Rare	90						210W	
PANAMA								
(U.S. GLASS)								
Goblet, Rare	135							
PANELLED CRUET								
One Size	95							
PANELLED DANDELION								
(FENTON)								
Pitcher.................................	400	425	550	575				
Tumbler	50	55	60	70				
Candle Lamp Whimsey,								
Rare				3,200				
Vase Whimsey, Rare				3,500*				
PANELLED DIAMOND AND BOWS								
(FENTON)								
Vase, 7"-14".........................	35	40	40	40	85		75	
Also called "Boggy Bayou"								
PANELLED HOBNAIL								
(DUGAN)								
Vase, 5"-10".........................	40	60	75		85		95	
PANELLED PALM								
(U.S. GLASS)								
Mug, Rare	95							
PANELLED PRISM								
Jam Jar w/lid	55							
PANELLED SMOCKING								
Sugar	50							
PANELLED SWIRL								
Rose Bowl............................	65							
PANELLED THISTLE								
(HIGBEE)								
Tumbler	100							
PANELLED TREE TRUNK								
(DUGAN)								
Vase, 7"-12", Rare................	70	90	110		150			
PANELS AND BALL								
(FENTON)								
Bowl, 11".............................	60						175W	
Also Called "Persian Pearl"								
PANELS AND BEADS								
Shade.................................							55VO	
PANSY								
(IMPERIAL)								
Bowl, 8¾"	40	95	85	110			80AQ	
Creamer or Sugar	25	40	45				50SM	
Dresser Tray........................	60	90	80				100SM	
Pickle Dish, Oval	30	50	40	95			60SM	
Nappy, Old Only	20		27					
Plate, Ruffled,								
Rare	80	195	120				100SM	

Parlor Panels

Peacock

Peacock and Grapes

Peacock Lamp

	M	A	G	B	PO	AO	Pas	R
PANTHER								
(FENTON)								
Bowl, Ftd, 10"	135	340	900	250		5,500NG	780W	
Bowl, Ftd, 5"	55		400				350W	1,450
Whimsey Bowl, 10½"	950			1,000				
PAPERWEIGHT								
Flower-Shaped,								
Rare							200	
PARLOR								
Ashtray				95				
PARLOR PANELS								
Vase, 4"-11"	50	190	250	200			450SM	
PASTEL HAT								
Various Sizes	50+						50+	
PASTEL PANELS								
(IMPERIAL)								
Pitcher							300	
Tumbler							75	
Mug, Stemmed							90	
Creamer or Sugar							65	
PEACH								
(NORTHWOOD)								
Bowl, 9"							150W	
Bowl, 5"							50W	
Butter							275W	
Creamer, Sugar, or								
Spooner, ea	275*						150W	
Pitcher				650			775W	
Tumbler				85EB			100W	
PEACH BLOSSOM								
Bowl, 7½"	60	75						
PEACH AND PEAR								
(DUGAN)								
Banana Bowl	70	95						
PEACHES								
Wine Bottle	45							
PEACOCK, FLUFFY								
(FENTON)								
Pitcher	500	600	700	800				
Tumbler	45	55	60	65				
PEACOCK								
(MILLERSBURG)								
Bowl, 9"	375	550	500				650CM	
Bowl, 5"	90	135	240	1,000				
Bowl, Vt, 7½"								
Rare	500	500	450					
Bowl, Vt, 6"								
Rare		150						
Ice Cream Bowl, 5"	60	90	140	390				
Plate, 6", Rare	900	800						
Spittoon Whimsey,								
Rare	5,600	7,000						
Proof Whimsey,								
Rare	300	270	300					
Rose Bowl Whimsey,								
Rare		4,600						
Bowl, 10", Ice Cream,								
Rare	500	700	1,000					
Banana Bowl, Rare		3,500						
PEACOCK AND DAHLIA								
(FENTON)								
Bowl, 7½"	50		125	100			150W	
Plate, 8½",								
Rare	390			450				
PEACOCK GARDEN								
(NORTHWOOD)								
Vase, 8", Rare	4,200						3,000*	
PEACOCK AND GRAPE								
(FENTON)								
Bow, Flat or Ftd, 7¾"	50	175	175	150	250		450V	795
Plate, 9" (Either Base),								
Rare	550	425		450			395	
PEACOCK LAMP								
Carnival Base	800	450	495				550W	750
PEACOCK, STRUTTING								
(WESTMORELAND)								
Creamer or Sugar								
w/lid		65	65					
PEACOCK TAIL								
(FENTON)								
Bon-bon	75	75	90	55				
Bowl, 4"-10"	40	50	60	55	650			1,800
Compote	35	45	60	50			55W	
Hat	30	40	55	50				
Hat, Advertising	40		50					
Plate, 9"	200	225		175				
Plate, 6"	70	80		70				

Peacock at the Fountain
(Northwood)

Peacock Tail

People's Vase

Perfection

	M	A	G	B	PO	AO	Pas	R
PEACOCK AND URN (FENTON)								
Bowl, 8½"	150	325	300	200				
Plate, 9"	650	500	900	800			550W	
Compote	55	70	90	75			125W	
Goblet, Rare	70	100		85			110W	
PEACOCK AND URN (NORTHWOOD)								
Bowl, 9"	200	475	650			500LV	500LV	
Bowl, Ice Cream, 10"	400	500	790	900		31,000	1,100IG	
Bowl, 5"	75	90	110					
Bowl, Ice Cream, 6"	350	160	185	125		2,700	250IG	
Plate, 11", Rare	2,100	1,200						
Plate, 6", Rare	450	550						
(Add 10% If Stippled)								
PEACOCK AND URN AND VTS. (MILLERSBURG)								
Bowl, 9½"	350	400	375	2,000*				
Compote, Large, Rare	1,350	1,500	1,350					
Bowl, Ice Cream, 10" Rare	500	700	2,600	2,000*				
Bowl, Ice Cream, 6" Rare	300	150	290	750				
Ruffled Bowl, 6"	190	145	210					
Plate, 10½", Rare	2,900							
Mystery Bowl, Variant, 8¾" Rare	350	450	390	1,350				
PEACOCK AT THE FOUNTAIN (DUGAN)								
Pitcher				600				
Tumbler		90		80				
PEACOCK AT THE FOUNTAIN (NORTHWOOD)								
Bowl, 9"	75	95	145	100			600IG	
Bowl, 5"	45	60	95	75			275W	
Orange Bowl, Ftd	450	650	3,500	900		10,000		
Punch Bowl w/base	450	550		600		30,000	5,200W	
Cup	30	45		55		1,400	125W	
Butter	265	345	400	325				
Sugar	200	300	370	250				
Creamer or Spooner	100	100	300	225				
Compote, Rare	375	450		500		3,800	1,400IG	
Pitcher	375	650	1,700	700			800W	
Tumbler	40	50	500	80			240W	
Spittoon Whimsey, Rare		4,200						
PEACOCK TAIL VT. (MILLERSBURG)								
Compote, Scarce	90	120	110					
PEACOCK TAIL AND DAISY								
Bowl, Very Rare	1,500	1,850*				2,200BO*		
PEACOCKS (ON FENCE) (NORTHWOOD)								
Bowl, 8¾"	300	450	600	450		3,300	1,000IG	
Plate, 9"	500	950	1,300	1,200EB		4,800	1,600IB	
PEARL AND JEWELS (FENTON)								
Basket, 4"							200W	
PEARL LADY (NORTHWOOD)								
Shade							90PG	
PEARL #37 (NORTHWOOD)								
Shade							100PO	
PEBBLE AND FAN (ENGLISH)								
Vase, 11¼", Rare				750*			750AM*	
PENNY								
Match Holder, Rare		250						
PEPPER PLANT (FENTON)								
Hat Shape				200				
PERFECTION (MILLERSBURG)								
Pitcher, Rare	4,000	4,000	4,500					
Tumbler, Rare	600	400	650					

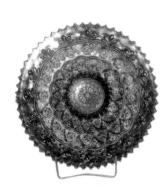

Persian Garden

Petal and Fan

Petals

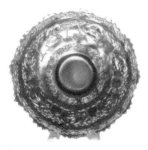

Peter Rabbit

	M	A	G	B	PO	AO	Pas	R
PERSIAN GARDEN (DUGAN)								
Bowl, Ice Cream, 11"	295	1,100	500	450	650		350W	
Bowl, Ice Cream, 6"	140	165	150	135	170		105W	
Bowl, Berry, 10"	190	220					300	
Bowl, Berry, 5"	50	60			80		100	
Plate, Chop, 13"								
Rare		11,000			4,800		2,200W	
Plate, 6",								
Rare	90	150					250W	
Fruit Bowl, w/base	110	420			500			
PERSIAN MEDALLION (FENTON)								
Bon-bon	35	55	60	50			200AO	1,000
Compote	75	400	190	85			650W	
Bowl, 10"	75	210	300	550				
Bowl, 5"	48	55	40	60				1,100
Bowl, 8¾"	60	90						950
Orange Bowl	95	300	250	275				
Rose Bowl	60	70	80	70				
Plate, 7"	50	250		200			700V	
Plate, 9½"		450		425			500W	
Hair Receiver	70	90		80			110	
Punch Bowl/Base	265	400	500	375				
Punch Cup	25	35	40	30				
PETAL AND FAN (DUGAN)								
Bowl, 10"	275	525	400		340		300	
Bowl, 5"	35	60	50		40		60	
Bowl, 8½"	65	95						
Plate, Ruffled, 6"		750						
PETALS (DUGAN)								
Bowl, 8¾"	40	55			110		70	
Compote	47	60					85	
Banana Bowl		90			110			
PETER RABBIT (FENTON)								
Bowl, 9", Rare	1,100		1,250	1,200				
Plate, 10", Rare	1,700		2,200	1,700			1,800AM	
PICKLE								
Paperweight, 4½"		65						
PIGEON								
Paperweight	190							
PILLAR AND DRAPE								
Shade					70MO		90W	750
PILLAR AND FLUTE (IMPERIAL)								
Compote	50						55SM	
Rose Bowl	60						75SM	
Creamer or sugar	35						40SM	
Celery Vase	60	90					85SM	
PILLOW AND SUNBURST (WESTMORELAND)								
Bowl, 7½"-9"	45	60			70		65AM	
PINCHED RIBS								
Vase	85				180			
PINE CONE (FENTON)								
Bowl, 6"	125	250	350	200			250W	
Plate, 6½"	150	175	275	125				
Plate, 8", Rare			250	225				
PINEAPPLE (ENGLISH)								
Bowl, 7"	60	70		67				
Bowl, 4"	40							
Creamer	70	100						
Sugar, Stemmed or Flat	75							
Compote	50	70		58				
Butter	85							
Rose Bowl	55							
PINEAPPLE, HEAVY (FENTON)								
Bowl, Ftd, 10" Rare	750			950			900W	
PIN-UPS (AUSTRALIAN)								
Bowl, 8¾", Rare	110	140						
PINWHEEL (DUGAN)								
Bowl, 6"	50				85			
Plate, 6½"	2,000							
PINWHEEL (ENGLISH)								
Vase, 6½"	100	120						
Vase, 8"	120	140						
Bowl, 8", Rare	50							
(Also Called Derby)								

Poinsettia (Imperial)

Plain Jane Basket

Pony

Pretty Panels

	M	A	G	B	PO	AO	Pas	R
PIPE HUMIDOR (MILLERSBURG)								
Tobacco Jar w/lid, Rare	5,000	7,000	6,500					
PLAID (FENTON)								
Bowl, 8¾"	120HA		350	200			950CeB	5,000
Plate, 9", Rare	350			450				7,900
PLAIN JANE								
Paperweight	90							
PLAIN JANE (IMPERIAL)								
Basket	60						75SM	
PLAIN PETALS (NORTHWOOD)								
Nappy, Scarce		85	90					
(Interior of Leaf and Beads Nappy)								
PLEATS AND HEARTS								
Shade							90	
PLUMS AND CHERRIES (NORTHWOOD)								
Sugar, Rare				1,750				
Spooner, Rare				1,750				
Tumbler				4,000*				
PLUME PANELS								
Vase, 7"-12"	50	70	80	65			150	850
POINSETTIA (IMPERIAL)								
Milk Pitcher	170	950	275				450SM	
POINSETTIA (NORTHWOOD)								
Bowl, Flat or Ftd, 8½"	400	575	750	1,000EB		4,000	3,500IB	
(Also Called Poinsettia & Lattice)								
POLO								
Ashtray	85							
POND LILY (FENTON)								
Bon-bon	45		65	60			75W	
PONY (DUGAN)								
Bowl, 8½"	120	260					1,100IG	
Plate, Age Questionable, 9", Rare,	450*							
POODLE								
Powder Jar w/lid	30							
POOL OF PEARLS								
Exterior pattern only								
POPPY (MILLERSBURG)								
Compote, Scarce	650	695	500					
Salver, Rare	1,200	1,450	1,600					
POPPY AND FISH NET (IMPERIAL)								
Vase, 6", Rare								750
POPPY SHOW (IMPERIAL)								
Vase, 12", Old Only	450	1,700	950				1,000SM	
Hurricane Whimsey		2,500					2,500W	
Lamp Whimsey	2,500*							
POPPY SHOW (NORTHWOOD)								
Bowl, 8½"	750	600	900	1,700			1,700IG	
Plate, 9", Rare	1,700	1,400	3,000	5,500EB			700W	
POPPY WREATH (NORTHWOOD)								
(Amaryllis Exterior Pattern)								
PORTLAND (U.S. GLASS)								
Bowl, 8½"							170	
POTPOURRI (MILLERSBURG)								
Milk Pitcher, Rare	2,000*							
PRAYER RUG (FENTON)								
Bon-bon, Rare					1,800IC			
(Iridized Custard Only)								
PREMIUM (IMPERIAL)								
Candlesticks, Pair	60	90					80	150
Bowl, 8½"	45	80					80	110
Bowl, 12"	55	75					90	130
Under Plate, 14"	50	90					120	150
PRETTY PANELS (FENTON)								
Pitcher w/lid								500
Tumbler, Handled	60							90IG

Primrose

Primrose and Fishnet

Prism and Daisy Band

Queen's Lamp

	M	A	G	B	PO	AO	Pas	R
PRETTY PANELS (NORTHWOOD)								
Pitcher	125		150					
Tumbler	60		70					
PRIMROSE (MILLERSBURG)								
Bowl, Ruffled, 8¼"	90	185	175	3,000			160CM	
Bowl, Ice Cream, 9", Scarce	110	190	190					
Bowl, Experimental, Goofus Exterior, Rare		900						
PRIMROSE AND FISHNET (IMPERIAL)								
Vase, 6", Rare								750
PRIMROSE PANELS (IMPERIAL)								
Shade							60	
PRIMROSE RIBBON								
Lightshade	90							
PRINCELY PLUMES								
Candle Holder		300						
PRINCESS (U.S. GLASS)								
Lamp, Complete, Rare		1,800						
PRISM								
Shakers, Pair	60							
Tray, 3"	50							
Hatpin		75						
PRISM BAND (FENTON)								
Pitcher, Decorated	175	350	395	410			350W	
Tumbler, Decorated	30	50	55	55			150W	
PRISM AND CANE (ENGLISH)								
Bowl, 5", Rare	45	65						
PRISM AND DAISY BAND (IMPERIAL)								
Vase	28							
Compote	35							
Bowl, 5"	18							
Bowl, 8"	30							
Sugar or Creamer, Each	35							
PRISMS (WESTMORELAND)								
Compote, 5", Scarce	50	90	100				150TL	
PROPELLER (IMPERIAL)								
Bowl, 9½", Rare	80							
Compote	35		45				55SM	
Vase, Stemmed, Rare	90							
PROUD PUSS (CAMBRIDGE)								
Bottle	85							
PULLED LOOP (DUGAN)								
Vase	40	60	50	110			650CeB	
PUMP, HOBNAIL (NORTHWOOD)								
One Shape, Age Questionable			850					
PUMP, TOWN (NORTHWOOD)								
One Shape, Rare	1,100	790	1,350					
PUZZLE (DUGAN)								
Compote	40	50	75	85	90		75W	
Bon-bon, Stemmed	40	50	90	125	100		80W	
PUZZLE PIECE								
One Shape				100*				
QUARTERED BLOCK								
Creamer	60							
Sugar	60							
Butter	125							
QUEEN'S JEWEL								
Goblet	55							
QUEEN'S LAMP								
One Shape, Rare			2,500					
QUESTION MARKS (DUGAN)								
Bon-bon	40	55			60		80IG	
Compote	40	70			75		70W	
Cake Plate, Stemmed, Rare		450*						
QUILL (DUGAN)								
Pitcher, Rare	2,000	3,500						
Tumbler, Rare	400	500						
RADIANCE								
Pitcher	240							
Tumbler	90							

	M	A	G	B	PO	AO	Pas	R
RAGGED ROBIN (FENTON)								
Bowl, 8¾", Scarce	75	100	100	100			150W	
RAINBOW (NORTHWOOD)								
Bowl, 8"..........................		80	95					
Compote..........................		110	150					
Plate, 9"..........................		135	160					
RAINDROPS (DUGAN)								
Bowl, 9"..........................	65	80			100			
Banana Bowl, 9¾"		150			165			
RAMBLER ROSE (DUGAN)								
Pitcher.............................	160	250	275	220				
Tumbler	30	50	55	45				
RANGER (MEXICAN)								
Creamer	40							
Nappy.............................	90							
Tumbler	290							
Milk Pitcher.....................	175							
Sugar	150							
Butter	190							
Breakfast Set, 2 Pieces	175							
Perfume, 5¼"	150*							
Pitcher, Rare......................	295							
Shot Glass, Rare.................	425							
RANGER TOOTHPICK								
Toothpick Holder	95							
Vase, 10"	50						65SM	
RASPBERRY (NORTHWOOD)								
Bowl, 9"..........................	60	70	75					
Bowl, 5"..........................	30	35	40					
Milk Pitcher.....................	150	225	275				2,000IB	
Sauce Boat, Ftd.................	90	150	275	190			350TL	
Pitcher.............................	165	275	295				2,200IB	
Tumbler	45	45	60				200IB	
Compote...........................	48	56	58					
RAYS (DUGAN)								
Bowl, 5"..........................	40	50	50		75			
Bowl, 9"..........................	55	90	90		125			
RAYS AND RIBBONS (MILLERSBURG)								
Bowl, Round or Ruffled, 8½"-9½"	65	90	90				300V	
Plate, Rare........................	1,100							
Banana Bowl, Rare.............			1,000					
Bowl, Tri-Cornered or Square	115	140	150					
RED PANELS (IMPERIAL)								
Shade................................								200
REGAL IRIS (CONSOLIDATED GLASS)								
"Gone With The Wind" Lamp, Rare	3,700							12,000*
REGAL SWIRL								
Candlestick, Each...............	75							
REX								
Pitcher.............................	375							
Tumbler	60							
RIB AND PANEL (FENTON)								
Vase	50	60		65		125		
Spittoon Whimsey...............	250							
RIBBED ELIPSE (HIGBEE)								
Mug, Rare							150HA	
RIBBED HOLLY (FENTON)								
Compote...........................	50	70		60				350
Goblet	75	100		85				390
RIBBED SWIRL								
Tumbler	60		80					
Bowl, 9"..........................	55		75					
RIBBON AND BLOCK								
Lamp, Complete	600							
RIBBON AND FERN								
Atomizer, 7"......................	90							
RIBBON AND LEAVES								
Sugar, Small......................	50							
RIBBON TIE (FENTON)								
Bowl, 8¾"	50	60	75	135				5,600
Plate, Ruffled, 9".................				175				7,500*
Plate, Flat, 9½"				360				

Ragged Robin

Raspberry

Rays

Ribbon Tie

Robin

Roman Rosette

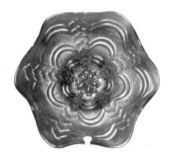

Rosalind

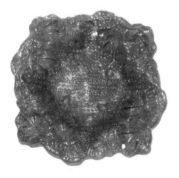

Rose and Greek Key

	M	A	G	B	PO	AO	Pas	R
RIBS								
(CZECHOSLOVAKIA)								
Ringtree	60							
Puff Box	95							
Pinbox.................................	75							
Perfume or Cologne	110							
Soap Dish...........................	60							
Dresser Tray.......................	110							
RINGS (JEANETTE)								
Vase, 8"	55							
RIPPLE								
(IMPERIAL)								
Vase, Various Sizes..............	60	150	190	110			350TL	
RISING SUN								
(U.S. GLASS)								
Butterdish	175							
Creamer	90							
Sugar	125							
Pitcher, 2 Shapes, Rare........	1,000*			2,000*				
Tumbler, Rare	400			600				
Tray, Rare				500				
Juice Tumbler, Rare	1,000							
ROBIN (IMPERIAL)								
Mug, Old Only	55						160	
Pitcher, Old Only, Scarce	300							
Tumbler, Old Only, Scarce ...	60							
ROCK CRYSTAL								
(McKEE)								
Punch Bowl w/base..............		600						
Cup.....................................		45						
ROCOCO								
(IMPERIAL)								
Bowl, 5"..............................	40		150				90SM	
Vase, 5½"............................	95		175				150SM	
ROLL								
Tumbler	40							
Cordial Set, Complete	350							
(Decanter, Stopper, 6 Glasses)								
Pitcher, Rare.......................							300CL	
Shakers, Rare, Each	45							
ROLLED RIBS								
Bowl (Marigold Opal)							150	
ROMAN ROSETTE								
(U.S. GLASS)								
Goblet, 6", Rare							110CL	
ROOD'S CHOCOLATES								
(FENTON)								
Advertising Plate..................		2,000*						
ROSALIND								
(MILLERSBURG)								
Bowl, 10" Scarce..................	175	260	325				500AQ	
Bowl, 5", Rare......................	200	295	575					
Compote, 6", Rare								
(Variant)		550	500					
Compote, Ruffled, 8",								
Rare	1,000							
Compote, Jelly, 9",								
Rare	1,800	2,000	2,000					
Plate, 9" Very Rare...............		2,500						
ROSE								
Bottle							130	
ROSE BAND								
Tumbler, Rare	700							
ROSE BOUQUET								
Creamer	60							
Bon-bon, Rare	75						400W	
ROSE COLUMN								
(MILLERSBURG)								
Vase, Rare	1,800	1,600	1,200	8,000				
Experimental Vase, Rare......		4,600						
ROSE GARDEN								
(SWEDEN)								
Letter Vase	180			190				
Bowl, 8¾"	80	80		75				
Vase, Round, 9"	385			250				
Pitcher, Communion,								
Rare	1,300			1,600				
Bowl, 6", Rare......................		90						
Butter, Rare.........................	450			445				
Rose Bowl, Small, Rare........	900							
Rose Bowl, Large, Rare				700				
ROSE AND GREEK KEY								
Square Plate,								
Rare							8,000AM*	
ROSE PANELS								
(AUSTRALIAN)								
Compote, Large	145							

Royalty

	M	A	G	B	PO	AO	Pas	R
ROSE PINWHEEL								
Bowl, Rare	1,900		2,200					
ROSE SHOW (NORTHWOOD)								
Bowl, 8¾"	500	600	3,000	800EB		2,400	1,900IB	
Plate	1,900	2,300	8,000	1,100	12,000MC	6,000	750W	
ROSE SHOW VARIANT (NORTHWOOD)								
Plate, 9"	1,800	1,900	2,200	3,800RenB	3,000		2,500IB	
Bowl, 8¾"	700	750		900			700W	
ROSE SPRAY (FENTON)								
Compote	175						190	
ROSE TREE (FENTON)								
Bowl, 10", Rare	1,150			1,200				
ROSE WINDOWS								
Tumbler, Rare	400							
ROSE WREATH (Basket of Roses) (NORTHWOOD)								
Bon-bon, Rare	275	350		350				
(Basketweave Exterior)								
ROSES AND FRUIT (MILLERSBURG)								
Bon-bon, Ftd, Rare	1,200	1,800	2,000	3,000				
ROSES AND RUFFLES (CONSOLIDATED GLASS)								
G-W-T-W Lamp, Rare	2,900							10,000
ROSETIME								
Vase	100							
ROSETTES (NORTHWOOD)								
Bowl, Dome Base, 9"	50	75						
Bowl, Ftd, 7"		80						
ROUND-UP (DUGAN)								
Bowl, 8¾"	100	180		140	175		180W	
Plate, 9", Rare	185	225		170	225		325W	
ROYALTY (IMPERIAL)								
Punch Bowl w/base	140							
Cup	30							
Fruit Bowl w/stand	100						140SM	
RUFFLED RIB (NORTHWOOD)								
Spittoon Whimsey, Rare	225							
Bowl, 8"-10"	50	70						
Vase, 7"-14"	70							
RUFFLES AND RINGS (NORTHWOOD)								
Exterior Pattern Only								
RUFFLES, RINGS AND DAISY BAND (NORTHWOOD)								
Bowl, Ftd, Rare, 8½"					1,000MO			
RUSTIC (FENTON)								
Vase, Funeral, 15"-20"	120	150	220	175				
Vase, Various Sizes	40	50	60	55	75		80	3,700
S-BAND (AUSTRALIAN)								
Compote	70	95						
S-REPEAT (DUGAN)								
Creamer, Small		75						
Punch Bowl w/base, Rare		1,800						
Cup, Rare		120						
Toothpick Holder (Old Only), Rare		85						
Tumbler	300							
Sugar, Rare (Very Light Iridescence)		250						
SACIC (ENGLISH)								
Ashtray	70							
SAILBOATS (FENTON)								
Bowl, 6"	38		75	70			125AM	550
Goblet	250	380	275	70			190	
Wine	35			100				
Compote	65			150				
Plate	470			400			350AM	
SAILING SHIP								
Plate, 8"	40							

Rosette

Rose Tree

Rose Spray Compote

Scale Band

Scottie

Scroll Embossed Variant

Sea Gulls Vase

	M	A	G	B	PO	AO	Pas	R
SAINT (ENGLISH)								
Candlestick, Each............	300							
SALAMANDERS								
Hatpin..............................		75						
SALT CUP (VARIOUS MAKERS)								
One Shape, Averaged..........	45	55	88RG				75CeB	
SATIN SWIRL								
Atomizer............................							75CL	
SAWTOOTH BAND								
Tumbler Rare	400							
SAWTOOTH PRISMS								
Jelly Jar	60							
SCALE BAND (FENTON)								
Bowl, 6".............................	35				80			
Plate, Flat, 6½"	45						85V	585
Plate, Dome Base, 7"	50							550
Pitcher..............................	125		400					
Tumbler	60		350					
SCALES (WESTMORELAND)								
Bon-bon	40	48			90	300	60TL	
Bowl, 7"-10"					90IM		46TL	
Deep Bowl, 5"		40						
Plate, 6"...........................	45	58					65TL	
Plate, 9"...........................		95			110	260	140	
SCARAB								
Hatpin..............................		100					150AM	
SCOTCH THISTLE (FENTON)								
Compote............................	46	60	75	50				
SCOTTIE								
Powder Jar w/lid	35							
Paperweight, Rare...............	250							
SCROLL (WESTMORELAND)								
Pin Tray	50							
SCROLL AND FLOWER PANELS (IMPERIAL)								
Vase, 10", Old Only.............	95	250		150				
SCROLL EMBOSSED (IMPERIAL)								
Bowl, 8½"	40	65						600
Dessert, Round or Ruffled, Rare	90	275	150					
Plate, 9".............................		325	200				90TL	
Compote, Large	50	450					100AQ	
Compote, Small	40	75	60					
Sauce	35	55						
SCROLL EMBOSSED VT. (ENGLISH)								
Handled Ashtray, 5"	45	60						
Plate, 7".............................	165							
SEACOAST (MILLERSBURG)								
Pin Tray, Rare	500	550	425				900CM	
SEAFOAM (DUGAN)								
Exterior Pattern Only								
SEAGULL (CZECH)								
Vase, Rare	1,150							
SEAGULLS (DUGAN)								
Bowl, 6½", Scarce	80							
SEAWEED								
Lamp, 2 Sizes	250							
Lamp Vt., 8½", Rare.............							395IB	
SEAWEED (MILLERSBURG)								
Bowl, 5", Rare.....................	400		470					
Bowl, 9", Rare.....................	275		375	1,600			400CM	
Plate, 10", Rare...................	1,000	1,100	1,000					
Bowl, 10½", Ruffled, Scarce	350	400	350				300CM	
Bowl, Ice Cream, 10½", Rare.....	400	450	500					
SERRATED RIBS								
Shaker, Each......................	60							
SHARP								
Shot Glass..........................	50						70SM	
SHELL								
Shade................................							75	
SHELL (IMPERIAL)								
Bowl, 7"-9"	45	250	75				90SM	
Plate, 8½"	190	1,050	375					
SHELL AND BALLS								
Perfume, 2½"	65							

Singing Birds

Single Flower Framed

Six Petals

Small Rib

	M	A	G	B	PO	AO	Pas	R
SHELL AND JEWEL (WESTMORELAND)								
Creamer w/lid	55	65	60				90W	
Sugar w/lid	55	65	60				90W	
SHERATON (U.S. GLASS)								
Pitcher							170	
Tumbler							50	
Butter							130	
Sugar							90	
Creamer or Spooner							75	
SHIP AND STARS								
Plate, 8"	40							
SHRINE (U.S. GLASS)								
Champagne							180CL	
Toothpick Holder		650					200CL	
SIGNET (ENGLISH)								
Sugar w/lid, 6½"	75							
SILVER AND GOLD								
Pitcher	150							
Tumbler	50							
SILVER QUEEN (FENTON)								
Pitcher	200							
Tumbler	70							
SINGING BIRDS (NORTHWOOD)								
Bowl, 10"	60	75	85					
Bowl, 5	30	35	40					
Mug	225	250	325	290		1,800	750W	
Butter	185	300	325					
Sugar	110	140	150					
Creamer	80	100	125					
Spooner	80	100	125					
Pitcher	350	375	550					
Tumbler	45	75	150					
Sherbet, Rare	300							
SINGLE FLOWER (DUGAN)								
Bowl, 8"	35	40	45		55			
Hat	30	40	40					
Handled Basket Whimsey, Rare	225				900			
Banana Bowl, 9½", Rare					350			
SINGLE FLOWER FRAMED (DUGAN)								
Bowl, 8¾"	65	90	80		130			
Bowl, 5"	40	50			75			
Plate		275			250			
SIX PETALS (DUGAN)								
Bowl, 8½"	40	125	70	80	75		60	
Plate, Rare	90	200	150		195			
Hat	45	50	60		80		150BA	
SIX-SIDED (IMPERIAL)								
Candlestick, Each	165	300	250				200SM	
SKATER'S SHOE (U.S. GLASS)								
One Shape	120							
SKI-STAR (DUGAN)								
Bowl, 8"-10"	60	95		175	150			
Bowl, 5"	40	50	60	55	80			
Basket, Handled, Rare					500			
Banana Bowl		125			290			
Plate, 7½"					160			
Hand Grip Bowl, 8"-10"					140			
Rose Bowl, Rare					600			
SMALL BASKET								
One Shape	50							
SMALL BLACKBERRY (NORTHWOOD)								
Compote	50	60	60					
SMALL PALMS								
Shade	45							
SMALL RIB (DUGAN)								
Compote	40	45	45				55AM	
Rose Bowl, Stemmed	40	45	50				55AM	
SMALL THUMBPRINT								
Creamer	60							
Toothpick Holder	70							

	M	A	G	B	PO	AO	Pas	R
SMITH REAL ESTATE								
Bowl	1,400							
SMOOTH PANELS (IMPERIAL)								
Bowl, 6½"	30						35PM	
Plate, 9¼"							90CL	
Tumbler							45PM	
Vase	40						250SMG	250
Pitcher	90		175					
SMOOTH RAYS (NORTHWOOD)								
Bon-bon	30						25CL	
SMOOTH RAYS (NORTHWOOD-DUGAN)								
Compote	40	50	55					
Rose Bowl	50	60			60			
Bowl, 6"-9"	45	90			80			
Plate, 7"-9"	60							
SMOOTH RAYS (WESTMORELAND)								
Compote			75				70AM	
Bowl, 7"-9", Flat	40	55	50		75		125BO	
Bowl, Dome Base, 5"-7½"			55		75		80TL	
SNOW FANCY (McKEE)								
Bowl, 5"			50					
Creamer or Sugar	50							
SODA GOLD (IMPERIAL)								
Candlestick, 3½", Each	55						60SM	
Bowl, 9"	45						60SM	
Pitcher	240						325SM	
Tumbler	40						75SM	
SODA GOLD SPEARS (DUGAN)								
Bowl, 8½"	40						40CL	
Bowl, 4½"	30						30CL	
Plate, 9"	50						160CL	
SOLDIERS AND SAILORS (FENTON)								
Plate (Illinois), Rare	1,000	1,600		1,750				
Plate (Indianapolis), Rare				3,500				
SOUTACHE (DUGAN)								
Bowl, 10"					200			
Plate, 10½", Rare					375			
Lamp, Complete	350							
SOUTHERN IVY								
Wine, 2 Sizes	45							
SOUVENIR BANDED								
Mug	85							
SOUVENIR BELL (IMPERIAL)								
One Shape, Lettering	180							
SOUVENIR MINIATURE								
One Shape, Lettering	50							
SOUVENIR MUG (McKEE)								
Any Lettering	65							
SOUVENIR PIN TRAY (U.S. GLASS)								
One Size							75	
(Same as Portland Pattern)								
SOUVENIR VASE (U.S. GLASS)								
Vase, 6½", Rare	100	135			150	400		
SOWERBY FLOWER BLOCK (ENGLISH)								
Flower Frog	60							
SOWERBY WIDE PANEL (SOWERBY)								
Bowl	45							
SPHINX (ENGLISH)								
Paperweight, Rare							595AM	
SPIDERWEB (NORTHWOOD)								
Candy Dish, covered							40SM	
SPIDERWEB (NORTHWOOD-DUGAN)								
Vase, 8"	50						80	
SPIDERWEB AND TREEBARK (DUGAN)								
Vase, 6"							65	
SPIRAL (IMPERIAL)								
Candlestick, Pair.	165	185	195				170SM	

Soda Gold

Soldiers and Sailors (Ill.)

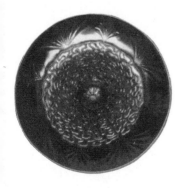

Soutache

Stag and Holly

Star of David

Star of David and Bows

Star and Fan Cordial Set

	M	A	G	B	PO	AO	Pas	R
SPIRALEX (ENGLISH)								
Vase, Various Sizes	50	65	70	60			80	
SPIRALLED DIAMOND POINT								
Vase, 6"	90							
SPLIT DIAMOND (ENGLISH)								
Creamer, Small....................	40							
Sugar, Open	40							
Butter, Scarce	65							
SPOKES (FOSTORIA)								
Bowl, 10".............................							100	
SPRING BASKET (IMPERIAL)								
Handled Basket, 5"	50						65SM	
SPRING OPENING (MILLERSBURG)								
Plate, 6½", Rare		1,600						
SPRINGTIME (NORTHWOOD)								
Bowl, 9"...............................	80	200	250					
Bowl, 5"...............................	40	55	75					
Butter	375	450	475					
Sugar	300	400	425					
Creamer or Spooner	275	350	400					
Pitcher, Rare.......................	750	1,000	1,250				1,800	
Tumbler, Rare	75	120	200				300	
STERLING FURNITURE (NORTHWOOD)								
Bowl....................................		700						
STRETCHED DIAMONDS & DOTS								
Tumbler	175							
SQUARE DAISY AND BUTTON (IMPERIAL)								
Toothpick Holder, Rare							125	
SQUARE DIAMOND								
Vase, Rare				750				
STAG AND HOLLY (FENTON)								
Bowl, Ftd, 9"-13"	150	300	400	425	1,700		790AQ	3,000
Rose Bowl, Ftd	350		800	1,000				
Plate, Ftd, 13".....................	1,000							
Plate, Ftd, 9".......................	700	1,000		1,800				
STANDARD								
Vase, 5½".............................	50							
STAR								
Paperweight, Rare................							295	
STAR (ENGLISH)								
Bowl, 8"...............................	50							
STAR CENTER (IMPERIAL)								
Bowl, 8½"	30	40					50	
Plate, 9"...............................	60	80					90	
STAR OF DAVID (IMPERIAL)								
Bowl, 8¼", Scarce	70	100	200				100SM	3,000*
STAR OF DAVID AND BOWS (NORTHWOOD)								
Bowl, 8½"	50	60	75				150AM	
STAR AND DIAMOND POINT								
Hatpin.................................		75						
STAR AND FAN								
Vase, 9½", Rare....................	250			200				
(Note: Same as curved Star Pattern)								
STAR AND FAN (ENGLISH)								
Cordial Set	1,500							
(Decanter, 4 Stemmed Cordials and Tray)								
STAR AND FILE (IMPERIAL)								
Bowl, 7"-9½"	35							
Vase, Handled	50							
Compote..............................	45							
Creamer or Sugar	30							
Pitcher................................	185							
Decanter w/stopper.............	110							
Rose Bowl............................	75	100	115				100AM	
Wine....................................	75						250IG	
Spooner...............................	30							
Sherbet	35							
Custard Cup	30							
Plate, 6"..............................	65							
Pickle Dish	40							
Tumbler, Rare	275							
Bon-bon	35							

	M	A	G	B	PO	AO	Pas	R
STAR AND HOBS								
Rose Bowl, 9",								
Rare				350				
STAR MEDALLION								
(IMPERIAL)								
Bon-bon	45							
Bowl, 7"-9"	30						40	
Compote	45							
Butter	100							
Creamer, Spooner or Sugar								
Each	60							
Milk Pitcher	80		95					
Goblet	45						60	
Tumbler	30		50				55	
Plate, 5"	60						45	
Plate, 10"							50	
Handled Celery	80						65	
Celery Tray	60						50	
Ice Cream, Stemmed,								
Small	35							
Pickle Dish	40							
Vase, 6"	40						45	
Custard Cup	20							
STAR AND NEARCUT								
Hatpin		60						
STAR AND ROSETTE								
Hatpin		75						
STAR SPRAY								
(IMPERIAL)								
Bowl, 7"	35						45SM	
Bride's Basket,								
Complete, Rare	90						125SM	
Plate, 7½", Scarce	75						95SM	
STARBRIGHT								
Vase, 6½"	40	45		50				
STARBURST								
Perfume w/stopper	65							
Spittoon	650							
STARFISH								
(DUGAN)								
Bon-bon, Handled, Rare		65			150		850	
Compote	40	65	75		125			
STARFLOWER								
Pitcher, Rare	3,200			2,750				
STARLYTE								
(IMPERIAL)								
Shade	40							
STARS AND BARS								
(CAMBRIDGE)								
Wine, Rare	150*							
STARS AND STRIPES								
(OLD GLORY),								
Plate, 7½", Rare	150*							
STIPPLED ACORNS								
Candy dish w/lid, Ftd	75	95		80				
STIPPLED DIAMOND SWAG								
(ENGLISH)								
Compote	45		65	60				
STIPPLED FLOWER								
(DUGAN)								
Bowl, 8½"					85			
STIPPLED PETALS								
(DUGAN)								
Bowl, 9"		75			90			
Handled Basket		150			165			
STIPPLED RAMBLER ROSE								
(DUGAN)								
Nut Bowl, Ftd	75			90				
STIPPLED RAYS								
(FENTON)								
Bon-bon	35	45	55	40				425
Bowl, 5"-9"	40	50	60	50				450
Compote	35	45	50	45				
Creamer or Sugar, Each	30	40	45	45				425
Plate, 7"	50	50	100	45				560
STIPPLED RAYS								
(IMPERIAL)								
Creamer, Stemmed	40		50				55SM	500
Sugar, Stemmed	40		50				55SM	500
Sugar Whimsey,								
Rare								600
STIPPLED RAYS								
(NORTHWOOD)								
Bowl, 8"-10"	45	55	65					
Compote	50	60	65					
STIPPLED SALT CUP								
One Size	45							

Starflower

Stippled Rays (Fenton)

Stippled Rays (Imperial)

Stippled Rays (Northwood)

Stork ABC Plate

Stork and Rushes

Strawberry (Fenton)

Strawberry (Millersburg

	M	A	G	B	PO	AO	Pas	R
STIPPLED STRAWBERRY (JENKINS)								
Tumbler	60							
Creamer or Sugar	35							
Spittoon Whimsey, Rare	225							
Syrup, Rare	250							
Butter	85							
Bowl, 9", Rare	90	200						
STORK (JENKINS)								
Vase	60							
STORK ABC								
Child's Plate, 7½"	60							
STORK AND RUSHES (DUGAN)								
Butter, Rare	145	165						
Creamer or Spooner, Rare	80	90						
Sugar, Rare	90	120						
Bowl, 10"	40	50						
Bowl, 5"	30	30						
Mug	35	50		350				
Punch Bowl w/base, Rare	190	300		325				
Cup	20	30		35				
Hat	25			30				
Handled Basket	60							
Pitcher	250			400				
Tumbler	30	60		75				
STRAWBERRY (DUGAN)								
Epergne, Rare	1,000	900						
STRAWBERRY (FENTON)								
Bon-bon	55	50	65	60			90V	450
STRAWBERRY (MILLERSBURG)								
Bowl, 6½"	90	150	140					
Bowl, 8"-10", Scarce	285	450	400				1,300V	
Compote, Rare	575	300	325				1,950V	
Gravy Boat Whimsey, Rare							1,500V	
Banana Boat Whimsey, Rare		2,000*	2,000*				2,000V	
Bowl, 9½", Tri-Cornered	390	500	450					
STRAWBERRY (NORTHWOOD)								
Bowl, 8"-10"	75	90	85	90		2,200	1,100IG	
Bowl, 5"	45	60	70	80				
Plate, 9"	175	450	395	375		2,600		
Plate, Handgrip, 7"	190	250	275	230				
Stippled Plate, 9"	1,600	1,350	1,500					
STRAWBERRY INTAGLIO (NORTHWOOD)								
Bowl, 9½"	65							
Bowl, 5½"	30							
STRAWBERRY POINT								
Tumbler	150							
STRAWBERRY SCROLL (FENTON)								
Pitcher, Rare	1,900			2,500				
Tumbler, Rare	175			250				
STRAWBERRY SPRAY								
Brooch				175				
STRETCHED DIAMOND (NORTHWOOD)								
Tumbler, Rare	175							
STREAM OF HEARTS (FENTON)								
Bowl, Ftd, 10"	80			110				
Compote, Rare	95						135	
Goblet, Rare	200							
STRING OF BEADS								
One Shape	35		40					
STUDS (IMPERIAL)								
Tray, Large	65							
Juice, Tumbler	40							
Milk Pitcher	75							
STYLE								
Bowl, 8"		95						
SUMMER DAYS (DUGAN)								
Vase, 6"	60			70				
(Note: This is actually the base for the Stork and Rushes punch set.)								
SUN PUNCH								
Bottle	30						35	
SUNFLOWER (MILLERSBURG)								
Pin Tray, Rare	450	395	350					

Sun-Gold

Swan Pastel

Sunken Hollyhocks

	M	A	G	B	PO	AO	Pas	R
SUNFLOWER (NORTHWOOD)								
Bowl, 8½"	50	70	65	1,195ReB			1,900IB	
Plate, Rare	250		400					
SUNFLOWER AND DIAMOND								
Vase, 2 Sizes	75			110				
SUNGOLD (AUSTRALIAN)								
Epergne							450	
SUNK DIAMOND BAND (U.S. GLASS)								
Pitcher, Rare	150						250W	
Tumbler, Rare	50						75W	
SUNKEN DAISY (ENGLISH)								
Sugar	30			40				
SUNKEN HOLLYHOCK								
G-W-T-W Lamp, Rare	4,000							12,000
SUNRAY								
Compote		40			55			
SUNRAY (FENTON)								
Compote (Milk Glass Iridized)					90MO			
SUPERB DRAPE (NORTHWOOD)								
Vase, Rare						2,700*		
SWAN, PASTEL (DUGAN-FENTON)								
One Size	225	300	500TL*	190	375		125IG	
SWEETHEART (CAMBRIDGE)								
Cookie Jar w/lid, Rare	1,550		1,100					
Tumbler, Rare	650							
SWALLOWS								
Tumbler, Enameled	120.00							
SWIRL (NORTHWOOD)								
Pitcher	250		800					
Tumbler	110		150					
SWIRL (IMPERIAL)								
Mug, Rare	90							
Candlestick, Each	35							
SWIRL HOBNAIL (MILLERSBURG)								
Rose Bowl, Rare	295	375	650					
Spittoon, Rare	575	750	1,250					
Vase, 7"-10", Rare	250	300	300	500				
SWIRL VARIANT (IMPERIAL)								
Bowl, 7"-8"	30							
Epergne			200		45			
Vase, 6½"	35		45		200		65W	
Plate, 6"-8¾"	50		60		60		75	
Pitcher, 7½"	100							
Cake Plate							85CL	
Dessert, Stemmed	30							
Juice Glass	40							
SWIRLED FLUTE (FENTON)								
Vase, 7"-12"	35	40	50	45			70W	485
SWIRLED RIBS (NORTHWOOD)								
Pitcher	165							
Tumbler	70	75						
SWIRLED THREADS								
Goblet	95							
SWORD AND CIRCLE								
Tumbler, Rare	150							
SYDNEY (FOSTORIA)								
Tumbler, Rare	800							
TAFFETA LUSTRE (FOSTORIA)								
Candlestick, Pair, Rare		300	350	400			450AM	
Console Bowl, 11", Rare		150	150	175			180AM	
(Add 25% For Old Paper Labels Attached)								
Perfume w/stopper	90	125					160LV	
TALL HAT								
Various Sizes, 4"-10"	45+						50PK	
TARGET (FENTON)								
Vase, 7"-11"	45	55	60		95		55	
TEXAS								
Giant Tumbler				260				
TEXAS HEADDRESS (WESTMORELAND)								
Punch Cup	45							

Ten Mums

Thin Rib and Drape

Three Fruits

Three-In-One

	M	A	G	B	PO	AO	Pas	R
TEN MUMS								
(FENTON)								
Bowl, Ftd, 9", Rare	500							
Bowl, 8"-11"	95	125	120	150				
Plate, 10", Rare...................				975				
Pitcher, Rare......................	495			900			1,500W	
Tumbler, Rare	70			80			340W	
THIN RIB								
(FENTON)								
Candlestick, Pair	80							390
THIN RIB AND DRAPE								
(FENTON)								
Vase, 8"-14"......................	40	50	55					
THIN RIB								
(NORTHWOOD)								
AND VTS								
Vase, 6"-11"......................	35	40	50	55	70	235	70	
THISTLE								
(ENGLISH)								
Vase, 6"	45							
THISTLE								
(FENTON)								
Bowl, 8"-10"	90	140	160	150				
Plate, 9", Rare....................		1,650	2,800					
Compote...........................	60			70				
Advertising Bowl (Horlacher)...	125	225	200	200				
THISTLE								
Shade..............................	60							
THISTLE AND LOTUS								
(FENTON)								
Bowl, 7"............................	55		75	70				
THISTLE AND THORN								
(ENGLISH)								
Bowl, Ftd, 6"......................	50							
Creamer or Sugar, Each	60							
Plate, Ftd, 8½"	150							
Nut Bowl	75							
THISTLE, FENTON'S								
(FENTON)								
Banana Boat, Ftd, Scarce	300	400	500	475				
THREE DIAMONDS								
(DUGAN)								
Vase, 6"-10".......................	45	50	60	60	75		60	
THREE FLOWERS								
(IMPERIAL)								
Tray, Center Handle, 12"	60						70SM	
THREE FRUITS								
(NORTHWOOD)								
Bowl, 9"..............................	45	90	150	180		750	240	
Bowl, 5"..............................	30	40	70	80		150	70	
Bowl, Dome Base, 8⅝"		90						
Bon-bon, Stemmed..............	50	65	80	90		850	120	
Plate, Round, 9"..................	200	400	290	375		2,800	900IB	
(Add 50% if Stippled)								
Bowl, Stippled, 9"	150	250	1,000	395		1,400		
THREE FRUITS MEDALLION								
(NORTHWOOD)								
Bowl, Ftd, 8-10½", Rare								
(Meander Exterior)..............	120	195	240	285		1,400	500AQ	
THREE FRUITS VT.								
(DUGAN)								
Plate, 12-Sided	150	175	200				160	
THREE-IN-ONE								
(IMPERIAL)								
Bowl, 8¾"	30	40	40				45SM	
Bowl, 4½"	20	25	25				30SM	
Plate, 6½"	50						80SM	
Rose Bowl, Rare	200							
Banana Bowl Whimsey	100							
Toothpick Holder, Rare				85				
THREE MONKEYS								
Bottle, Rare							90	
THREE ROLL								
Bedroom Set (Tumble Up)	90							
THREE ROW								
(IMPERIAL)								
Vase, Rare	900	1,200					1,100SM	
THUMBPRINT AND OVAL								
(IMPERIAL)								
Vase, 5½",								
Rare	600	850						
THUMBPRINT AND SPEARS								
Creamer	50		60					
THUNDERBIRD								
(AUSTRALIAN)								
Bowl, 9½"	350	395						
Bowl, 5".............................	60	75						

Tomahawk

Tracery

Tornado

Tree Bark

	M	A	G	B	PO	AO	Pas	R
TIERED THUMBPRINT								
Bowls, 2 Sizes......................	45							
Candlestick, Pair	120							
TIGER LILY								
(IMPERIAL)								
Pitcher............................	125	350	275					
Tumbler	35	60	40	350			90AM	
TINY BERRY								
Tumbler, 2¼"			45					
TINY HOBNAIL								
Lamp...............................	110							
TOBACCO LEAF								
(U.S. GLASS)								
Champagne							160CL	
TOLTEC								
(McKEE)								
Butter (Ruby Iridized), Rare		375						
Pitcher, Tankard, Very Rare...........................	2,600*							
TOMOHAWK								
(CAMBRIDGE)								
One Size, Rare				1,850				
TOP HAT								
Vase							50	
TOP O' THE MORNING								
Hatpin		50						
TOP O' THE WALK								
Hatpin		100						
TORNADO								
(NORTHWOOD)								
Vase, Plain.......................	450	550	500	1,200			1,200W	
Vase, Ribbed, 2 Sizes	495	575	550	1,150			1,500IB	
Vase Whimsey							1,300WS	
TORNADO VT.								
(NORTHWOOD)								
Vase, Rare	1,450							
TOWERS								
(ENGLISH)								
Hat Vase...........................	65							
TOY PUNCH SET								
(CAMBRIDGE)								
Bowl Only, Ftd....................	60							
TRACERY								
(MILLERSBURG)								
Bon-bon, Rare		650	650					
TREE BARK								
(IMPERIAL)								
Pitcher, Open Top	60							
Pitcher w/lid	70							
Tumbler, 2 Sizes	25							
Bowl, 7½"	20							
Pickle Jar, 7½"	35							
Candlestick, 7", Pair	50							
Sauce, 4".........................	10							
Candlestick, 4½", Pair.........	30							
Candy Jar w/lid	35							
TREEBARK VT.								
Candleholder on stand	85							
Pitcher............................	60							
Tumbler	20							
Planter	60							
Juice	25							
TREE OF LIFE								
(IMPERIAL)								
Bowl, 5½"	30							
Handled Basket..................	30							
Plate, 7½"	40							
Tumbler	25							
Pitcher............................	60							
Perfumer w/lid	40							
Vase Whimsey (From Pitcher)..						150CL		
TREE TRUNK								
(NORTHWOOD)								
Vase, 7"-12"........................	75	150	95	100		1,200	250IB	
Funeral Vase, 15"-20"	950	1,500	1,250	1,400	2,800*MO	6,500	6,000IG	
Jardinere Whimsey, Rare.....	2,000	2,500						
TREFOIL FINE CUT								
(MILLERSBURG)								
Exterior pattern only								
TRIAD								
Hatpin		55						
TRIANDS								
(ENGLISH)								
Creamer, Sugar or Spooner	50							
Butter	65							
Celery Vase.......................	55							

	M	A	G	B	PO	AO	Pas	R
TRIPLETS (DUGAN)								
Bowl, 6"-8"	35	40	45		55			
Hat....................................	30	35	38					
TROPICANA (ENGLISH)								
Vase, Rare	1,600							
TROUT AND FLY (MILLERSBURG)								
Bowl, 8¼", Various Shapes	500	600	750				1,100LV	
Plate, 9", Rare....................		7,500						
TULIP (MILLERSBURG)								
Compote, 9", Rare...............	750	850	800					
TULIP AND CANE (IMPERIAL)								
Wine, 2 Sizes, Rare	85							
Claret Goblet, Rare	110							
Goblet, 8 oz, Rare	75							
Compote	45							
TULIP SCROLL (MILLERSBURG)								
Vase, 6"-12", Rare................	275	400	300					
TUMBLE-UP (FENTON-IMPERIAL)								
Plain, Complete	85						90	
Handled, Complete, Rare	295						320	
TWINS (IMPERIAL)								
Bowl, 9".............................	40		50				45	
Bowl, 5".............................	25		30				35	
Fruit Bowl w/base	60							
TWITCH (BARTLETT-COLLINS)								
Cup...................................	30							
Creamer	30							
Sherbet	35							
TWO FLOWERS (FENTON)								
Plate, 13", Rare	1,100							7,000
Bowl, Ftd, 5"-8"	60	70	70	55				
Bowl, Spatula, 8".................	90	110	135	120			250W	2,200
Rose Bowl, Rare	195		225	200				
Bowl, Ftd, 8"-10"	75	175	250	275			375W	5,800
Plate, Ftd, 9"......................	600		675	650				
TWO FRUITS (FENTON)								
Divided Bowl, 5½" Scarce	75	90	115	95			120W	
TWO ROW (IMPERIAL)								
Vase, Rare		1,100						
URN								
Vase, 9"	65							
US DIAMOND BLOCK (U.S. GLASS)								
Compote, Rare.....................	65				90			
Shakers, Pair.......................	80							
UMBRELLA PRISMS								
Small Hatpin		45						
Large Hatpin		70						
UNIVERSAL HOME BOTTLE								
One Shape..........................	125*							
UNSHOD								
Pitcher...............................	85							
UTILITY								
Lamp, 8", Complete	90							
VALENTINE								
Ring Tray	80							
VALENTINE (NORTHWOOD)								
Bowl, 10", Rare....................	500							
Bowl, 5", Rare......................	125	200						
474 VARIANT (SWEDEN)								
Compote, 7".........................			90					
VENETIAN (CAMBRIDGE)								
Vase, (Lamp Base), 9¼", Rare...	1,500		1,300					
Creamer, Rare	550							
Sugar, Rare	550							
Butter, Rare........................	950							

Tulip and Cane

Twins

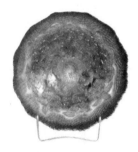

Two Flowers

Two Fruits

	M	A	G	B	PO	AO	Pas	R
VICTORIAN								
Bowl, 10"-12", Rare		500			2,500			
VINEYARD (DUGAN)								
Pitcher.........................	90	300			950			
Tumbler	25	50					300W	
VINEYARD AND FISHNET								
(IMPERIAL)								
Vase, Rare								750
VINEYARD HARVEST								
(AUSTRALIAN)								
Tumbler, Rare	250							
VINING LEAF AND VT.								
(ENGLISH)								
Spittoon, Rare	350							
Vase, Rare	225							
Rose Bowl, Rare	250							
VINING TWIGS (DUGAN)								
Bowl, 7½"	35	45	50				55	
Hat...............................	40	50					60W	
VINTAGE (FENTON)								
Epergne, One Lily, 2 Sizes ...	100	135	150	150				
Fernery, 2 Varieties	55	70	100	95			200AM	980
Bowl, 10".......................	45	60	90	125			85	4,800
Bowl, 8".........................	40	45	50	50		1,000	70	3,600
Bowl, 6½"......................	30	40	45	45			60	2,500
Bowl, 4½"......................	25	35	40	40			55	
Plate, 7¾"	280	185	200	130			45	
Whimsey Fernery................		200						
Card Tray	40							
Punch Bowl w/base.............	275	400	450	465				
(Wreath of Roses Exterior)								
Cup.............................	25	35	37	40				
Rose Bowl.......................	55			60				
Compote........................	40	50	55	60				
Plate, 7".........................	115			240				
Plate, Ruffled, 11"...............	200		275	295				
VINTAGE (DUGAN)								
Powder Jar w/lid	70	120		150				
Dresser Tray, 7" x 11"..........	85							
VINTAGE								
(U.S. GLASS)								
Wine............................	40	50						
VINTAGE								
(MILLERSBURG)								
Bowl, 5", Rare	500		600	800				
Bowl, 9", Rare..................	600	900	800	3,500				
VINTAGE BANDED								
(DUGAN)								
Mug..............................	35						45SM	
Tumbler, Rare	600							
Pitcher..........................	250	550						
VINTAGE LEAF								
(FENTON)								
Bowl, 8½"	50	75	85	70				
Bowl, 5½"	25	35	40	30				
VINTAGE VT.								
(DUGAN)								
Plate............................	300	400						
Bowl, Ftd, 8½"..................			100				450WS	
VIOLET								
Basket, Either Type	50	65		75				
VIRGINIA BLACKBERRY								
(U.S. GLASS)								
Pitcher, Small, Rare				250				
(Note: Tiny Berry Miniature								
Tumbler May Match This.)								
VOTIVE LIGHT								
(MEXICAN)								
Candle Vase, 4½", Rare	450							
WAFFLE BLOCK								
(IMPERIAL)								
Handled Basket, 10"............	50						165TL	
Bowl, 7"-9"	40							
Parfait Glass, Stemmed	30						45	
Fruit Bowl w/base..............							200CM	
Vase, 8"-11"	40						55	
Nappy...........................							40PM	
Pitcher..........................	120						170CM	
Tumbler	200						215CM	
Rose Bowl, Any Size...........	70							
Plate, 10"-12", Any Shape	85						170SM	
Sherbet							35CL	
Punch Bowl	175						225TL	
Cup.............................	20						30TL	
Shakers, Pair...................	75							
Creamer	60							
Sugar	60							

Vineyard

Wheat

Vintage Banded

Votive Light

Waterlily and Cattails

Water Lily and Dragonfly

Webbed Clematis

Whirling Leaves

	M	A	G	B	PO	AO	Pas	R
WAFFLE BLOCK AND HOBSTAR (IMPERIAL)								
Basket	250						265SM	
WAFFLE WEAVE								
Inkwell	95							
WAR DANCE (ENGLISH)								
Compote, 5"	120							
WASHBOARD								
Creamer, 5½"	45							
WATER LILY (FENTON)								
Bon-bon	40	50	55	50			60	
Bowl, Ftd, 5"	50	90	300	100			150V	1,600
Bowl, Ftd, 10"	90	140	400	250			175BA	3,700
Chop Plate 11", Very Rare	4,500*							
WATER LILY AND CATTAILS (FENTON)								
Toothpick Whimsey	75							
Bon-bon	60	85		90				
Pitcher	340							
Tumbler	95							
Butter	175							
Sugar	100							
Creamer or Spooner	75							
Bowl, 5"	35	50		50				
Bowl, 7"-9"	50							
Spittoon Whimsey, Rare	2,400							
WATER LILY AND CATTAILS (NORTHWOOD)								
Pitcher	400			6,000				
Tumbler	110	200		2,700*				
WATER LILY AND DRAGONFLY (AUSTRALIAN)								
Float Bowl, 10½", Complete	150	185						
WAVEY SATIN								
Hatpin		95						
WEBBED CLEMATIS								
Vase, 12½"	250							
WEEPING CHERRY (DUGAN)								
Bowl, Dome Base	90	130			220		100	
Bowl, Flat Base	75	110			190		90	
WESTERN DAISY (WESTMORELAND)								
Bowl	50	60			200MO			
Hat	45	50						
WESTERN THISTLE								
Tumbler, Rare	340							
Vase, Rare	250							
WESTMORELAND JESTER'S CAP								
Vase	40	50	55	60	75	225	85	
WHEAT (NORTHWOOD)								
Sweetmeat w/lid, Rare		9,000	9,500					
Bowl w/lid, Rare		8,000						
WHEELS (IMPERIAL)								
Bowl, 9"	50							
WHIRLING HOBSTAR (U.S. GLASS)								
Punch Bowl w/base	125							
Cup	20							
Pitcher	190							
WHIRLING LEAVES (MILLERSBURG)								
Bowl, 9"-11", Round or Ruffled	95	400	450				250CM	
Bowl, 10", Tri-Cornered	300	500	500				550V	
WHIRLING STAR (IMPERIAL)								
Bowl, 9"-11"	40							
Compote	55		85					
Punch Bowl w/base	135							
Cup	20							
WHITE ELEPHANT								
Ornament, Rare							350W	
WHITE OAK								
Tumbler, Rare	300							
WICKERWORK (ENGLISH)								
Bowl w/base, Complete	275							
WIDE PANEL (U.S. GLASS)								
Salt	50							

Wide Rib Vase

Wild Blackberry

Wildflower (Northwood)

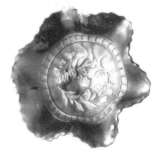

Wildflower

	M	A	G	B	PO	AO	Pas	R
WIDE PANEL (NORTHWOOD-FENTON-IMPERIAL)								
Bowl, 9"	45	90					80SM	
Compote	40							
Epergne, 4 Lily, Rare	1,000	1,600	1,700	2,000		28,000	1,900W	
Console Set, 3 Pieces	110						135	
Goblet	40							290
Cake Plate, 12"-15", Rare	150UP	250UP					270UP	400
Punch Bowl	115							1,175
Cup	20							150
Lemonade, Handled	30						75W	
Compote, Miniature	40							
Covered Candy	40	60						390
Spittoon Whimsey	500							
Vase	30	40	45	60			70	700
WIDE PANEL (WESTMORELAND)								
Bowl, 7½"							70TL	
Bowl, 8¼"							75TL	
WIDE PANEL BOUQUET								
Basket, 3½"	75							
WIDE PANEL SHADE								
Lightshade			175					
WIDE PANEL VT. (NORTHWOOD)								
Pitcher, Tankard	200	275	300					
WIDE RIB (DUGAN)								
Vase	55	60	70	70	90	300	85	
WILD BERRY								
Jar w/lid	250							
WILD BLACKBERRY (FENTON)								
Bowl, 8½", Scarce	65	90	110					
Bowl, "Maday" Advertising, Rare		1,250*	1,500*					
WILD FERN (AUSTRALIAN)								
Compote	165	240						
WILDFLOWER (MILLERSBURG)								
Compote, Ruffled, Rare	1,000	1,200	1,500					
Compote, Jelly, Rare		1,600						
WILDFLOWER (NORTHWOOD)								
Compote (Plain Interior)	300	350	350					
WILD GRAPE								
Bowl, 8¾"	60							
WILD LOGANBERRY (WESTMORELAND)								
Cider Pitcher, Rare							520IM	
Compote, Covered, Rare							295IM	
Creamer, Rare							150IM	
Sugar, Rare							100IM	
Wine	145							
Goblet					150			
(Note: Also Known as Dewberry)								
WILD ROSE (NORTHWOOD)								
Bowl, Flat, 8"	40	50	45					
Bowl, Ftd, Open Edge, 6"	45	65	75				150BA	
WILD ROSE (MILLERSBURG)								
Small Lamp, Rare	1,000	1,200	1,100					
Medium Lamp, Rare	1,200	1,500	1,200					
Lamp, Marked "Riverside," Very Rare			3,000*					
Medallion Lamp, Rare	2,000	2,500	2,300					
WILD ROSE								
Syrup, Rare	700							
WILD ROSE SHADE								
Lightshade	95							
WILD STRAWBERRY (DUGAN)								
Bowl, 9"-10½"	200	300	300		375			
Plate, 7"-9", Rare		375						
Bowl, 6", Rare	60	95			140			
WINDFLOWER (DUGAN)								
Bowl, 8½"	95			85				
Plate, 9"	165			160				
Nappy, Handled	85	95		185			95PK	
WINDMILL (IMPERIAL)								
Bowl, 9"	35	40	40				140V	
Bowl, 5"	20	25	25					
Fruit Bowl, 10½"	40		40					
Milk Pitcher	60	170	110					
Pickle Dish	25		45					
Tray, Flat	35		65				80	
Pitcher	70	200	160				425	
Tumbler	25	95	45				175AM	
WINDSOR (IMPERIAL)								
Flower Arranger, Rare	90						90IB	

Wishbone Flower Arranger

Woodlands Vase

Wreath of Roses Variant

Zig-Zag

	M	A	G	B	PO	AO	Pas	R
WINE AND ROSES (FENTON)								
Cider Pitcher, Scarce	665							
Wine..............................	90			95		550	120AO	
WINGED HEAVY SHELL								
Vase, 3½"..............................							95	
WINKEN								
Lamp................................	135							
WISE OWL								
Bank	50							
WISHBONE (IMPERIAL)								
Flower Arranger..................	90						90	
WISHBONE (NORTHWOOD)								
Bowl, Flat, 8"-10"	190	150	160	370			900IB	
Bowl, Ftd, 9"......................	200	170	190				1,300SM	
Epergne, Rare.....................	400	550	850				1,700W	
Plate, Ftd, 9", Rare	900	400						
Plate, Flat, 10", Rare...........	500	875	900					
Pitcher, Rare......................	800	1,000	990					
Tumbler, Scarce	95	170	200				400PL	
WISHBONE AND SPADES (DUGAN)								
Bowl, 8½"		395			200			
Bowl, 5".............................		250			190			
Plate, 6", Rare....................		395			300			
Plate, 10½", Rare		1,100			1,350			
WISTERIA (NORTHWOOD)								
Bank Whimsey, Rare							2,500W	
Pitcher, Rare......................							7,500IB	
Tumbler, Rare							900IB	
WITCHES POT								
One Shape, Souvenir	850							
WOODEN SHOE								
One Shape, Rare	275							
WOODLANDS								
Vase, 5", Rare.....................	300							
WOODPECKER (DUGAN)								
Wall Vase...........................	55		90				115V	
WOODPECKER AND IVY								
Vase, Rare			1,900				2,100V	
WREATH OF ROSES (FENTON)								
Bon-bon	40	45	50	45			65	
Bon-bon, Stemmed.............	45	50	50	50			65	
Compote............................	45	50	50	45				
Punch Bowl w/base.............	2,000	350	375	390	2,000			
Cup..................................	25	30	35	40	320			
WREATH OF ROSES VT. (DUGAN)								
Compote............................	55	65	65	60				
WREATHED BLEEDING HEARTS (DUGAN)								
Vase, 5¼"...........................	110							
WREATHED CHERRY (DUGAN)								
Oval Bowl, 10½"..................	90	140		300			225W	
Oval Bowl, 5"......................	40	40		75			60W	
Butter	110	160					195W	
Sugar	70	100					110W	
Creamer or Spooner	65	95					100W	
Toothpick, Old Only.............		175						
Pitcher..............................	240	425					775W	
Tumbler	40	55					170W	
ZIG ZAG (FENTON)								
Pitcher, Decorated, Rare	250			450			575IG	
Tumbler, Decorated	40			50			75IG	
ZIG ZAG (MILLERSBURG)								
Bowl, Round or Ruffled, 9½" ...	275	350	375					
Bowl, Tri-Cornered, 10".......	450	575	575					
Card Tray, Rare..................			900					
ZIPPER LOOP (IMPERIAL)								
Hand Lamp, Rare	1,300						1,500SM	
Medium Lamp, Rare	600						600SM	
Large Lamp, Rare	500						500SM	
ZIPPER STITCH (CZECH)								
Cordial Set (Tray, Decanter, 4 Cordials), Complete	1,700							
ZIPPER VT. (ENGLISH)								
Sugar w/lid	50							
ZIPPERED HEART								
Bowl, 9".............................	70	110						
Bowl, 5".............................	40	50						
Queen's Vase, Rare	4,000	3,800						
Pitcher (Not Confirmed)	1,000*	1,500*						
Tumbler (Not Confirmed)	120*	150*						
ZIP ZIP (ENGLISH)								
Flower Frog Holder	60							